UN Peace Operations

This book assesses the UN Peace Operations in Haiti and establishes what lessons should be taken into account for future operations elsewhere.

Specifically, the book examines the UN's approaches to security and stability, demobilisation, disarmament and reintegration (DDR), police, justice and prison reform, democratisation, and transitional justice, and their interdependencies through the seven UN missions in Haiti. Drawing on extensive fieldwork and interviews conducted in Haiti, it identifies strengths and weaknesses of these approaches and focuses on the connections between these different sectors. It places these efforts in the broader Haitian political context, emphasises economic development as a central factor to sustainability, provides a civil society perspective, and discusses the many constraints the UN faced in implementing its mandates. The book also serves as a historical account of UN involvement in Haiti, which comes at a time when the drawdown of the mission has begun. In an environment where the UN is increasingly seeking to conduct security sector reform (SSR) within the context of integrated missions, this book will be a valuable contribution to the debate on intervention, UN peace operations and SSR.

This book will be of interest to students of peace operations and peacekeeping, conflict studies, security studies and IR in general.

Eirin Mobekk is a Policy Director at the Norwegian Agency for Development Cooperation (NORAD). She holds a PhD in War Studies from King's College London, and is co-author of *Peace and Justice: Seeking Accountability After War* (2007).

Cass Series on Peacekeeping

General Editor: Michael Pugh

This series examines all aspects of peacekeeping, from the political, operational and legal dimensions to the developmental and humanitarian issues that must be dealt with by all those involved with peacekeeping in the world today.

A full list of titles in this series is available at: www.routledge.com/strategicstudies/series/CSP

Recently published titles:

Statebuilding and Justice Reform
Post-conflict reconstruction in Afghanistan
Matteo Tondini

Rethinking the Liberal Peace
External models and local alternatives
Edited by Shahrbanou Tadjbakhsh

Peace Operations and Organized Crime
Enemies or allies?
Edited by James Cockayne and Adam Lupel

Corruption and Post-Conflict Peacebuilding
Selling the peace?
Edited by Christine Cheng and Dominik Zaum

South America and Peace Operations
Coming of age
Edited by Kai Michael Kenkel

Peace Operations in the Francophone World
Global governance meets post-colonialism
Edited by Bruno Charbonneau and Tony Chafer

Cooperative Peacekeeping in Africa
Exploring regime complexity
Malte Brosig

Evaluating Peacekeeping Missions
A typology of success and failure in international interventions
Sarah-Myriam Martin-Brûlé

UN Peace Operations
Lessons from Haiti, 1994–2016
Eirin Mobekk

UN Peace Operations

Lessons from Haiti, 1994–2016

Eirin Mobekk

LONDON AND NEW YORK

First published 2017
by Routledge
2 Park Square, Milton Park, Abingdon, Oxon OX14 4RN

and by Routledge
711 Third Avenue, New York, NY 10017

Routledge is an imprint of the Taylor & Francis Group, an informa business

© 2017 Eirin Mobekk

The right of Eirin Mobekk to be identified as author of this work has been asserted by her in accordance with sections 77 and 78 of the Copyright, Designs and Patents Act 1988.

All rights reserved. No part of this book may be reprinted or reproduced or utilised in any form or by any electronic, mechanical, or other means, now known or hereafter invented, including photocopying and recording, or in any information storage or retrieval system, without permission in writing from the publishers.

Trademark notice: Product or corporate names may be trademarks or registered trademarks, and are used only for identification and explanation without intent to infringe.

British Library Cataloguing-in-Publication Data
A catalogue record for this book is available from the British Library

Library of Congress Cataloging-in-Publication Data
Names: Mobekk, Eirin, author.
Title: UN peace operations : lessons from Haiti, 1994-2016 / Eirin Mobekk.
Other titles: United Nations peace operations
Description: Abingdon, Oxon ; New York, NY : Routledge, 2017. |
Series: Cass series on peacekeeping | Includes bibliographical references and index.
Identifiers: LCCN 2016026339| ISBN 9780415480864 (hardback) | ISBN 9781315881638 (ebook)
Subjects: LCSH: United Nations--Haiti. | United Nations--Peacekeeping forces--Haiti. | Peace-building--Haiti--International cooperation. | Haiti--Politics and government--1986-
Classification: LCC JZ6374 .M627 2017 | DDC 972.9407/3--dc23
LC record available at https://lccn.loc.gov/2016026339

ISBN: 978-0-415-48086-4 (hbk)
ISBN: 978-1-315-88163-8 (ebk)

Typeset in Times New Roman
by HWA Text and Data Management, London

Printed and bound by CPI Group (UK) Ltd, Croydon, CR0 4YY

'This is an important and timely contribution to the burgeoning literature on UN peace operations. Mobekk's analysis does much to explain why Haiti has become a graveyard for UN-led efforts to reform conflict-strewn and deeply divided societies.'

— *Mats Berdal, King's College London, UK*

'A much-needed analysis from Eirin Mobekk based on extensive direct knowledge gained from long-term involvement in Haiti and informed by her extensive experience of other major conflict zones. UN peacekeeping is evolving rapidly and becoming far more multi-dimensional. As an organisation it faces many demands and even more challenges and if it is to greatly improve its peacekeeping operations it must learn from recent experience. This book is a singularly valuable contribution to that laudable aim.'

— *Paul Rogers, University of Bradford, UK*

'This is a commanding book. It is about the history of UN operations in Haiti, but it is also about lessons for international interventions generally. Mobekk sharply argues the need for justice – criminal justice reinforcing judicial reform and police reform at the same time, and politics in international interventions. Political responsibility of the locals (in this case Haitians) as well as internationals is vital – all the technocratic, institution-building, bureaucratic reforms that the UN and others bring "neutrally" to interventions are doomed to underperformance if there is no recognition that political problems need politics to deal with them. Eirin Mobekk has done a brilliant job of showing this.'

— *James Gow, King's College London, UK*

Contents

Acknowledgements   *viii*
Abbreviations   *ix*

1   UN peace operations   1

2   The Haitian backdrop   14

3   (In)security and (in)stability   34

4   Disarmament, demobilisation and reintegration and the defence reform that never was   56

5   Police reform   81

6   Judicial and prison reform   110

7   Justice and reconciliation   139

8   Democratisation: strengthening good governance   156

9   Violence, democracy and development: concluding thoughts   189

Appendix A: UN missions to Haiti   *195*
Appendix B: Haiti timeline: a chronology of key events   *198*
Index   *202*

Acknowledgements

This book has been many years in the making. It is the product of years of working on UN peace operations, security sector reform and the rule of law, as well as a consistent engagement with Haiti from the mid-1990s. I first went to Haiti in 1996 and have continued to engage with the country ever since. The book has gone through many phases and reflects the development of my own thinking on these topics.

Many have provided their support to this process, but I would like especially to thank Professor James Gow who supported me diligently through my first years of working on Haiti. Thanks also go to Ruby Sandhu who read several chapters of this book and offered her insightful comments, as well as to Michael Deibert who through the years has been a sounding-board for my thoughts and deliberations on Haiti. I would also sincerely like to thank *Democratization*, *Small Wars and Insurgencies*, and *International Relations* for letting me use parts of my articles published previously in these journals.

The interviews undertaken in Haiti and in New York over many years were of critical importance to this book. I would like to thank Haitian civil society, politicians, government representatives, women's groups and all other individuals and organisations who shared their vast experiences and knowledge with me, as well as all UN and UNDP staff both in New York and in Haiti, and other international organisations working in and on Haiti, who all generously gave their time – without their input this book would not have been possible. Moreover, thanks to all my friends in Haiti without whom I would not have been able to access and conduct all these interviews. Any omissions, errors or inaccuracies are of course my own.

Finally, heartfelt thanks to all at Routledge, and especially to Hannah Ferguson for her patience and tolerance of missed deadlines. And, last but not least, a big thank you to my friends and family in Norway, the UK and elsewhere who have listened to my monologues on Haiti for a long time, and of course as always to my parents.

Abbreviations

APENA	Administration pénitentiaire nationale
APN	National Popular Assembly
BID	Banque interaméricaine de developpement (Inter-American Development Bank)
CARICOM	The Caribbean Community
CAU	Corrections Advisory Unit
CDCs	Community Development Committees
CEP	Conseil Electoral Provisional (Provisional Electoral Council)
CID	Cruel, inhumane and degrading treatment
CIDA	Canadian International Development Agency
CIMO	Compagnie d'Intervention et Maintien d'Ordre
CNDDR	Commission Nationale de Désarmement, de Démantèlement et de Réinsertion
CNG	Conseil National de Gouvernement (National Council of Government)
CPVDs	Committees for the Prevention of Violence and for Development
CSPJ	Conseil Superieur du Pouvoir Judiciaire
CVR	Conflict Violence Reduction
DAC	Development Assistance Committee
DAP	Direction de l'Administration Pénitentiaire
DCPJ	Direction centrale de la Police judiciaire (Central Directorate of the Judicial Police)
DDR	Demobilisation, Disarmament and Reintegration
DFID	United Kingdom Department for International Development
DPKO	Department of Peacekeeping Operations
EMA	L'École de la Magistrature
ENP	L'École National de Police
EU	European Union
FAd'H	Forces armées d'Haïti
FL	Famni Lavalas
FNCD	Front National pour le Changement et la Democratie (National Front for Change and Democracy)

FRAPH	Le Front pour l'Avancement et Progres d'Haiti (Front for the Advancement and Progress of Haiti)
GDP	Gross Domestic Product
GFP	Global Focal Point
GNP	Gross National Product
GOH	Government of Haiti
HIPC	Heavily Indebted Poor Countries
ICF	Interim Cooperation Framework
ICITAP	International Criminal Investigative Training and Assistance Program (US)
ICRC	International Committee of the Red Cross
IDA	International Development Association
IDEA	International Institute for Democracy and Electoral Assistance
IDPs	Internally displaced people
IG	Inspector General
IMF	International Monetary Fund
INGO	International non-governmental organisation
IOM	International Office for Migration
IPMs	International Police Monitors
ISF	Integrated Strategic Framework
JMAC	Joint Mission Analysis Centre
LAC	Latin American and Caribbean
MANUH	Mission Nations Unies en Haiti (United Nations Mission in Haiti)
MICAH	International Civilian Support Mission in Haiti
MICIVIH	Mission Civile Internationale en Haiti (International Civilian Mission in Haiti)
MIDH	Mouvement pour l'Instauration de la Democratie en Haïti (Movement for the Establishment of Democracy in Haiti)
MIF	Multinational Interim Force
MINUSTAH	Mission des Nations Unies pour la stabilisation en Haïti (UN Stabilisation Mission in Haiti)
MIPONUH	Mission de Police de Organisation des Nations Unies au Haiti
MNF	Multinational Force
MOJPS	Ministry of Justice and Public Security
MPP	Mouvman Péyizan Papaye (Papaye Peasant Movement)
NCD	National Disarmament Commission
NCDDR	National Commission on Disarmament, Demobilisation and Reintegration
NCHR	National Coalition for Haitian Rights
NGO	Non-Governmental Organisation
NTJC	National Truth and Justice Commission
OAS	Organisation of American States
OECD	Organisation for Economic Cooperation and Development
OIF	Organisation of La Francophonie

OPL	Organisation Politique Lavalas/Organisation du Peuple en Lutte (Political Organisation of Lavalas/Organisation of People in Struggle)
OTI	Office of Transition Initiatives
PIO	Public Information Office
PNH	Police Nationale d'Haïti (Haitian National Police)
QIP	Quick Impact Projects
RAMIDEM	Rassemblement des Militaires Démobilisés (Organisation of Demobilised Soldiers)
RAMIRESM	Rassemblement des Militaires Révoqués Sans Motif (Organisation of Soldiers Dismissed without a Reason)
RDNP	Rassemblement des Democrates Nationalistes et Progressistes (Assembly of Progressive National Democrats)
ROE	Rules of Engagement
ROLIP	UN Rule of Law Indicator Project
SG	Secretary-General
SGBV	Sexual and gender-based violence
SRSG	Special Representative of the Secretary-General
SSR	Security Sector Reform
TC	Truth Commission
UDMO	Unités Départmentales de Maintien d'Ordre
UNDP	United Nations Development Programme
UNDPKO	United Nations Department for Peacekeeping Operations
UNHCR	United Nations High Commission for Refugees
UNHQ	United Nations Headquarters
UNMIH	UN Mission in Haiti
UNODC	United Nations Office on Drugs and Crime
UNOG	United Nations Office at Geneva
UNPOL	United Nations Police
UNSC	United Nations Security Council
UNSMIH	UN Support Mission in Haiti
UNTMIH	UN Transition Mission in Haiti
USAID	United States Agency for International Development
USIP	United States Institute for Peace
VSN	Voluntaires de Securité Nationale
WFP	World Food Programme

1 UN peace operations

Since the early 1990s, there has been an immense evolution in peace operations, in policies, mandates, scope and function. Where traditional peacekeeping previously focused on ensuring security and stability – now restructuring the security sector; protecting civilians; supporting disarmament, demobilisation and reintegration of ex-combatants; increasing democratic space, institution-building and good governance – are all core to the UN mandates – in short building peace. In addition, there has been a drive towards more 'robust' peacekeeping. Similarly, the expectations of the UN to solve conflicts have altered. There has been a growth both vertically and horizontally of multi-dimensional peacekeeping challenges and thus the need for sophisticated solutions. The policy developments and capacities to address these challenges have increased in the UN, yet in tandem there remains considerable policy-operational gaps.

In the simplest terms, UN peace operations are about ensuring security and stability to provide an environment to transition from conflict to peace. The means by which to achieve this will vary according to context and operations, but in most cases they will include conducting support for DDR, defence, police, justice and penal reform, democratisation, economic development and transitional justice in addition to conducting more traditional peacekeeping. This book addresses these aspects of peace operations and their relationship, through the peace operations in Haiti 1994–2016. Peace operations strive to create the conditions where democracy can develop. However, frequently even if initial stability and democratisation have been achieved, it has often proven more difficult to achieve the longer term objectives of creating sustainable security intuitions and a stable democracy, repeatedly resulting in a return of conflict.

The evolution, change and improvement in UN and international policy and discourse on peace operations have been significant, yet implementation has continued to lag behind. The discourse has tended to focus on either one specific variable (e.g. police reform), or the relationship between two of the variables (e.g. police and justice reform) or state building, peacebuilding, democratisation or conflict and development in one or several countries. This book examines the UN's approaches to security and stability, DDR, police, justice and prison reform, democratisation, and transitional justice and their interdependencies through the seven UN missions in Haiti. It identifies strengths and weaknesses of these approaches, and focuses on the connections between these different sectors. It places these efforts in the broader Haitian political context; emphasises economic development as a central factor to sustainability; provides a civil society perspective, and discusses the many constraints the UN faced in implementing its mandates. The book is also a historical account of the UN in Haiti, which comes at a time when the drawdown of the mission has begun. Therefore, this book provides a contribution to the discourse by explicitly highlighting the interdependencies between these variables and in particular drawing attention to the lack of strong political mandates in complex national political environments. Thus, the aim of this book is to examine, using Haiti as an example, why after long-term peace operations and other international and bilateral support so many countries revert into violence, poor governance and undemocratic practices even when substantial progress has been made in several areas. What this book establishes is that when the interdependencies of these variables are not cohesively addressed it undermines progress in core areas; and that the national political context can have a considerable negative impact upon progress in programme implementation.

It has been acknowledged, and perhaps best exemplified through the development of UN integrated missions, that to achieve the objectives of any peace operations a crosscutting, comprehensive and cohesive approach is needed. Yet in practice, this has been difficult to implement in many contexts. In a world where everyone is increasingly specialised, addressing the interdependencies of each sector in a peace operation is complex. It is extremely difficult to find people that can tackle defence reform, as well as economic development and transitional justice, but this is where cooperation, communication and coordination, ideally integration, become ever so important. This has too often been absent.

However, there needs to be an understanding of what UN missions can and cannot do. UN peace operations are frequently an easy target for criticism by international and national stakeholders without an adequate understanding of the restrictions such operations function within. For example, there has been increasing pressure to expand mandates and meet peacekeeping challenges yet adequate human and financial resources have not always been provided, thus limiting the missions' abilities to implement the mandate effectively. In addition, a UN peace operation takes place within a broader national and international political context and is often constrained by this. For example, there may be strong national resistance to UN strategies for change and international actors, rather than supporting a peace operation's objectives, in some instances, have effectively hindered the UN's ability to implement its mandate, through promoting their own national interests.

An evolution in policy

There has been an evolution in policy guidance supporting and developing peace operations. These polices, that have and will guide UN peace operations then, now and in the future, include, for example, the Agenda for Peace, the Brahimi report, the Secretary-General's reports on Rule of Law and Transitional Justice, the Secretary-General's reports on Security Sector Reform, the Secretary-General's reports on the protection of civilians (POC), the Secretary-General's report on peacebuilding in the immediate aftermath of conflict, the Capstone doctrine and the CivCap review.[1] This has led to a comprehensive framework for peace support operations. For example, it has meant more effective ways in which to conduct police reform, to promote local ownership, and to ensure a framework for more robust peacekeeping and peace enforcement, to mention but a few.

Although this evolution in consolidating policies in peace operations and how to improve them has taken place, two issues in particular have remained. First, there is an operational–policy gap, where implementation in areas such as security sector reform and the rule of law have not adequately reflected progress in policy. Second, these efforts are not firmly rooted in a political strategy, but are often separate interventions in promoting, supporting and enhancing the different aspects of building peace. Cohesiveness of the various support efforts is frequently lacking and not placed within the political context. This has also meant that, for example, when more robust peacekeeping opens up a stability dividend it has not always adequately been taken advantage of. Both these issues are exemplified well by Haiti.

As the relationship between different development efforts is core to this book, the concepts of integrated missions and security sector reform are central. Although neither was developed until after the end of the first set of missions in Haiti (2001), parts of security sector reform were embedded in all mandates 1994–2001, in particular policing and coordination efforts were acknowledged as central to the missions.

The UN developed the concept of integrated missions as a response to multi-dimensional peacebuilding challenges. In the period discussed in this book the concept of integrated missions was trialled and tested with resulting birthing pains. Haiti was in many ways a test case for integration of UN missions, particularly in demobilisation, disarmament and reintegration (DDR). The Capstone Doctrine offers the following definition of integrated missions: 'An integrated mission is one in which there is a shared vision among all United Nations actors as to the strategic objectives of the United Nations presence at the country-level. This strategy should reflect a shared understanding of the operating environment and agreement on how to maximize the effectiveness, efficiency, and impact of the United Nations overall response.'[2] It is intended to ensure that the UN mission together with the UN country team and agencies work within a strategic framework to deliver responses to multi-dimensional peacekeeping challenges.

Security sector reform is acknowledged to be at the core of peacebuilding activities, as it is essential for continued stability in post-conflict societies – with the establishment of integrated UN missions the links between SSR, rule of law and DDR was also emphasised by the UN.[3] There has been considerable development on the issue of SSR within the UN, including the establishment of an SSR unit in the DPKO and two reports by the UN Secretary-General on the role of the UN supporting SSR, an inter-agency task force on SSR and a Security Council Resolution on the challenges and opportunities of SSR.[4] A broad definition of security sector has emerged, which incorporates 'traditional' (or core) security actors (e.g. defence forces, police, border guards, intelligence services), justice institutions (e.g. judiciary, prosecution services), non-statutory security forces (e.g. PMCs, rebel groups), and management and oversight bodies (e.g. ministries, parliament).[5] The UN Secretary-General's report defines security sector reform as 'a process of assessment, review and implementation as well as monitoring and evaluation led by national authorities that has as its goal the enhancement of effective and accountable security for the State and its peoples without discrimination and with full respect for human rights and the rule of law'. The objective is good governance: a security sector that is accountable, legitimate and transparent in the provision of internal and external security and rule of law. By mid-2016, seven[6] UN operations had taken place in Haiti, with what effectively was a mandate of SSR, although SSR was never specifically mentioned.

Crosscutting elements: enablers and inhibiters

Several crosscutting elements are discussed in the following chapters: contextual understanding; local ownership; political will; external influences; coordination; economic development and civil society; and how they affect support to disarmament, demobilisation and reintegration, SSR, democratisation, transitional justice and security and stability. These elements are not posited here as 'new', as many have been discussed since the early 1990s; but sadly they remain as vital today as they were in 1994 and improvement in effectively addressing them has only been marginal.

Any of these elements can be either enablers or inhibiters to the successful implementation of the mandates in a peace operation. They were crucial in relation to Haiti and are arguably central to most other peace operations. Although depending on context, some may be of greater importance and have more influence than others, and there may be in other peace operations additional crosscutting elements to the ones discussed here.

Contextual understanding

Understanding the context of a country is critical to the success of UN missions, from goal setting and programme design to achieving more strategic objectives. UNDPKO has long acknowledged this. There are however many problems with ensuring a sufficient level of understanding prior to deployment as there is ensuring consistency in that knowledge. This does not suggest that all or indeed any staff member has to be a specialist on any given mission country – it does mean however that basic knowledge about the political, ethnic, socio-economic and conflict structures that underpin the country is essential. As the oft-cited adage goes, to change the future we must understand the past. That past may rest in the most recent history or be buried hundreds of years hence. For any UN mission, broader politics matter and why they came to be thus often shows a pattern, which needs to be understood in order to be addressed.

In the early 1990s the 'one-size-fits-all' approach to peace and security was regularly applied and models were liberally adapted from one context to another.

As lessons were learnt, the importance of in-depth contextual understanding grew and model transference was accepted as a flawed system. Nonetheless there have continued to be issues around contextual knowledge, including insufficient understanding, knowledge retention, institutional memory, and updating when the context changes. There has been a tendency to focus on immediate conflict analysis rather than broader political understanding. The overarching political context and changes within it have a profound effect upon operational support. Haiti, as elaborated in the following chapters, is an example where contextual understanding or a lack thereof, had a direct negative impact upon implementation and support.

National political will and politics matter

If there is no national political will to change, it is almost impossible to affect change. This book defines political will broadly. It is not only about the government, but also about parliament, as well as leadership within each sector (police, justice, penal, armed forces) and, in Haiti, the will among the political opposition and political and economic elites to change. Political will and with it politics, becomes a strong inhibiter when the government is undermining the very mandate of the mission, leaving the UN to balance between pressuring the government for change and simultaneously being dependent upon them to remain as they are there at the government's invitation.

Political will is also constantly shifting, frequently rooted in an ever-changing political landscape in a post-conflict environment. Thus in all peace operations politics matter enormously.[7] Any UN mission needs to be flexible and have the ability to respond to these shifts and more importantly foresee the potential changes, thus ensuring that it has contingency planning in all sectors of its mandate. Subsequent chapters explore the complexities of dealing with a multi-faceted and ever-changing political environment.

Local ownership

Support for democratisation, transitional justice, and security sector reform in post-conflict countries has repeatedly lacked local ownership and met only the objectives of donor requirements instead of those of the recipient country. However, since the late 1990s more emphasis has been placed on the importance of local ownership of these processes. The United Nations Secretary-General stated that 'we must learn better how to respect and support local ownership, local leadership and a local constituency for reform, while at the same time remaining faithful to United Nations norms and standards'.[8] Considerable experience has shown that unless there is local ownership, support processes will not succeed. For example, the UN Secretary-General has stated that 'broad national consultation lies at the heart of national ownership' and that success is dependent upon: 'a nationally led and inclusive process in which national and local authorities, parliaments and civil society, including traditional leaders, women's groups and others, are actively engaged'.[9] There is therefore seemingly a consensus on the virtues of local ownership. Yet operationally the meaning of the concept is often unclear and ambiguous. Thus, implementation has lagged behind. While advances in policy frameworks have underscored the importance of broad local ownership of support, a minimalist approach has often been applied, reducing ownership to consultations with the government, political and economic elites and security sector leadership. In Haiti local ownership, or at times a lack thereof, underscores all these issues.

Local ownership must be viewed in context. It will vary according to whether the country is in a phase of stabilisation, peacebuilding, post-authoritarian transition, poverty reduction and development or in a fragile state. Local ownership is a process and not something that can always be present in a predetermined and predefined form. In saying that ownership is a process, it is not to suggest that there are circumstances under which there should be no ownership, but rather that local ownership will develop and change over time. Ownership is influence over, capability and responsibility for the different phases of planning, implementation, policymaking and execution. Not all of these facets will be present simultaneously, to the same degree or from the start in all contexts. Viewing local ownership as an evolutionary process better reflects the different contexts. However, without local ownership support will ultimately fail.

Civil society

Civil society's central role in building peace is uncontested. But the UN's ability to draw on civil society, particularly in the areas of security sector reform and the rule of law, has not been consistent. This was also reflected in Haiti, even though civil society was strong and vibrant. Moreover, a part of civil society was very negative to UN efforts. This affected the missions' relationship with civil society throughout different periods. It was further complicated because NGOs, in particular, became increasingly political after the mid-1990s.

In addition, parts of civil society were in effect substituting the government's role in providing services to citizens where the government was unable to. This also led to a complicated dynamic between the government

External influences

UN peace operations do not operate in a vacuum of support to governments, and the UN is rarely the primary donor in the areas examined in this book. It is impossible to discuss UN reform efforts without reference to other donors and their efforts. This book does not go into detail about these programmes but mentions them when relevant. The issue is how they affect each other positively or negatively, including their (in)ability to coordinate and have a similar strategic vision.

Bilateral donors' national interests always have an impact upon programme implementation in UN peace operations. They affect, and in some instances restrict, what the UN can do, and complicate the role the UN can play. This is rarely sufficiently emphasised as a restrictive element for the UN. In Haiti, the US as the major donor played a central role; this was a result of many factors including drug trafficking, migrants and it being within the purview of the US 'backyard'. For example, historically US influences for better or worse have always played an essential part in Haiti's political processes – and, as is explored in subsequent chapters, this affected the UN missions in various ways.

Coordination

There is a consensus that to maximise efficiency and impact while minimising duplication of support efforts there needs to be coordination, yet rarely does anybody want to be coordinated. Donors have different national agendas inhibiting coordination.

Fundamentally, there are different objectives and often no agreement on the means to achieve those objectives. The objective broadly may be stability and security, or the even more elusive 'peace', but what that means for different actors may be vastly different. Coordination is in particular difficult for the issues discussed in this book. In other areas such as humanitarian aid, education, and health coordination is easier, as having similar strategic objectives is less contentious. However, the rule of law and democratisation are more politically sensitive and donors as well as different UN agencies have been much more reluctant to coordinate efforts.

Cooperation frameworks are always established in post-conflict societies, but traditionally they have tended not to work well for issues such as defence, police, justice and penal reform, as there are frequently many national interests at play. In Haiti, several such frameworks were established, however, mostly after 2004. These included the Interim Cooperation Framework (ICF), drawn up in July 2004 as a joint effort between the international community and the transitional government, which established needs and targets in over 16 sectors. It set forth a strategy for the stabilisation and reconstruction of Haiti. Participating in creating the ICF were government representatives from over 35 countries, NGOs, international organisations, the UN and Haitians (civil society, political parties, government and press).[10] This framework included a focus on DDR, police, justice and prisons.[11] The aim was for donors and MINUSTAH to avoid duplication and to put resources where most needed. A framework for all UN agencies was also established: the Integrated Strategic Framework for Haiti. This was developed in 2010 for an initial 18-month period and subsequently extended by a revised ISF. The framework was organised around institutional, territorial, economic and social rebuilding pillars and an 'enabling environment' pillar. These frameworks aimed to integrate humanitarian, development and stabilisation priorities aligned with the Haitian government's own strategic development plans.[12]

Economic development

The economic development of a fragile state has a profound impact upon the sustainability of in particular DDR, police, justice, penal reform and democratisation efforts. The ability to conduct interventions effectively in all these

8 *UN peace operations*

areas is closely intertwined with economic development. It is a critical component and part of the missing political strategic objective in peace operations. Often it is not flaws in the support to, for example, police reform, but insufficient economic development that creates the major problems. These connections are highlighted in the subsequent chapters.

This book does not focus in much detail on Haiti's economic development during the period from 1994 until today. Nor will it undertake an economic analysis of Haiti. It only highlights the lack of cohesion between the economic programming and support on the one hand and programmes targeted at ensuring security, safety, SSR and democratisation on the other. It establishes that without a streamlined and comprehensive approach to post-conflict interventions, especially within the UN family, the chances of improved stability decrease and the levels of change that these programmes can have are influenced.

This book – UN peace operations in Haiti

With a near-consistent presence of UN peace operations since 1994, a large number of mandates and changing political contexts, Haiti is an excellent case to explore the six core elements of this book: DDR; police, judicial and penal reform; transitional justice; and democratisation. Haiti was one of many cases of its time that spurred the evolution of policies and approaches that changed the face of peace operations.

Haiti was also a test-case for new polices tackling multi-dimensional peacekeeping challenges. It was the first UN peace operation that was specifically designed to restore democracy, and proved the difficulties with doing so. Moreover, Haiti was not at war or in a traditional post-conflict situation. It was a violent transition. Security and stability was core to all of the mandates in Haiti. It framed all operations. Yet how the UN approaches security and stability has changed massively in the last twenty or so years; these changes have sometimes been rooted in the practitioner's own ideologies, views and understanding of security and therefore implementation has varied considerably, even if the mandate remained the same.

Haiti has experienced two phases of UN peace operations: 1994–2001 and 2004–present day. The 1994–2001 operation was the first of its kind explicitly mandated to 'restore democracy' and the 2004 intervention followed the breakdown in democratic governance and a rebellion that forced the president out of office.

The first mission's mandates (1994–2001) were limited in scope, predominately focusing on the establishment of a police force, support for the democratisation process and ensuring security and stability. The mandates after 2004 differed considerably from the preceding period in that they concentrated much more extensively on support for different sectors of peacebuilding including DDR, justice and penal reform. The international community paid more attention to Haiti post-2004, as it was evident that the previous intervention had failed. This took many forms in terms of both clearer and stronger mandates, as well as high profile appointments.[13] The UN Stabilisation Mission in Haiti (MINUSTAH's) presence underwent three phases from 2004 to 2016: 2004–06 ensuring security and stability and supporting security sector reform under a transitional government; 2006–10 renewed stabilisation and reform efforts and enforcement operations; post-earthquake 2010 reconstruction, rebuilding and stability and security.

Humanitarian disasters have had a vast impact upon the peace operations in Haiti. There have regularly been hurricanes bringing about untold devastation, for example, in 2008 there were four consecutive hurricanes. However, the earthquake had the most significant impact. On 12 January 2010, a 7.0 magnitude earthquake hit Haiti. The earthquake was a massive humanitarian disaster; there were 200,000 to 300,000 injured and over 220,000 people died, and an estimated 1.5 million were left homeless and internally displaced. There was extensive devastation to infrastructure and the state apparatus; an estimated 30 per cent of civil servants perished; prisons, police stations and public buildings were destroyed. The UN and partners established settlement sites and support refocused on reconstruction activities; it was not until the end of 2013 that 90 per cent displaced by the earthquake had left the resettlement camps. MINUSTAH also suffered. Over 100 United Nations staff lost their lives, including the Special Representative of the Secretary-General (SRSG) and the Deputy SRSG and other senior mission personnel. Many were injured. This was not only a devastating humanitarian tragedy for Haiti, it also significantly affected support to the areas discussed in this book in the subsequent years.

Chapter outline

Haiti, once hailed as the world's first independent black republic with the promise of equality and freedom, was very far from achieving that goal over 200 years later. Chapter 2 provides a brief outline the history of Haiti. This is by no means intended as an in-depth analysis of Haitian history, but a brief look at central factors, which continued to have an impact upon Haitian society at the time of both interventions. It discusses the history of authoritarianism and that there had never been a democratically elected government until 1991; the development of social and economic differences and how this put in place a system that strongly influenced politics, conflict and violence; the armed forces' role in the governance; and the crosscutting issue of international involvement and influence, particularly the role of the US. The chapter also provides an overview of the contexts at the times of deployment of the UN missions (1994 and 2004).

Chapter 3 elaborates on instability and insecurity in Haiti. The types of insecurity and violence changed through time in Haiti, as will happen in most longer term peace operations' contexts. This chapter does not detail all violence and instability in Haiti, but rather emphasises the political nature of much of the violence and links it to the issues in the subsequent chapters. It discusses both the criminal and political nature of the violence, the new threats that emerged post-2004 through armed gangs and the changed nature of some of crimes committed, such as kidnapping, and places civil unrest within the socio-economic context. How providing security came to be defined during the various peace operations

10 *UN peace operations*

in Haiti changed considerably over time from a very minimalist 'force protection' approach to stabilisation and a 'new experience' in peacekeeping. The chapter thus also explores the change in the peace operations dealing with shifting insecurity.

Initially insecurity and instability was in many ways linked to flawed disarmament, demobilisation and reintegration processes, discussed in Chapter 4. It has long been recognised that disarmament, demobilisation and reintegration are central in reducing violence in post-conflict societies. It is one factor in ensuring sustainable peace and stability. The chapter analyses both the periods of DDR in Haiti, and establishes the Haitian view of these. It elaborates on MINUSTAH's reorientation from DDR towards a community violence reduction programme, which reflected a more nuanced understanding of the context and solutions needed.

Chapter 5 contends with the various police reform processes. The police reform process underwent three distinct phases from 1994 to 2015: the establishment of an interim police force; the creation of a new civilian Haitian police force; and after its demise, the re-establishment of the Haitian National Police (PNH)[14] after 2004. The latter phase incorporated the new challenges faced by the PNH and the UN in the aftermath of the earthquake. This chapter discusses the difficulties of establishing the PNH in a politically charged environment; and the re-establishment of the PNH during a transitional government, political stalemates and limited resources, whilst highlighting issues such as local ownership and coordination.

The rule of law is critical to ensure security and stability in a post-conflict society, and essential for democracy. However, an imbalance has been created by the UN and bilateral donors, in concentrating support on police development whilst marginalising judicial and penal reform. The judicial and penal systems in Haiti from 1994 through to 2016 could only be described as dysfunctional at best. Chapter 6 discusses the judicial and prison reform processes in Haiti. It focuses predominately on post-2004 when the UN mission had a clear mandate to support judicial and penal reform.[15] It establishes that Haitian will to conduct reform in the judicial sector was limited and undermined efforts achieved with the police, and that penal reform remained weak. The chapter emphasises that efforts in the criminal justice system should have been placed in the context of earlier authoritarianism and argues that years of authoritarianism still affected the justice system and its flaws were firmly rooted in the political system and a collapsing democratisation process.

Chapter 7 examines transitional justice and discusses the National Truth and Justice Commission and democratic prosecutions. Although transitional justice was not part of any of the UN mandates in Haiti, this chapter argues that, particularly after 1994, its absence was linked to the continued insecurity. The chapter establishes that reconciliation did not occur in the period between 1994 and 2000 and that the absence of some form of criminal justice was a key contributing factor. Due to the change in the type of violence, transitional justice was not on the agenda after 2004. This chapter thus focuses on post-1994 efforts. Because transitional justice was not consolidated, it contributed to the gradual unravelling of the democratic process discussed in Chapter 8.

During all peace operations in Haiti, the restoration of and support for democracy was a central feature. Chapter 8 provides an overview of the first restoration of democracy; discusses the expectations of Haitians versus democracy restored; analyses the gradual unravelling of the democratic process and identifies democratic deficiencies. Subsequently the chapter analyses the political legitimacy of the post-2004 governments, tracing gradual limitations on the democratic process from repeatedly flawed elections and lacking participation to disillusion. It highlights the interdependencies between democracy, socio-economic development, security, and political will in a context of the history of authoritarianism and abuse of power. Finally, Chapter 9 draws together the different areas of the book and offers some concluding thoughts.

A note on methodology

In addition to primary and secondary research material, this book is based on extensive qualitative interviews conducted in Haiti with government officials, national NGOs, civil society, politicians, business representatives, INGOs, UN staff and other international and national stakeholders at different times in the period 1996–2015. In-person and telephone interviews were also conducted with UNDPKO staff in New York in the same period.

Notes

1 Report of the Secretary-General, 'An Agenda for Peace', A/47/277, 17 June 1992. General Assembly and Security Council, 'Report of the Panel on United Nations Peace Operations', A/55/305-S/2000/809, 21 August 2000. Report of the Secretary-General, 'The rule of law and transitional justice in conflict and post-conflict societies', S/616/2004, 23 August 2004. Report of the Secretary-General, 'The rule of law and transitional justice in conflict and post-conflict societies', S/2011/634, 12 October 2011. Report of the Secretary-General, 'Securing peace and development: the role of the United Nations in supporting security sector reform', A/62/659-S/2008/39, 23 January 2008. Report of the Secretary-General, 'Securing states and societies: Strengthening the UN's comprehensive support to SSR', A/67/970-S/2013/480, 13 August 2013. Security Council Resolution, 'The maintenance of international peace and security: SSR challenges and opportunities', S/RES/2151, 28 April 2014. There have been regular Secretary-General's reports on POC the first: Report of the Secretary-General, 'The protection of civilians in armed conflict', S/1999/957, 8 September 1999 to the current last Report of the Secretary-General, 'The protection of civilians in armed conflict', S/2015/453, 18 June 2015. Report of the Secretary-General, 'Peacebuilding in the immediate aftermath of conflict', A/63/881-S/2009/304, 11 June 2009. UNDPKO, UN Peacekeeping Operations, Principles and Guidelines (Capstone Doctrine), 2008. 'Civilian Capacity in the aftermath of Conflict: independent report of the Senior advisory Group', March 2011. The report of the high-level independent panel on UN peace operations, 'Uniting our strengths for peace – politics, partnership and people' 16 June 2015 (Hippo) was also developed during this time, but due to the timeframe discussed in this book is of lesser relevance. Stabilisation is also a term that came to be developed and increasingly promoted, particularly by the US and the UK in this time period. The UN has authorised several stabilisation missions including in CAR, DRC, Mali and Haiti. Yet the term 'stabilisation' has never been clearly defined or agreed upon by the UN. Stability and security are the terms used in resolutions, even if the missions are called stabilisation missions.

12 *UN peace operations*

2 Capstone Doctrine, 2008, p.53.
3 Statement of the President of the Security Council, S/PRST/2005/30, 12 July 2005.
4 Report of the Secretary-General, 'Securing peace and development: the role of the United Nations in supporting security sector reform' A/62/659-S/2008/39, 23 January 2008. Report of the Secretary-General, 'Securing states and societies: Strengthening the UN's comprehensive support to SSR.' A/67/970-S/2013/480, 13 August 2013. Security Council Resolution, 'The maintenance of international peace and security: SSR challenges and opportunities', S/RES/2151, 28 April 2014. The Secretary-General established an Inter-Agency SSR Task Force that is co-chaired by DPKO and UNDP with representation from 14 UN entities engaged in SSR. The goal of the Task Force is to enhance UN capacity to deliver more effective support to national SSR efforts. 'Delivering as one UN', <http://www.un.org/en/peacekeeping/issues/security.shtml> (accessed 5 April 2016).
5 OECD DAC Handbook on Security System Reform, Supporting Security and Justice, 2007. Note that the discourse on SSR frequently refers to transformation or security sector development. This book will use security sector reform; or refer to police reform, justice reform etc. This is because the UN uses the concept of SSR and not transformation or security sector development.
6 See list of missions in Appendix A.
7 See also J.-M. Guehenno, *The fog of peace, a memoir of international peacekeeping in the 21st century*, Washington DC: Brookings Institution Press, 2015, p. 225.
8 Secretary-General Report on the Rule of Law and Transitional Justice in Conflict and Post-Conflict Societies, UN Doc. S/2004/616/ 3 August 2004, para.17. Local ownership was also significantly underlined in the Presidential Statement, 'Security Council stresses importance, urgency of restoring rule of law in post-conflict societies', Security Council 5052nd Meeting, SC/8209, Press Release, 6 October 2004. For academic discourse on local ownership see e.g. T. Donais (ed.), Local Ownership and Security Sector Reform, Hamburg: Lit Verlag, 2008; L. Nathan, No Ownership, No Commitment: A Guide to Local Ownership of Security Sector Reform, University of Birmingham, Birmingham 2007.
9 UN Secretary-General's Report on SSR, A/62/659-S/2008/39 23 January 2008, para.36.
10 OCHA Situation Report no. 15, *Haiti Socio-Political Crisis*, 24 June 2004, paras. 8–11.
11 *Interim Cooperation Framework*, July 2004, paras.54–66. However, the Framework was initially criticised because of its slow implementation and limited civil society participation. See e.g. Oxfam report, 'Mid-term reflections on the Interim Cooperation Framework', July 2005, p.3. For other lessons see also L. Campeau, 'Haiti: Lessons from the ICF from 2004–06 and extended and revised ICF from 2006 onwards', Worldbank, Sourcebook, second edition, 2009.
12 See e.g. SG report, S/2012/128, 29 February 2012, para.46, and SG report, S/2013/139, 8 March 2013, para.50.
13 For example appointing US President Bill Clinton as Special Envoy of the UN Secretary-General, as well the involvement of Peter Collier, Jeffery Sachs and George Soros.
14 The term 'police force' as opposed to 'police service' is purposefully used throughout – the aim was to establish a service, but although improved at the time of writing, the police still constituted a force rather than a service.
15 The term prison and prison reform is used throughout; the more commonly used term is corrections and correctional reform, however during the time in question there were no correctional facilities in Haiti – they were and continue to be prisons. Penal and prison reform is used interchangeably.

Bibliography

Campeau, L., 'Haiti: Lessons from the ICF from 2004–06 and extended and revised ICF from 2006 onwards', Worldbank, Sourcebook, second edition, 2009.

Donais, T. (ed.), *Local Ownership and Security Sector Reform*, Hamburg: Lit Verlag, 2008.

General Assembly and Security Council, 'Report of the Panel on United Nations Peace Operations', A/55/305-S/2000/809, 21 August 2000.

Guehenno, J.-M., *The Fog of Peace, A Memoir of International Peacekeeping in the 21st Century,* Washington DC: Brookings Institution Press, 2015.

High Level Independent Panel on Peace Operations, 'Uniting our strengths for peace – politics, partnership and people' 16 June 2015.

Interim Cooperation Framework, Republic of Haiti, Interim Cooperation Framework, 2004–2006, Summary Report, July 2004.

Nathan, L., 'No ownership, no commitment: A guide to local ownership of security sector reform', University of Birmingham, Birmingham 2007.

OCHA (Office for the Coordination of Humanitarian Affairs) Situation Report no. 15, *Haiti Socio-Political Crisis*, 24 June 2004.

OECD DAC *Handbook on Security System Reform, Supporting Security and Justice*, 2007.

Oxfam, 'Mid-term reflections on the Interim Cooperation Framework', July 2005.

President of the Security Council, Statement, S/PRST/2005/30, 12 July 2005.

Security Council 5052nd Meeting, SC/8209, Press Release, 6 October 2004.

Security Council Resolution, 'The maintenance of international peace and security: SSR challenges and opportunities', S/RES/2151, 28 April 2014.

Security Sector Reform, 'Delivering as one UN', n.d. <http://www.un.org/en/peacekeeping/issues/security.shtml> (accessed 5 April 2016).

Senior Advisory Group, 'Civilian capacity in the aftermath of conflict', March 2011.

SG report, 'An agenda for peace', A/47/277, 17 June 1992.

SG report, 'The protection of civilians in armed conflict', S/1999/957, 8 September 1999.

SG report, 'The rule of law and transitional justice in conflict and post-conflict societies', S/616/2004, 23 August 2004.

SG report, 'Securing peace and development: the role of the United Nations in supporting security sector reform' A/62/659-S/2008/39, 23 January 2008.

SG report, 'Peacebuilding in the immediate aftermath of conflict', A/63/881-S/2009/304, 11 June 2009.

SG report, 'The rule of law and transitional justice in conflict and post-conflict societies', S/2011/634, 12 October 2011.

SG report, 'Securing states and societies: Strengthening the UN's comprehensive support to SSR.' A/67/970-S/2013/480, 13 August 2013.

SG report, 'The protection of civilians in armed conflict', S/2015/453, 18 June 2015.

UNDPKO, UN Peacekeeping Operations, Principles and Guidelines (Capstone Doctrine), 2008.

2 The Haitian backdrop

Haitian history has been characterised by authoritarianism, external influences in domestic affairs, politicised armed forces, social and economic divides, and economic under-development and poverty. Haiti's history and its legacies played a noteworthy part in the country's situation after 1994 and what led to the establishment of so many UN peace operations. It is, therefore, essential to consider it, before dwelling on the operations themselves. This is by no means intended as an in-depth analysis of Haitian history, but a brief look at central factors which continued to have an impact upon Haitian society at the time of both interventions.[1]

This chapter focuses on factors which affected the implementation of the UN mandates: the history of authoritarianism and the fact that there had never been a democratically elected government until 1991; the development of social and economic differences and how this put in place a system that strongly influenced politics, conflict and violence; the role of the armed forces in governance; and the crosscutting issue of international involvement and influence, particularly the role of the US. Historically, international influences, for better or worse, have always been an essential part of Haiti's political processes. These variables are not presented as explanatory factors for the failings in governance and democratisation at various times, problems with an inefficient police force, or issues within the judicial system. They were however among the influencing elements on UN programmes and support, and impeded UN progress at times. This chapter also provides an overview of the contexts at the times of deployment of the UN missions (1994 and 2004), including the economic situation.

A history of authoritarianism

The French acquisition of Saint-Domingue in 1697 was to be the beginning of a trend of brutality in Haiti, through their introduction of a ruthless system of slavery. In 1791 the slaves revolted, and after thirteen years the Napoleonic forces were defeated and independence was declared on 1 January 1804 by Jean-Jacques Dessalines.[2] Victory came at great cost. Agriculture was destroyed and an estimated one third of the population had perished. Haiti was also forced to pay 150 million francs in indemnity to France.[3]

Not long after independence a civil war erupted, and Haiti split into a southern republic and a northern state. In 1820 Haiti was united under General Jean-Pierre Boyer, who was not ousted until 1843. After Boyer, and until the American intervention in 1915, there was a string of generals none of whom lasted very long, or made much of a difference in alleviating the misery of the people of Haiti.[4]

The American occupation

The American occupation of Haiti began on 25 July 1915 and lasted for nineteen years. It was precipitated by the decapitation of President Vilbrun Guillaume Sam,[5] who had declared himself President and led an abusive regime.[6] The occupation had few but vital effects upon Haiti's political, military and economic structure, effects which were still visible at the end of the 1990s. Some features introduced by the French were reinforced during the occupation, and others, obliterated by the revolution in 1804, were reinstated. Changes were introduced, which created an everlasting impact on the development of the country. There were three key legacies: the occupation reinstated the power of the elite,[7] reinforcing social and economic divisions; centralised political and economic power in the capital, entrenching a rural/urban divide; and established the Gendarmerie.

Limiting, if not eradicating, the political power of the elite had been an objective after independence. But the occupation reinstated their power. This deepened old social, political and economic divisions. It gave the educated elite greater political and economic power and ensured that they held public office. Closely tied to this, and also reinforcing divisions, was the reconstitution of an old corvee law, a labour law by the Marines. This law constituted forced labour, where men were compelled to work to improve the road network. This was perceived as restoring slavery.[8] It sparked a revolt, the Caco War,[9] which lasted from 1918 to 1922.[10]

Another outcome of the occupation was the centralisation and control of all political and economic power in Port-au-Prince. This reinforced the strong division between urban and rural areas, effectively creating 'two republics'. Subsequent governments reinforced this centralisation. This alienated the majority of the population not only from all decision-making processes, but also from knowing about them. Lastly the occupation established the Gendarmerie with the purpose of making it a non-politicised force. However, its structure and the military departments established with it served as an effective control mechanism for the political system.[11]

Post-occupation – a string of dictatorships

The period from 1934 to the ousting of Jean-Claude Duvalier in 1986 can be divided into three: 1934–1957 an era of great unrest, numerous presidents and the army as the unprecedented power holder; 1957–1971 François Duvalier's presidency, which ended with his death; and 1971–1986 Jean-Claude Duvalier's rule. Throughout all periods what has been termed *la politique de class et colour* was central.

In the period from 1934 until François Duvalier's (Papa Doc) rule there were four presidents. Stenio Vincent had come to power during the occupation, and represented the power of the elite that the occupation had reinstated. He was followed by Elie Lescot who further increased division through, for example, conducting a campaign to eradicate vodoun.[12] He also created discord within the army.[13] Subsequently Dumarsais Estimé came to power, and with him Noirisme was introduced into government – an ideology promoting black supremacy.[14] He promoted black people into government and civil service, among them François Duvalier. Colonel Paul Magloire led a coup against Estimé and ruled from 1950 to 1956. Following a well-established pattern, Magloire attempted to hold on to power, but was unsuccessful. Magloire promoted the elite's interests, but an elite led by a black president. This became known as *la politique de doublur*,[15] a black puppet president with the mulatto elite holding the strings. In the following period Haiti had five governments in six months. Elections were held and Duvalier was elected on 22 September 1957.[16] The validity of his election has been disputed.[17] Duvalier had the support of the army, and the army was at the time supreme 'kingmaker'.

Duvalier's regime was characterised by torture, corruption and murder. With extreme brutality, he set about minimising all types of opposition. He reduced the political power of the military so they could no longer control or 'elect' Presidents; and he established the *Tonton Macoutes*[18] under his direct control to ensure the armed forces could not challenge his presidency. All groups that could be perceived to threaten his power had their own power reduced or eradicated.[19] After only seven months in office all of Duvalier's opponents were driven underground or into exile.[20] This policy of terror and political killings continued throughout his regime.[21] Duvalier declared himself president for life in 1964 and changed the constitution so that his son could inherit the presidency. Duvalier and his regime were throughout his time in office supported by the US.

The brutal years of corruption, torture and murder did not come to an end with Duvalier's demise. Jean-Claude Duvalier (Baby Doc) came to power in 1971, at nineteen years old. His presidency was approved by 2,391,916 votes to 1. He held numerous mock elections and referenda, which were deemed positive steps by the US State Department.[22] Corruption grew to incredible new heights during his regime, as did dissent. It was a popular rebellion that drove Baby Doc out of Haiti, although his ouster was greatly assisted by the fact that the US finally withdrew its support for the regime.[23] By 1986, it was clear that Jean-Claude could no longer hold on to power and he went into exile. A troubled era for Haiti had ended and another began.

A step towards change?

A new junta, *Conseil National de Gouvernement* (CNG), led by General Henri Namphy, seized power. The CNG consisted primarily of old Duvalierists. Namphy had survived two Duvalier regimes and had risen in rank. The Haitian people, therefore, severely doubted his democratic aspirations. The US government backed the CNG.[24]

It was, nonetheless, during this period that the first steps towards democratisation began. For example, a new constitution was written, unprecedented in its liberalism. It stated that a Civilian Electoral Council (CEP) should plan and execute all elections, and that the 'zealous partisans of the Duvalier regimes' were barred from elections for ten years.[25] The constitution separated the police from the army, and stated that civilian courts could try soldiers for criminal offences.[26] It also reduced the powers of the presidency.[27] A referendum on the constitution was held. The turnout was around 50 per cent and 98 per cent voted in favour it.[28] Naturally the CNG and the army were against such a liberal constitution, which limited their power; and as a result the first careful steps towards democracy were abruptly halted.

The CEP was dissolved in summer 1987 and the scheduled elections were cancelled after a massacre at the polling booths, reportedly killing 34 people.[29] During this period the CNG was severely repressive, killings and assassinations happening with some regularity.[30] Although aid was suspended after the election-day massacre, the US administration continued to work with the regime, providing aid and military equipment.[31] This created hostile anti-American feelings in the Haitian population. The US was seen as the only reason why the CNG was able to hold on to power.[32]

A presidential election was held on 17 January 1988 and Leslie Manigat was elected president, with 450,000 voters and 1,062,016 votes cast.[33] This was a Duvalieresque election and Manigat was more selected than elected. Nevertheless, Manigat turned out to be less the army's man than Namphy must have expected. He challenged the army and tried to make reforms.[34] He consequently only lasted for 19 weeks; with Duvalier gone the army once again turned into 'kingmaker'. Without a strong president there was no one to control the army, which had dramatic consequences. Namphy declared himself president, dissolved the National Assembly and proclaimed the constitution invalid.[35] He emphasised that the constitution had introduced 'elements that are foreign to Haiti's history and traditions'.[36] Violence grew out of all proportions and, according to one source, the CNG killed more Haitians in a year of government than Baby Doc had done during 15 years in power.[37]

During CNG's rule Jean-Bertrand Aristide became the leader of the grassroots and Lavalas[38] and a symbol of the opposition to the military regime. He was working within *Ti Legliz* (little church), which was a base of opposition. He attacked Duvalierism and *macoutism* as well as the elite, the US and the Catholic Church hierarchy.[39] Namphy, who continued his policies of terror unabated, went too far by instigating a massacre in St Jean Bosco, Aristide's church, in September. As a result he was ousted from power by a group of enlisted soldiers.[40] To replace Namphy, these soldiers turned to Prosper Avril, a true Duvalierist, who had risen in power during the Duvalier regimes.[41] This change of leader, therefore, did not change the policies pursued. On the contrary the human rights abuses steadily increased.[42] The situation was critical and volatile, but once again the regime went too far. A popular revolt erupted and the US put pressure on Avril to resign, which he did in March 1990.

An interim government was set up with Ertha Pascal-Trouillot as the interim president. Violence did not subside during her administration.[43] Nevertheless, elections were organised and finally held on 16 December 1990. Aristide won the elections with 67.7 per cent of the vote and was inaugurated on 7 February 1991. He was the first ever democratically elected president of Haiti – a new era had begun.

Social and economic divides: class, colour and caste by another name

In Haiti there have always been very sharp divisions between the economic and political elites and the vast majority of disenfranchised and marginalised poor. This is based on a mix of socio-economic differences, but is also related to that of colour. It is important to note that colour is not only about skin tone, but differences in culture, religious beliefs and access to education, jobs and money. Colour in Haiti is a relative concept and refers as much to education, property ownership and money as to the colour of the skin. Historically the French slave system created a separate caste, an economic elite, which established a structure – a disenfranchised majority versus that elite – that was reinforced at different times. Although it has its background in French colonialism, it is predominately based on economic structures. This structure was still there when Aristide was elected.

Laying the foundations

The bases for the divisions in Haitian society can be traced back to colonial times and the structures that the French put in place. The colony conducted extreme abuses of the slaves.[44] The turnover was immense, which was viewed as more profitable. It was cheaper 'to buy than to breed'.[45] The consequence of this was that the people of Haiti retained beliefs, language and culture from Africa.[46] It also meant that at the time of independence in 1804, half of the Haitian slaves were African born.[47] This would prove to be an important aspect in the development of Haiti.

The French treatment of slaves in Haiti is important because they left behind a class, caste and colour structure that continued to exist and was refined throughout the years. The French, moreover, left a system where military chieftains had near unbridled power.[48] This authoritarian military power and with it extensive corruption, were the two other features of the colony, which became entrenched in Haitian society.[49] In the 1990s this structure still permeated Haitian society, politics and economics.

It began with the French fathering children with African slaves. These fathers frequently acknowledged their offspring, provided them with an education and allowed them to inherit.[50] They evolved into a class that was above the slaves but below the *blancs* (whites) in status and position.[51] They were sometimes wealthier and had more education than a poor *blanc*, but they were still an 'undercaste'. The castes could be divided into three: *blancs*, *affranchis/anciens libre* and slaves.[52] Generally the *anciens libre* would be mulatto and the slaves black, although blacks could be found among the *affranchis* and vice versa.[53] Social distinctions generally followed colour, but not entirely, as it was possible to have blacks and mulattos in both groups.[54] The *affranchis* should have enjoyed the same legal rights as the *blancs*, yet they did not. They were excluded from numerous professions, they did not have the same civil liberties and they were not legally equal to a *blanc*.[55] They acquired wealth and possessions, but they lacked status and position.

There was a deep division between the *affranchis* and the blacks. The *affranchis* kept slaves and embraced France culturally. The *affranchis* did not support slave revolt, but supported revolt to acquire their own rights vis-à-vis the *blancs*.[56] The *affranchis* became a caste that culturally identified itself with France, but opposed the French because they deprived them of their rights. This disabled them from identifying with or seeking support in either group. However, it was the cooperation between the *affranchis* and the slaves that led to independence.[57]

Class, colour and caste reinforced each other, but not completely.[58] There were two important divisions: white versus non-white, and slave versus free.[59] Among the whites there were also distinctions: *grands blancs*, *petits blancs*, *blancs manants*, and within this distinction a difference between those who had been born in France and those born in the colony.[60] With the abolition of slavery in 1793, the caste system legally ended. However, a distinction between *anciens libre* (former *affranchis*) and *nouveaux libre* (liberated slaves) evolved and coincided more often than not with that of class.[61] This was a complex structure with numerous conflicts and differing interests embedded within it. It was not simply a distinction of colour, but something much more complex.

Post-independence – continued schisms

After independence the constitution reflected the importance of these divides (and initially a wish to abolish them). It stated that regardless of colour all Haitians were to be called 'black', including the German and Polish groups living on the island. It exemplifies the complexity of the concept of colour as used as a distinction in Haitian society. The significance of the constitution arose from another article. It stated that no white man could acquire or own property in Haiti. This made Haiti's foreign relations exceedingly difficult. The constitution provided a symbol of the difference between Haitians and the former colonial power.

It was also fundamental in the civil war, which was as much about class, cast and colour as it was about power. The south was considered mainly mulatto and governed by the mulatto General Alexandre Pétion, the north was predominantly black and was ruled by the black Henry Christophe. During Boyer's rule the class/caste/colour distinctions became ever more important and the differences were increasingly emphasised by the influential families.[62] The distinctions grew particularly because Boyer's regime concentrated wealth and power in the hands of the mulattos.[63]

These class, caste and colour divisions were also reinforced during the American occupation. For a while the occupation inspired unity between the elite and the rural peasants in a fight against the occupation, albeit only on the surface.[64] The American occupation restored the mulatto elite to power and into office. This reinforced and deepened the old lines of division. The new constitution, which once again allowed whites to own Haitian property, solidified these boundaries in Haitian society. From these strengthened lines of division grew Noirisme. It was initially a response to the monopoly of political and economic power of the mulatto elites. However, it became a radical ideology promoting black supremacy.

A strong proponent of Noirisme was François Duvalier, who, in time, would use it in his own politics during his dictatorship. He developed his thoughts on Noirisme during the American occupation. Haiti had, since the French, been a divided society and continued to be so after the revolution, but the occupation served to reinforce this, which would continue to dominate the social and political scene of Haiti in the subsequent years.

When Duvalier came to power he put his theories on Noirisme into practice. The mulatto elite's power in politics became, therefore, nearly completely eradicated during his time in power. The situation changed when Jean-Claude became president. Papa Doc had been destroying the elite, whereas Jean-Claude married into it.[65] With his marriage into an 'elite' family, the situation of power in relation to colour and class again changed in Haiti. The traditional elite regained political power.

With Aristide this changed yet again. He was perceived to threaten the elite's powerbase and his electoral victory frightened the elite. He emphasised equality, justice and participation.[66] His inaugural speech did not alleviate this fear, but alarmed the elite even further, since it was delivered in Creole and directed to the poor.[67] However, Aristide selected half his cabinet and several key advisers from the elite. This was perhaps an attempt to calm fears, although in so doing he agitated members of the traditional political parties, who were passed over and who had assisted him in his election campaign.[68] But the elite were not appeased by this act. They feared the change and what it might bring. As Dupuy argues: 'For most of its history, the Haitian bourgeoisie has been a visionless, retrograde social class concerned primarily with safeguarding its immediate wealth and privileges.'[69] Aristide was seen to threaten those privileges and not only rhetorically. His government fired a large number of public employees and began collecting taxes.[70] The threat became real.

The armed forces – a history of political interference and control

Politics and the military had always been closely intertwined in Haiti and the US occupation aimed to change that. The Marines set about changing the army and creating a new force. The policy was to create a smaller, but more efficient force with no political involvement.[71] This policy nearly destroyed the old army and created a centralised structure.[72] Yet, it was unable to reach the objective of a non-political force. To the contrary, in many ways the Marines laid the foundations for a politicised force. The president of Haiti took his orders directly from the leadership of the Marines, and during the period of Haitisation and gradual pull-out, this task was given to the Haitian army.[73] Instead of ensuring a non-politicised army, the military and politics became strongly entangled during the occupation and served to strengthen the link between army and politics instead of severing it.

The restructured force, the Gendarmerie (later named Garde d'Haiti), was used as a means of control. To simplify this task, the Marines divided Haiti into three departments to which a fourth was added in 1922. With the creation of these departments, it was possible for the Gendarmerie to have military presence throughout the country and to enforce strict arms control laws, minimising the possibility of rural revolt. While restructuring the army, the Marines also replaced the police structure. A system was created in which the army began effectively to serve as both army and police force.[74]

The lasting effects of the American occupation of Haiti were, first and foremost, enshrined in the army structure they left behind. It was an army that was to become 'kingmaker' in Haitian politics and change the face of Haitian politics for the rest of the century. It expanded into civilian spheres of interest and developed into a bureaucratic institution.[75] It made and ousted presidents at will. It ran Haitian political life. A president needed the support of the army to come to power and its continued support to stay there. The occupation created an army that became 'a political instrument that would in the future make and break presidents until Duvalier found a way to subordinate it to his will'.[76] The structure was so strong that even after Duvalier, it once more arose as 'kingmaker'. The army, it seemed, had been forever politicised. Moreover, the military departments established during the occupation were used by the Duvalier regimes to control the population, as they had been during the American occupation. There was no change in the structure of the police–army relationship after the occupation. Effectively, the army was still the only police force in Haiti until 1994. This was highly significant for the development of Haitian society as it left the army in complete control over the rule of law.

The ability of the army to completely control Haitian political life changed with Duvalier. He used the structures put in place by the French and reinforced by the US occupation, such as the *chefs de sections* and the military departments, which made control over the countryside easier. In addition, his establishment of the *Tontons Macoutes*,[77] as his own personal force, ensured control. This force, due to its structure with Duvalier in direct control, and its application 'attributed greatly to the disintegration of the army'.[78] Duvalier began to withdraw power from the army and he succeeded, partially by giving the presidential guard status as a military department, and storing an army arsenal in the palace.[79] This served as a counterweight to the other military departments and reduced significantly the possibility of armed revolt by the army. To root out any possibility of army betrayal he closed down the military academy in 1961. Duvalier had succeeded in 'unmaking' the Haitian army and controlled his forces by divide and rule. The army, once the 'kingmaker' (and indeed the maker of Duvalier), was allocated a more passive role. A new force had been created, which could not be controlled by the army or by anyone except Duvalier. The legacy of this change left its imprint on Haitian life.

As his father had been frightened of the power of the army and created the *Tontons Macoutes*, Jean-Claude Duvalier was frightened of the *Tonton Macoutes*. The *macoutes* despised Baby Doc and viewed him as a traitor due to his marriage into the elite.[80] To counter-balance the power of the *Tontons Macoutes*, he reopened the military academy, increased the power of the army and created a new counter-insurgency force, trained by the US, called the Leopards.

Acutely aware of the power of the military, when Aristide took office he retired the entire high command, set about dividing the army and the police and abolished the dreaded *chefs de section*.[81] Fighting corruption, drug trafficking and human rights abuses conducted by the military were in focus. Commissions to investigate massacres were established and several people arrested.[82] This set the army against him to such an extent that it was felt necessary for him to create a personal guard of civilians to stand between him and the army.[83] The army, which had had their powers renewed under Baby Doc, did not appreciate the rapid de-escalation of their importance, resulting in the ultimate consequence – another coup.

Another coup

The coup in September 1991 must be viewed in the context of a history of authoritarianism, social and economic divides and the role of the military in making and breaking Haitian presidents. President Aristide was ousted after only seven months in power. The military regime, led by Raoul Cédras, was exceptionally brutal towards Aristide supporters and conducted vast human rights abuses. The coup d'état violently put an end to the democratic aspirations of the Haitian population. The army and elite had similar goals in Haiti. The military wanted to maintain their position and power which had been threatened by the new government, and the elite wanted to retain their political and economic power in Haitian society.

It is estimated that 3,000 to 5,000 died as direct result of the military regime from 1991 to 1994. These were all civilians. The repression of the population was intense and was conducted throughout the country, but it was especially bad in the major urban centres.[84] The *chefs de section* who had been abolished under Aristide were reinstated. The army was supported by the paramilitary group *Front pour l'Avancement et le Progrès d'Haiti* (FRAPH) and *attachés* (armed gangs affiliated with the army) to suppress opposition. In the first few months over 100,000 fled across the border to the Dominican Republic.[85] By April 1992 the American coast guard had intercepted 20,000 refugees from Haiti. At the end of 1992 US intelligence estimated that 100,000 were about to take to the sea.[86] The international community was swift in condemning the coup, but action was slow.

Governor's Island and Port-au-Prince agreements

In July 1993 the international community enforced oil and arms embargoes, forcing Cédras to the negotiating table.[87] The result of these negotiations was the Governor's Island agreement.[88] The agreement included the nomination and confirmation of a Prime Minister, suspension of sanctions, assistance by the international community, an amnesty for the junta, the return to Haiti of Aristide and 'modernisation' of the Haitian Armed Forces. Sanctions were to be suspended immediately after the Prime Minister was confirmed and had assumed office.[89] Parts of the agreement were implemented, including Aristide's nomination of a new Prime Minister, as this was tied to the lifting of sanctions. After the agreement was concluded there was renewed violence by the army, and one of the largest massacres by the regime of the civilian population was conducted: the Rabouteau massacre in Gonaives.[90]

On 11 October 1993 the USS Harlan County attempted to dock at Port-au-Prince. It was filled with US troops and international observers, who, in accordance with UN Security Council Resolution 867, were to establish the UN Mission in Haiti (UNMIH). It was hindered from docking by a group of *attachés* and supporters of FRAPH.[91] The sanctions were immediately reinstated and new ones enforced. The International Civilian Mission in Haiti (MICIVIH) reported an increase of violence during the period that followed the Harlan County incident.[92] The targets were Aristide supporters and the MICIVIH concluded that the guilty parties were members of FRAPH, *attachés* with support of the army or members of the armed forces.[93]

By 15 September 1994, it was evident that all other means had been exhausted and that an intervention was imminent. As international forces were on their way to Haiti, Cédras signed the Port-au-Prince agreement with a US delegation led by former US president Jimmy Carter. According to a source close to Cédras, he wanted the intervention as much as Aristide did.[94] The agreement gave de facto amnesties to the military junta and meant that the intervention could be conducted without loss of lives. But contrary to the amnesties stipulated in the Governor's Island agreement, the Port-au-Prince agreement only referred diffusely to 'certain military officers'.[95] None of these were mentioned by name. It could be interpreted to mean all the military officers connected with the coup. It was a very contentious document as the elected government of Haiti was not party to it.

The Port-au-Prince agreement affected the situation in the country thereafter. The return of Aristide and the elected government was not referred to in the agreement. It stipulated that the Haitian army would work in 'close cooperation' with the US military mission to implement the agreement, which was to promote 'freedom and democracy'.[96] It also emphasised that the US mission would be coordinating with the Haitian military high command.[97] The intervention rhetoric before the agreement was emphasising the legality of the intervention based on the illegality of the de facto regime and the protection of democracy. This created problems on the ground for the US forces; because of the agreement foe had become friend overnight. UN Security Council Resolution 940, which gave the mandate for intervention, referred to the implementation of the Governor's Island agreement. These agreements, chiefly the Port-au-Prince agreement, as discussed in the following chapters, made mandate implementation more complicated.

At the time of the first UN mission, violence was clearly political and actors easily identified: the Forces Armées d'Haiti (FAd'H), *attachés*, the FRAPH and their supporters in the elite; and the supporters of Aristide – Lavalas. There were also divisions within the elite and these were predominately political – some of whom supported a democratic Haiti, others who worked vehemently against it. During the first period of UN peace operations this began to change.

Re-emerging authoritarianism

During the latter part of the 1990s the political landscape and the nature of the use violence began to change. *Famni Lavalas*, as well as other political and non-political groups, began to rely on young armed men to control the community – anything from providing security to ensuring that no other groups operated in those areas. After the departure of the last UN mission in 2001, political groups of all shades used the disenfranchised and poor youths to further their own agendas, and the relations between actors and armed gangs whose allegiance sometimes could be bought started to become murkier. In early 2004 the armed gangs included Aristide loyalists, former officials of the Lavalas government, unofficial pro-Aristide armed gangs, gangs who participated in the 1991 coup (including FRAPH members), former military officers, former police officers, former rural police (*chefs de section*), and non-political armed groups.[98] Most of these groups acted as law enforcers during 2004.

The period after 2000 was characterised by violence and instability.[99] There were regular demonstrations against Aristide and his government, as well as clashes between the opponents and supporters of Aristide. Some mayors and local authorities used illegal security forces instead of turning to the police. In November 2000 this problem was exacerbated when it was condoned by the central government. The Prime Minister had stated that these groups were illegal, but after the violence and bombs leading up to the presidential elections he called for vigilante groups to help to restore order.[100] These groups committed a notable number of human rights abuses.[101] Throughout 2003 there was increasing opposition to Aristide's regime and by late 2003 an opposition movement comprising political, private and civil society actors demanded his resignation. During this period the police turned increasingly political and there was an internal struggle within the force.

Violence in Haiti has changed over the years. Describing the violence as political violence reflecting the pro- and anti-Aristide factions is too simplistic. Haiti was never only a conflict of political factions fighting for power. Polarisation and the violence it has engendered in Haiti are multi-layered. The conflict was based on political and economic factors. The entrepreneurs of violence and their private economic interests were key in the conflict. These actors were both societal actors, that is armed gangs, including former armed forces, and also state actors, including corrupt security services, a president that used armed gangs for particular purposes, as well as corrupt government officials. The recruitment process to the different parties to the conflict varied, but can broadly be said to have been a combination of political support as well as financial in terms of payment for support and participation.

The violence in Haiti during 2000–04 was both criminal and political in nature. It is therefore difficult to estimate the number of causalities during this period that were a direct result of the political violence or what was a result of criminal armed violence. Data on deaths and injury in Haiti are scarce, the Ministry of Health lacks a functioning system for tracking and collection by civil society organisations is limited.[102]

Prior to 2004 the majority of the violence and instability had taken place in urban centres. The civilian population was affected since the majority of violence took place in urban areas and overcrowded slums. There were refugees to the

Dominican Republic, the US and the Bahamas; how many of these refugees were a direct result of the violence or because of the extreme poverty in Haiti is difficult to estimate. The United Nations High Commission for Refugees (UNHCR) states that the total refugee population from Haiti to the US, France and Canada in 2004 was 9,208, and there were 6,953 asylum applicants to the same countries in that period. In 2003 it was 7,547 and 5,061 respectively and in 2005 13,542 and 9,622. This does not include illegal non-registered refugees or the ones that were turned back and is therefore not an accurate overview of the refugee population.

The Caribbean Community (CARICOM) mediated between the parties and submitted a Prior Action Plan on 31 January 2004, which was followed by an implementation plan established by the Group of Six (Canada, France, US, EU, OAS, Bahamas). Several diplomatic initiatives taken by the Organisation of American States (OAS) and CARICOM followed. The peace plan which outlined a power-sharing agreement with Aristide, a new prime minister and legislative elections, was rejected outright by the rebels and opposition leaders who insisted on Aristide's departure. Aristide agreed to the peace plan, but insisted he would not step down until 2006. The US stated they would continue to press for the peace plan and held talks with the parties to gain acceptance for it. They were unsuccessful.

The political instability and insecurity that had continued to mar Haiti after the departure of the UN reached its peak in February 2004 when fighting broke out in Gonaives. Armed gangs, former soldiers and police seized the town and gradually took control over most of the north of the country until they were threatening to enter Port-au-Prince. President Aristide left the country on 29 February 2004. The circumstances surrounding Aristide's departure are disputed; Aristide argues he was forcibly removed while the US military claims he left voluntarily.[103] An interim president, Boniface Alexandre, was sworn in and a thirteen-member transitional government, led by Gerard Latortue, was formed – to be in power until free and fair elections could be held. A Consensus on the Political Transition Pact was signed by the transitional government, members of the *Conseil des Sages*, political groups and civil society organisations. *Fanmi Lavalas* denounced the pact. The UN Security Council authorised a Multinational Interim Force (MIF) to intervene, to be replaced by the UN Stabilisation Mission in Haiti (MINUSTAH) on 1 June 2004.

The context in which the new UN mission was deployed was therefore considerably different to the situation in 1994, the landscapes of politics and violence had changed substantially, with alliances fluctuating, and new actors entering the scene – the new UN mission entered a changed context of political and economic violence. It was a more complex environment where multi-dimensional peacebuilding was needed. As is established in the following chapters, some innovative strategies were put in place to address non-traditional peacekeeping conflict scenarios.

Economic destitution

Placing the peace operations within the broader context of the economic[104] situation in Haiti is critical as this is so closely linked with instability and insecurity, as well as with issues such as DDR, democratisation, police reform and justice. One of

26 *The Haitian backdrop*

the arguments throughout this book is that without a coherent approach to these issues placed firmly within a broader economic development framework they are hard pressed to succeed. Unfortunately programming in these areas is rarely, if ever, linked up with programming in the security and democratisation sectors. The economic situation at the start of both periods of peace operations in Haiti was dire; the paragraphs below highlight the economic situation in the country at the start of each period of peace operations (1994 and 2004), establishing that little progress had happened in the ten years between.

Haiti has been the poorest country in the western hemisphere for decades. In 1994, 70 per cent of Haitians were unemployed; the vast majority, over 70 per cent, lived in rural areas; in large parts the government was unable to provide basic services, and there were very few health care facilities, and poor access to education, sanitation, clean water and electricity. It was estimated that 70 to 80 per cent lived below the poverty line, surviving on less than US$2 per day.

The World Bank estimates that over the 1980–91 period real Gross National Product (GNP) per capita was falling by about 2 per cent per year. The economy went into even worse decline during the military regime, exacerbated by the US, OAS and UN sanctions. A period of economic stagnation followed the coup in September 1991. Economic growth rates turned negative and inflation soared. For example, GDP growth was at –8.3 per cent in 1994. Consumer prices grew at 39.3 per cent in 1993 and 10.9 per cent in 1994. The real minimum wage fell to 44.4 per cent of its 1990 level. By 1994 exports were down to 131 million dollars, affected by the trade embargo, which had severe consequences to unemployment levels. The World Bank estimates that, by May 1994, employment in the export-oriented assembly sector had fallen to 8,000 compared with 44,000 in September 1991. Construction and manufacturing were also severely affected: imports of manufactured articles fell by 50 per cent and imports of machinery and transport equipment fell by 71 per cent in the year following the coup. A similar situation prevailed in the agricultural sector. For example, output of coffee for exports was down to 21,000 tons in 1994 from 37,000 in 1991, output of bananas for domestic consumption decreased from 510,000 tons to 362,000 tons.

Five years after the 1994 intervention not much had improved when in 1999 the Gross Domestic Product (GDP) per capita was approximately US$250 compared with the average of US$3,320 for Latin America and the Caribbean region.[105]

In 2004, according to the World Food Programme, 76 per cent of Haitians lived on less than US$2 per day, and 55 per cent lived on less than US$1 per day.[106] Moreover, a small minority controlled the vast majority of the country's assets. This was compounded by an increase in population from an estimated 7.7 million in 1994 to 9.1 million in 2004 (10.7 million in 2015). The GDP per capita according to the World Bank in 2003 was an estimated US$400 and the human development index ranking was 150. There were extreme differences between the capital, other urban areas and rural areas; in the capital 20 per cent lived in extreme poverty, whilst in other urban areas this increased to 50 per cent and in the rural areas to 59 per cent.[107] Compared with the average Latin American and Caribbean (LAC) countries Haiti had a life expectancy in 2004 of 49.4 years, whilst in neighbouring countries in 2005 it was an average of 71.9. Infant mortality at birth (per 1,000) was 79 in 2004, whereas LAC had an average of 27 in 2005. The percentage of population that was undernourished was 49 per cent in 2004, whilst in LAC it was 10 per cent in 2005.[108] Haiti was in 2003–04, as in 1994 and in 2016, largely agrarian with two-thirds of the population subsistence farmers. This reality and thus poverty was compounded by Haiti's environmental degradation.

Haiti's environmental degradation is both a reflection of and a contribution to poverty. In 1925, 60 per cent of the island was covered by forest. By 2008 only 1.5 per cent remained.[109] A combination of factors contributed to the environmental degradation, but it is rooted in socio-economic pressures. Deforestation came about as a result of the high unemployment and little income. Making charcoal through cutting trees was a key way of earning a living and necessary for fuel. As a result of deforestation Haiti became much more vulnerable to tropical storms and hurricanes. It has also had a significant impact on agricultural production as the topsoil washed out into the rivers and seas, leaving poor soil for growth.

The most important donors in Haiti in these years have been the UN, the UNDP, the World Bank, the IMF, the Inter-American Development Bank (BID), the EU, the US and Canada. The US has consistently been the largest donor followed by Canada. Haiti's major trading partner is the US; other countries include Canada and Dominican Republic. The difference between exports and imports in Haiti has been persistently large, for example in 2006, according to US State Department data, exports were in total US$494.4 million and imports US$1,548.3 billion. The economy has for decades been effectively supported by considerable remittances from the Haitian diaspora, particularly in the US, France and Canada. For example, according to the World Bank remittances in 2002 were US$650 million, which had more than doubled from 1997 and represented 19 per cent of Haiti's GDP.[110] In 2006 according to BID estimates the Haitian diaspora sent more than US$1.65 billion to Haiti, representing one-third of the country's GNP.[111] The World Bank stated that there were US$1.07 billion recorded remittances to Haiti in 2006 – the equivalent of 21.6 per cent of GDP. But the World Bank acknowledged that the true size of remittances was larger.[112]

High unemployment and poor subsistence farming meant extreme poverty in many rural areas. This led to rapid urbanisation and migration to, in particular, Port-au-Prince. This contributed to instability in urban areas; 'the combination of high unemployment, rapid urbanisation and economic stagnation created an explosive social situation in Port-au-Prince'.[113] This in turn, as is explored in more depth in subsequent chapters, undermined security and stability, and affected UN efforts in all areas discussed in this book.

Conclusion

The historical legacies continued to mark contemporary Haiti at the start of and during both sets of peace operations. The legacies of authoritarianism, social and economic divides, and politicised security forces had left an imprint upon society that continued to shape it.

28 *The Haitian backdrop*

These legacies are not posited to be the sole reasons for failings in governance, security sector reform, democratisation or justice. Those failings, discussed throughout the book, rested on a number of interconnected variables, both internal and external to Haitian society. Therefore, this historical context is not suggested to provide a set of explanatory factors for all that ails contemporary Haiti. It did, however, have a significant impact upon Haitian society at the time of UN deployments. Thus any support in the sectors emphasised in this book needed to take this into consideration when planning for programming. It is within this context and history that international support took place, yet seemingly only the more recent historic events were given credence or heeded.

Subsequent chapters show that some flaws in programming had their origins in poor historic and contemporary knowledge. This insufficient knowledge can, for example, help to explain problems encountered with implementation of key mandated tasks, or wrongly mandated tasks, such as a classic approach to DDR. Many lessons were learnt and applied during the various UN missions in Haiti, whereas some were not. Any support and programming needs to be placed within the historic and contemporary context or the potential for failure increases.

Notes

1 For a timeline of Haitian history see Annex B.
2 Dessalines was a general under Toussaint Louverture, a leader of the Haitian independence movement, who died during the revolution.
3 It was later reduced to 90 million.
4 From independence until the American occupation there were 26 leaders of Haiti, in addition there were five provisional presidents during this time. For an overview of this period see: L. Paquin, *Les Haitiens, Politique de Classe et de Couleur*, Port-au-Prince: Imprimerie le Natal, 1988.
5 R. Prince, *Haiti Family Business*, Nottingham: Russell Press, Latin America Bureau, 1985, p.20. J.H. McCroklin, *Garde d'Haiti, Twenty Years of Organization and Training by the United States Marine Corps,* Annapolis: The US Naval Institute, 1956, p.16.
6 For example, he executed 167 political prisoners in the summer after taking power. McCrocklin, *Garde d'Haiti* p.15, E. Abbott, *Haiti, the Duvaliers and Their Legacy*, London: Robert Hale, 1991, p.33.
7 This is discussed more in detail in the section 'The armed forces' in this chapter.
8 R. Heinl & N. Heinl, *Written in Blood: The Story of the Haitian People 1492–1971*, Boston: Houghton Mifflin Company, 1978, pp.449–451.
9 Caco is a bird of prey and the rebellious groups adopted this name. The bird is recognisable by its red feathers, and the caco rebels wore a piece of red cloth to indicate that they were cacos. See McCrocklin, *Garde d'Haiti*, p.8.
10 One of the leaders of the revolt was Charlemagne Péralte. He was killed by the Marines. He became a symbol of the fight against the Marines, and was likened to the Christ figure because he was crucified. For an overview see: G. Michel, *Charlemagne Péralte*, Port-au-Prince: Le Natal, 1989. Before the occupation the cacos had more or less acted as bandits, assisting one president to power, then ousting him to support another who paid them. McCrocklin, *Garde d'Haiti*, p.7. The occupation changed this and they became guerrilla fighters. The estimated number of cacos killed during the revolt varies from 2,250 to 15,000, whereas the Marines and the Gendarmerie sustained 98 casualties. P. Farmer, *Aids and Accusation*, Berkeley: University of California Press, 1992, p.181. There also existed cacos of discourse, who did not use

The Haitian backdrop 29

violence, but who supported their aim and expressed it through speeches, literature and discussion. M.S. Laguerre, *The Military and Society in Haiti*, London: Macmillan, 1993, p.70.
11 See the section 'Another coup' for more details.
12 Abbott, *Haiti*, p.54.
13 Laguerre, *Military*, p.88.
14 M.R. Trouillot, *Haiti: State Against Nation: The Origins and Legacy of Duvalierism*, New York: Monthly Review Press, 1990, p.133.
15 A.P. Maingot, 'The political rot from within', *Current History*, vol.94, no.2 1995, p.60.
16 For a detailed account of Duvalier see: B. Diederich & A. Burt, *Papa Doc and the Tonton Macoutes*, Editions Henri Deschamps, 1986.
17 See e.g. Abbott, *Haiti*, p.75. P. Farmer, *The Uses of Haiti*, Maine: Common Courage Press, 1994, p.107.
18 A civilian militia officially called Volontaries de la Securité Nationale established by François Duvalier in 1959.
19 D. Nicholls *From Dessalines to Duvalier: Race, Colour and National Independence in Haiti*, London: Macmillan, 1996, p.212.
20 Diederich & Burt, *Papa Doc*, p.111.
21 Estimates have been as high as 50,000 killed during his time in power. Prince, *Family Business*, p.36.
22 P. Bellgarde-Smith, *Haiti. The Breached Citadel*, London: Westview Press, 1990, p.104.
23 Farmer, *Uses*, pp.124–125.
24 Ibid., p.127.
25 The Haitian Constitution, article 291, 1987.
26 Ibid. articles 263 and 267.3 respectively.
27 Ibid. Chapitre III, article 133, sections A & B.
28 G. Chamberlain, 'Up by the roots: Haitian history through 1987', in D. McFadyen (ed.), *Haiti: Dangerous Crossroads*, Boston: South End Press, 1995, p.21.
29 G.A. Fauriol (ed.), *The Haitian Challenge, US Policy Considerations*, Washington: Center for Strategic and International Studies, 1993, p.51. Another report stated 22 dead and 67 wounded. A. Dupuy, *Haiti in the New World Order, The Limits of the Democratic Revolution*, Oxford: Westview Press, 1997, p.57.
30 Farmer, *Uses*, p.139. For an overview of the abuses committed by this regime and the following regimes and of the justice situation until the elections of Aristide see, Lawyers Committee for Human Rights, The Americas, *Paper Laws, Steel Bayonets: Breakdown of the Rule of Law in Haiti*, November 1990.
31 W.I. Robinson, *Promoting Polyarchy. Globalization, US Intervention and Hegemony*, Cambridge: Cambridge University Press, 1996, p.281. Chamberlain, 'Roots', p.27.
32 Chamberlain, 'Roots', p.27.
33 Abbott, *Haiti*, p.365.
34 Chamberlain, 'An Interregnum. Haitian History from 1987 to 1990', in McFadyen (ed.) *Haiti*, p.36.
35 Farmer, *Uses*, p.145.
36 Dupuy, *Haiti*, p.59.
37 Farmer, *Uses*, p.129.
38 Lavalas is Creole for 'the flood', the name of the supporters of Aristide, later Aristide's political party.
39 Dupuy, *Haiti*, p.73.
40 Lawyers Committee, *Paper Laws*, p.7.
41 Chamberlain, 'Interregnum', p.37.
42 Lawyers Committee, *Paper Laws*, p.9.
43 Ibid.
44 For examples of abuse see M. Smartt Bell, *All Souls' Rising*, London: Granta Books, 1995.

The Haitian backdrop

45 P. Bellgarde-Smith, *Haiti. The Breached Citadel*, London: Westview Press, 1990, p.40.
46 Abbott, *Haiti*, p.11.
47 Bellgarde-Smith, *Haiti*, p.33.
48 Ibid. p.35.
49 R. Prince, *Haiti Family Business*, Nottingham: Russell Press, Latin America Bureau, 1985, pp.13–14.
50 S.W. Mintz, 'Can Haiti Change?', *Foreign Affairs*, vol.74, no.1, Jan/Feb, 1995, p.76.
51 The use of the word *blanc* later evolved to not only mean white but to encompass all foreigners regardless of colour.
52 Nicholls, *Dessalines*, p.20. *Affranchis* can be defined as 'freed people'. They consisted of mostly mulattoo and a few thousand blacks, they were also known as *gens de couleur*. Bellegarde-Smith, *Haiti*, pp.37–38.
53 Ibid.
54 There was an elaborate classification based on colour, which included over 200 combinations. Bellgarde-Smith, *Haiti*, p.38.
55 Abbott, *Haiti*, p.13.
56 Mintz, 'Can Haiti change?' p.77.
57 Bellgarde-Smith, *Haiti*, p.39.
58 D. Nicholls, *Haiti in Caribbean Context: Ethnicity, Economy and Revolt*, London: Macmillan, 1985, p.23.
59 Ibid., p.24.
60 Bellgarde-Smith, *Haiti*, p.36.
61 Nicholls, *Haiti*, p.24.
62 Nicholls, *Dessalines*, p.21.
63 Ibid., p.72.
64 Nicholls, *Dessalines*, p.163.
65 G. Chamberlain, 'Up by the Roots. Haitian History through 1987', in D. McFadyen (ed.), *Haiti: Dangerous Crossroads*, Boston: South End Press, 1995, p.15.
66 Ibid. p.202 and p.140.
67 Chamberlain, 'Haiti's Second Independence. Aristide's Seven Months in Office', in McFadyen (ed.), *Haiti*, p.52.
68 Ibid.
69 Dupuy, *Haiti*, p.122.
70 Ibid. p.119.
71 Nicholls, *Dessalines*, p.148.
72 Laguerre, *Military*, p.63.
73 Ibid., p.80.
74 Ibid., p.74.
75 Laguerre, *Military*, p.90.
76 Abbott, *Haiti*, p.47.
77 The estimated numbers of macoutes vary widely, Robinson states that there were 300,000 of them, who depended on the continuance of the Duvalier dictatorship, since they survived by terrorising and extorting money from the population. W.I. Robinson, *Promoting Polyarchy, Globalization, US Intervention and Hegemony*, Cambridge: Cambridge University Press, 1996, p.269. However Rotberg emphasises that it is doubtful if they ever numbered more than 10,000. R.I. Rotberg, *Haiti, The Politics of Squalor*, Boston: Houghton Mifflin, 1971, p.213.
78 Laguerre, *Military*, p.119.
79 Ibid., pp.108–111.
80 Ibid.
81 Farmer, *Uses*, pp.164–169. In fact many *chefs de section* operated as previously. Dupuy, *Haiti*, p.117.
82 Dupuy, *Haiti*, p.118.
83 Chamberlain, 'Haiti's', p.55.

84 For statistics on torture, abuse and killings see e.g., G. Danroc and D. Roussière, *La Répression au Quotidien en Haiti 1991–1994*, Port-au-Prince: H.S.I 1995, and Commission Nationale de Verité et de Justice, *Si M Pa Rele*. Port-au-Prince, 1995.
85 Farmer, 1994, *Uses*, p.190.
86 R.I. Perusse, *Haitian Democracy Restored 1991–1995*, London: University Press of America, 1995, pp.39–40.
87 Perusse, *Haitian*, p.47.
88 For a full text of the agreement see Governor's Island Agreement reprinted in Perusse, *Haitian*, pp.49–50.
89 Governor's Island agreement para.4. 13 days after the signing of the Governor's Island agreement, the New York Pact was agreed upon and signed. This pact reiterated the basics of the Governor's Island agreement, but included a political truce that was stipulated to last for six months. It also called for an end to repression practices and to establish a Compensation Commission for the victims of the coup. Report of the Secretary-General, *S/26397* 13 August 1993, para.1, para.2(c), (f) respectively. This pact was, as the Governor's Island agreement, not complied with by the junta.
90 This massacre took place in April 1994.
91 Perusse, *Haitian*, pp.56–57.
92 SG report, S/1994/1363, 30 November 1994.
93 Ibid.
94 Interview by author, Port-au-Prince, October 1997.
95 Port-au-Prince agreement, para.3.
96 Port-au-Prince agreement para.2 and para.1, respectively.
97 Ibid., para.4.
98 Amnesty International, 'Haiti: Armed Groups still active', Findings of Amnesty International Delegation, 8 April 2004.
99 For more detailed overview of the 2000–04 period see e.g. M. Deibert, *Notes From the Last Testament: The Struggle for Haiti*, 2005. R. Robinson, *An unbroken agony, Haiti from revolution to the kidnapping of a president*, New York: BasicCivitas, 2007. Amnesty International yearly reports and Human Rights Watch yearly reports. For human rights abuse in Haiti from 1957 to 2004 see also A.S. Thompson, 'Haiti's tenuous human rights climate', in Y. Shamsie and A.S. Thompson (eds), *Haiti hope for a fragile state*, Wilfrid Laurier University Press, 2006.
100 There was a wave of violence up the presidential elections in November 2000. Eleven bombs went off in Port-au-Prince, four bombs were disarmed the day before the elections. Several people were wounded and two children killed.
101 Amnesty International, Haiti, 8 April 2004.
102 See e.g. Oxfam, Haiti: Violence Impact Study, 2006.
103 Much has been written about Aristide's departure and how it came about; for this discussion see e.g. N. Chomsky, P. Farmer, & A. Goodman, *Getting Haiti right this time, the US and the coup*, Maine: Common Courage Press, 2004. R. Robinson, *An unbroken agony: Haiti from revolution to the kidnaping of a president*, New York: BasicCivitas books, 2007. R. Fatton Jr, 'Haiti's unending crisis of governance: food, the constitution and the struggle for power', in J. Heine and A.S. Thompson, *Fixing Haiti MINUSTAH and beyond*, Tokyo: UNU, 2011.
104 It must be noted that there are serious problems with national accounts in Haiti, including incomplete coverage and the questionable accuracy of raw data.
105 UN Report E/1999/103, 2 July 1999.
106 World Food Programme, <http://www.wfp.org/country_brief/indexcountry.asp?country=332#Facts%20&%20Figures> (accessed 15 July 2008).
107 Faubert, p.15.
108 Ibid. p.15.
109 S. Meharg and A. Arnusch, 'Security sector reform: A case study approach to transition and capacity-building', Strategic Studies Institute, January 2010, p.79.

110 P. Fagan, 'Remittances in Crisis – A Haiti Case Study', HPG-ODI Background Paper, April 2006.
111 BID, 'Remittances to Haiti topped $1.65 billion in 2006', Press Release, 5 March 2007. <http://www.iadb.org/news/articledetail.cfm?language=en&artid=3637> (accessed 8 January 2016). See also BID, Inter-American Development Bank Haiti Survey, <www.bendixenandassociates.com/studies/Public_Opinion_Survey_of_Remittances_to_Haiti.pdf> (accessed 8 January 2016).
112 World Bank, <siteresources.worldbank.org/INTPROSPECTS/Resources/334934-1199807908806/Haiti.pdf> (accessed 5 January 2016)
113 D. Verner and A. Heinemann, 'Social resilience and state fragility in Haiti, breaking the conflict-poverty trap', World Bank, *En Breve*, no.94, September 2006, p.2.

Bibliography

Abbott, E., *Haiti, the Duvaliers and Their Legacy*, London: Robert Hale, 1991.
Amnesty International, 'Haiti: Armed Groups still active', Findings of Amnesty International Delegation, 8 April 2004.
Bellgarde-Smith, P., *Haiti. The Breached Citadel*, London: Westview Press, 1990.
Chomsky, N., *Year 501. The Conquest Continues*, London: Verso, 1995.
Chomsky, N., Farmer, P. and Goodman, A., *Getting Haiti right this time, the US and the coup*, Monroe, ME: Common Courage Press, 2004.
Commission Nationale de Verité et de Justice, *Si M Pa Rele*, Port-au-Prince: CNVJ, 1995.
Coordination Europe-Haïti, 'Haiti's Poverty Reduction Strategy Paper (PRSP) process and the limited participation of civil society', 13 November 2007.
Danroc, G., and Roussière, D., *La Répression au Quotidien en Haiti 1991–1994*, Port-au-Prince: H.S.I, 1995.
Deibert, M., *Notes From the Last Testament: The Struggle for Haiti*, New York: Seven Stories Press, 2005.
Diederich, B. and Burt, A., *Papa Doc and the Tonton Macoutes*, Port-au-Prince: Editions Henri Deschamps, 1986.
Dupuy, A., *Haiti in the New World Order, The Limits of the Democratic Revolution*, Oxford: Westview Press, 1997.
Fagan, P., 'Remittances in crisis – A Haiti case study', HPG-ODI Background Paper, April 2006.
Farmer, P., *Aids and Accusation*, Berkeley, CA: University of California Press, 1992.
Farmer, P., *The Uses of Haiti*, Monroe, ME: Common Courage Press, 1994.
Fauriol, G.A. (ed.), *The Haitian Challenge, US Policy Considerations*, Washington, DC: Center for Strategic and International Studies, 1993.
Haitian Constitution, 1987.
Heine J., and Thompson, A.S., *Fixing Haiti MINUSTAH and Beyond*, Tokyo: United Nations University, 2011.
Heinl, R. and Heinl, N., *Written in Blood: The Story of the Haitian People 1492–1971*, Boston, MA: Houghton Mifflin, 1978.
Inter-American Development Bank, 'Remittances to Haiti topped $1.65 billion in 2006', Press Release, 5 March 2007. <http://www.iadb.org/news/articledetail.cfm?language=en&artid=3637> (accessed 8 January 2016).
Inter-American Development Bank, Haiti Survey, <www.bendixenandassociates.com/studies/Public_Opinion_Survey_of_Remittances_to_Haiti.pdf> (accessed 8 January 2016).

International Development Associate and International Monetary Fund, 'HIPC and MDRI – Status of implementation', 27 September 2007.
Laguerre, M.S., *The Military and Society in Haiti*, London: Macmillan, 1993.
Lawyers Committee for Human Rights, The Americas, *Paper Laws, Steel Bayonets: Breakdown of the Rule of Law in Haiti*, November 1990.
Maingot, A.P., 'The political rot from within', *Current History*, vol.94, no.2, 1995.
McCroklin, J.H., *Garde d'Haiti, Twenty Years of Organization and Training by the United States Marine Corps*, Annapolis, VA: The US Naval Institute, 1956.
McFadyen, D. (ed.), *Haiti: Dangerous Crossroads*, Boston, MA: South End Press, 1995.
Meharg, S., and Arnusch, A., 'Security sector reform: A case study approach to transition and capacity-building', Carlisle, PA: Strategic Studies Institute, January 2010.
Michel, G., *Charlemagne Péralte*, Port-au-Prince: Le Natal, 1989.
Ministry of Planning and External Cooperation, 'Growth and poverty reduction strategy paper', <http://siteresources.worldbank.org/INTPRS1/Resources/Haiti-PRSP(march-2008).pdf> (accessed 21 April 2008).
Mintz, S.W., 'Can Haiti Change?', *Foreign Affairs*, vol.74, no.1, Jan/Feb., 1995.
Nicholls, D., *Haiti in Caribbean Context: Ethnicity, Economy and Revolt*, London: Macmillan, 1985.
Nicholls, D., *From Dessalines to Duvalier: Race, Colour and Independence in Haiti*, London: Macmillan, 1996.
Oxfam, 'Haiti: Violence impact study', 2006.
Paquin, L., *Les Haitiens, Politique de Classe et de Couleur*, Port-au-Prince: Imprimerie le Natal, 1988.
Perusse, R.I., *Haitian Democracy Restored 1991–1995*, London: University Press of America, 1995.
Prince, R., *Haiti Family Business*, Nottingham: Russell Press, Latin America Bureau, 1985.
Robinson, R., *An Unbroken Agony: Haiti from Revolution to the Kidnapping of a President*, New York: BasicCivitas, 2007.
Robinson, W.I., *Promoting Polyarchy. Globalization, US Intervention and Hegemony*, Cambridge: Cambridge University Press, 1996.
Rotberg, R.I., *Haiti, The Politics of Squalor*, Boston, MA: Houghton Mifflin, 1971.
Shamsie, Y., and Thompson, A.S,. (eds), *Haiti Hope for a Fragile State*, Warterloo, ON: Wilfrid Laurier University Press, 2006.
Smartt Bell, M., *All Souls' Rising*, London: Granta Books, 1995.
Trouillot, M.R., *Haiti: State Against Nation: The Origins and Legacy of Duvalierism* New York: Monthly Review Press, 1990.
Verner, D., and Heinemann, A., 'Social resilience and state fragility in Haiti, breaking the conflict-poverty trap', World Bank, *En Breve*, no.94, September 2006.
World Bank, Haiti, <siteresources.worldbank.org/INTPROSPECTS/Resources/334934-1199807908806/Haiti.pdf > (accessed 5 January 2016).
World Food Programme (WFP), 'Facts and figure'<http://www.wfp.org/country_brief/indexcountry.asp?country=332#Facts%20&%20Figures> (accessed 15 July 2008).

UN documents

SG report, S/26397, 13 August 1993.
SG report, S/1994/1363, 30 November 1994.
UN Report E/1999/103, 2 July 1999.

3 (In)security and (in)stability

Security and stability is at the core of UN peace operations' mandates. At its most basic level security is a 'state of being free from danger or threat'. But it is in what can be described as a co-dependent relationship where security and stability is essential to establishing a viable democratisation process, state and institution building and sustainable peace, but where stability and security also rest on issues such as transitional justice, socio-economic development, security sector reform, democratisation and the rule of law. Ensuring a secure and stable environment was core to all the UN mandates in Haiti.

The types of insecurity and violence[1] changed through time in Haiti, as they will do in most long-term peace operations contexts. Therefore the means and approaches through which to address them need to be adapted accordingly. How provision of security came to be defined during the various peace operations in Haiti changed over time from a very minimalist 'force protection' approach to stabilisation and a 'new experience' in peacekeeping, from risk avoidance to active pursuit of a security agenda, where peacekeepers engaged the elements of destabilisation.

This chapter is not meant to detail all violence and instability in Haiti,[2] but rather to emphasise the political nature of much of the violence and link it to the issues discussed in the subsequent chapters. It also explores the change in the peace operations dealing with shifting insecurity. It discusses the nature of the violence; the new threats that emerged post-2004 through different armed gangs; the 'new experience' in peacekeeping; the changed nature of some of crimes committed, such as kidnapping; and places civil unrest within the socio-economic context.

Criminal or political violence?

UN Security Council Resolution 940 mandated the UN mission to ensure a 'secure and stable' environment in Haiti. The actors of insecurity and instability were at the time of deployment clearly identifiable: former armed forces and their supporters. Security was heightened after the UN intervention, but because of the large numbers of weapons circulating, problems within the new police force, dissatisfied former soldiers, poverty, and a lack of justice, public insecurity was still prevalent.

When the Multinational Force (MNF) transferred their mandate to the UN it declared the environment safe and stable. But the situation was feared to be an impending crisis[3] and a UN report stated that insecurity and fear remained significant in Haiti.[4] This insecurity had not changed notably at the time of transfer of power from President Aristide to President Préval in 1996. The situation was described as 'insecurity is more present than democracy'.[5]

This does not indicate that the environment was not made *safer*; it was. There was no longer organised political repression or institutionalised violence. People no longer feared the army and there was freedom of speech and assembly. However, the supporters of the coup were active during the UN missions and were a destabilising factor. In the rural areas insecurity persisted, where, for example, rural magistrates controlled the areas much as before.[6]

Initially one problem with making Haiti secure and stable partly rested in the UN's rules of engagement (ROEs). United Nations Mission in Haiti's (UNMIH) rules of engagement stated: 'Interventions to prevent death or grievous bodily harm at the hands of a hostile group, will only be authorised by the Force Commander in order to defend the mandate of the mission.'[7] This led to a couple of incidents where the UN peacekeeping forces did not intervene to protect civilians, which was met with strong negative reactions in Haitian society. As a result the ROE for the United Nations Support Mission in Haiti (UNSMIH) was changed to: 'Use of force, up to and including deadly force, may be authorised by the Force Commander/on scene commander to defend any person against a hostile act or hostile intent when Haitian authorities are not available nor able to render immediate assistance.'[8] This was an important improvement since the on scene commander could make the decision and they could defend any person, even against the *intent* of hostility. It massively widened the opportunities available to the peacekeeping forces to actively create a more secure environment in Haiti, although to what extent it did is debatable, as much of the violence perpetrated went unaddressed.

Haitians became very dissatisfied with the UN's ability to provide security and stability.[9] This critique was rebutted by the UN stating that the insecurity was not political, but criminal in nature; and that it was not the UN's mandate to tackle crime.[10] Defining violence as crime was based on the initial limited ROEs, an unwillingness by the missions to get actively involved in protecting civilians combined with a genuine incomplete understanding of the political nature of the violence. This was exacerbated by the more complex nature of conflict. There were no armed factions fighting for power, but armed groups supported by various political and economic actors perpetrating assassinations, killings and violence that destabilised and undermined the democratisation process. It was not a traditional peacekeeping environment. From the onset of the MNF intervention to the departure of the UN peace operations, and beyond, there were acts that can only be defined as politically motivated. For example, President Préval's own security agents made threats to his life, and they were also allegedly involved in the assassinations of two leaders of an opposition party.[11] The UN Secretary-General's report in May 1998 concluded that there had been some incidents, but that they did not 'appear to reflect any specific pattern of unrest or politically motivated violence'.[12] Still, politically motivated murders were never fully absent. There might not have been a pattern of unrest, or *organised* political violence, but there were regular politically motivated incidents throughout UN presence in Haiti (1994–2001).

Defining the violence as non-political can in part be explained by a shift in insecurity after the deployment of the UN mission. During the coup era, insecurity had predominantly been present in poor neighbourhoods, where the army and the paramilitaries had suppressed any support for a democratic Haiti. After the intervention, insecurity also became prevalent in other neighbourhoods; the elite too became a target. The elite were, therefore, especially harsh in their critique of the UN's inaction. There was more focus on this type of insecurity than there was on the insecurity that existed in the poor areas, which was underreported both by the victims and the media.[13] This shift lent support to the claims that violence and crime was not politically motivated, but financially driven. However, it could be interpreted to be partially political, since a majority of the elite had actively or tacitly supported the junta. The increase of insecurity in these areas could therefore be interpreted as a type of retribution. It is difficult to differentiate between acts motivated by politics and those driven by other objectives in a post-conflict state. In a country where there has been a prolonged crisis, distinctions are blurred and 'criminal' activity often has a political motivation or a political implication.

Nonetheless insecurity was also profound within slum areas, such as Cité Soleil, where armed gangs flourished. Defining this insecurity as criminality did not take into consideration the fact that it was in the poor areas that Aristide and Lavalas had their support. These areas were highly politicised; and former *Forces Armées d'Haïti* (FAd'H) and *Le Front pour l'Avancement et Progres d'Haiti* (FRAPH) members were not disarmed or demobilised. Therefore, the insecurity that persisted in these sectors was, in part, politically driven. Haitians argued that the insecurity was political with *an aspect* of criminality and that the character of the violence was political.[14] The absence of public security was not all due to political factors, but even non-political acts can be used to destabilise. Criminal acts for gain performed by gangs led by, for example, former FAd'H members increased insecurity. Anti-democratic groups used this as a means of destabilising the new democracy. A wave of violence was reported by the UN in 1997 and it was acknowledged that the people behind it 'have access to weapons and the funds necessary to carry out acts of destabilisation'.[15] In a fragile situation like the one that existed in Haiti, few things are apolitical. This did not change after the second deployment of UN peacekeepers.

A 'new experience' in peacekeeping

The primary cause of insecurity, after the deployment of the UN Stabilisation Mission in Haiti (MINUSTAH), was armed gangs, irrespective of their political affiliation or lack thereof. In early 2004 the armed gangs included Aristide loyalists, former officials of the Lavalas government, unofficial pro-Aristide armed gangs, gangs who participated in the 1991 coup (including FRAPH members), armed political groups allied to different anti-Aristide and anti-Lavalas political parties and/or economic elites, former military officers, former police officers, and former rural police (*chefs de section*), private security sometimes acting as private militia, and non-political armed groups.[16]

The conflict between the armed pro-Aristide gangs and those in support of his ouster continued to escalate in the presence of MINUSTAH. Although MINUSTAH had established a presence throughout the country by 2005, security in Port-au-Prince deteriorated, due to a rise in killings and kidnappings. MINUSTAH was at the time not operating at mandated strength, which undermined its capacity to tackle the violence and the gangs.[17] Credible statistics on violence in Haiti are very difficult to find due to limited state capacity to collect such data, but one estimate suggests 1,600 were killed from February 2004 to October 2005.[18] But it was not simply a matter of political violence with different factions fighting for power. The face of violence in Haiti changed during MINUSTAH's presence – violence transformed from overt political violence to urban gang violence, both political and non-political, overwhelmingly present in Port-au-Prince. The violence and conflict had their origins in politics but were rooted in a mix of politics and economics, which continued to thrive due to the continued absence of state authority and lack of socio-economic development. Political and economic elites used the armed gangs to further political objectives, providing them with arms and protecting them from arrest. They were habitually using kidnappings, perpetrating gang-on-gang killings and fighting for urban territory and some were without political affiliation. Moreover, youths and children in the poor areas were drawn into the gangs. Earlier armed groups did not have the same tendency of using youths; they did not fight over urban territory or use kidnapping as a tool (see subsection on kidnapping below). Armed groups were also involved in murder, drug and weapons trafficking. They were also present in the countryside operating as self-imposed and self-elected law enforcement. Yet the phenomenon of gang-on-gang violence and kidnappings was not seen to the same extent as in the capital. This was further complicated because armed gangs in some districts of Port-au-Prince looked after their communities by distributing money and offering protection, which led some communities to protect the gangs since they saw the benefits, as well as simply out of fear.[19] In 2006 they operated with impunity. After the earthquake in 2010 the gangs and territories changed. New alliances were forged, old gangs split, new gangs formed and territories changed hands – the gangs' territorial borders in the communities became porous.[20] This was largely a result of the internally displaced (IDP) resettlement camps and the movement of people.

Although armed gangs in Haiti changed over time and had their roots in politics, it is wrong to assume they were no longer political after 2006–07. They were perhaps not ideological, as one would define insurgents, but they functioned as part of the political instability as they were influenced and supported by political and economic actors. Many had shifting allegiances. Not all had a clearly defined political agenda, but were nonetheless paid to wreak political havoc. Criminal networks and political armed gangs in Haiti were not mutually exclusive. This created an environment where the armed gangs' role in destabilisation and undermining the democratisation process became much more complex.

MINUSTAH was initially strongly criticised for what was viewed by many Haitians as inaction against the armed gangs.[21] MINUSTAH had to address two ostensibly reinforcing objectives: supporting the transitional government and creating a secure and stable environment. However, rather than being reinforcing these objectives were incompatible as the transitional government actively supported armed gangs to undermine support for Aristide in key areas of Port-au-Prince in particular. Parts of the economic and political elite also reinforced this. Therefore, due to these political constraints MINUSTAH did not set out a strategy for dealing with armed gang violence. In addition, MINUSTAH did not have the resources to face these non-traditional peacekeeping threats to security. Although the violence perpetrated during 2000–04 was between armed gangs of different political ilk, the deployment was that of a traditional peacekeeping operation; these other security threats were seemingly not anticipated or planned for.

During and after the presidential elections in 2006 there was a self-imposed truce by the armed gangs, and the biggest obstacle to change – the transitional government – was removed. But violence escalated again in June 2006. Gang rivalry and fights over territory led to large numbers of casualties, for example, in January 2007 in one neighbourhood 29 bodies were found.[22] With the change in government MINUSTAH was able to respond more robustly to the violence.

In response to the deteriorating security situation in late 2006 and early 2007, MINUSTAH began a new process of dealing with the armed gangs which at the time was unheard of in peace operations. This action was described as a 'new experience in UN peacekeeping',[23] since it dealt with armed gangs, who were criminal as well as political in nature, rather than rebel groups or state actors, and who conducted urban gang-warfare. MINUSTAH and the Haitian National Police (PNH) conducted co-joint security operations and the UN peacekeeping forces arrested several hundred gang members, kidnap victims were released, and weapons and ammunition seized. MINUSTAH was able to notably reduce the level of violence and kidnappings in early 2007 by this crackdown on armed gangs in the capital. This removed the main gang leaders and led to the arrests of around 850 alleged gang members by the end of July 2007.[24] Security increased markedly, which resulted in schools, shops and markets reopening, and residents returning to high violence areas.[25] This strategy became important to ensure security and stability through active robust[26] peacekeeping. The joint patrols and active security work by MINUSTAH was much welcomed and positively received by all sectors and created greater stability. It was a new approach and innovative in a difficult and increasingly insecure context which could not be defined within the traditional parameters of peacekeeping.

The joint patrols and security operations targeting armed gangs and their leaders continued for the next couple of years. Unfortunately these efforts were severely affected by the earthquake when an estimated 5,000 to 6,000 prisoners[27] escaped, including many gang leaders and gang members. They returned to their neighbourhoods and contributed greatly to the lawlessness that followed in the wake of the earthquake. Over a year later, only 8 per cent of the prisoners had been rearrested.[28] There was a general trend of greater insecurity in Haiti from 2009 to 2011[29] – this trend had therefore begun prior to the earthquake and was not only a consequence of it. A MINUSTAH report underscored that some of these armed gangs had connections with political parties and drug traffickers.[30] After the earthquake the joint patrolling continued; for example in July 2011 three areas were targeted and several gang members arrested.[31] These operations continued throughout 2015.

Making the 'new experience' possible

It was sensitive for a UN mission to proactively engage armed gangs in this manner and a 'new approach'. There were three main factors that made the implementation of this new security approach possible in Haiti: the election of the new government that supported action against armed gangs in combination with civilian support; the establishment of the Joint Mission Analysis Centre; and the change of Force Commander in MINUSTAH.

MINUSTAH's ability to more effectively engage was facilitated by the election of President Préval and a willingness by the Haitian government to confront the gangs. There was also broad support in Haitian society for MINUSTAH to take a more proactive role in ensuring security. MINUSTAH, the government and civil society agreed that the armed gangs were a destabilising factor and a spoiler for sustainable peace, and posed a threat to civilians. This afforded the mission to pursue a security agenda that had until then not been possible.

Central to the mission's ability to conduct these operations was the establishment of the Joint Mission Analysis Centre (JMAC). They very effectively supported and provided intelligence-led operations. The Haiti JMAC has been termed to have set 'the gold standard' for supporting enforcement of a mandate.[32] The JMAC was established in 2005. Although it was to be an analytical unit it also took on an operational role, collecting and analysing data on the size of gangs, leadership, locations, weapons etc.[33] As a result this type of JMAC has been attempted in other contexts, albeit not with similar results. The JMAC in Haiti was provided with both strong support from UN Department of Peacekeeping Operations (UNDPKO) and mission leadership to conduct this role, which facilitated their activities. It also meant that the mission could take an effective lead in the joint operations as they relied on their own intelligence gathering capacity, rather than on the PNH. The PNH could not be entirely relied upon (see Chapter 5) as they had poor intelligence gathering capacities and some officers were part of the criminal networks.

Lastly, it was only when a new Force Commander was appointed in January 2007 that MINUSTAH was able to launch more effective operations. The previous Force Commander had been urging caution – which was further complicated by some troop contingents' inability to be deployed in this manner.[34] This underscores the importance of defining the mission clearly from the start and understanding the context. MINUSTAH had viewed this as a peacekeeping operation and therefore changing and evolving this perspective met with resistance. It also shows how the gangs were part of the political environment undermining political stability; it demonstrates how individuals can obstruct necessary changes and approaches within a mission; and how cohesion at leadership level is critical to affect change. Importantly, it underscores the SRSG's and DPKO's understanding of the issues and context and willingness to try a new approach to solve the conflicts and to ensure stability and security in Haiti.

Operational deficits

There were several shortfalls of these operations. A number of civilians were wounded during these operations. For example, one survey found that 52 per cent of respondents reported 'that family members, friends, or neighbours… were killed or wounded during the fighting with the gangs'.[35] The SRSG Edmond Mulet admitted that there had been 'collateral damage'.[36] Nevertheless 97 per cent of Haitians surveyed perceived the strategy to be justified.[37] One argument against these operations was that they 'appeared in some cases both to disperse and simultaneously to radicalise youth and so-called gangs'.[38] It has also been viewed as 'a military solution to address…a social, economic and cultural problem'.[39] It also created a strong dependency upon the mission as a security provider; especially since only a small percentage were joint operations (9 per cent in 2015). But these operations notably increased security in gang-held territories at least for a period of time. The longevity and sustainability was undermined by the absence of linking this to other interventions and reform both in the police and in the development sector. It would be impossible to solve the issue of armed gang violence separately from the political and economic agendas in Haiti.

The connection to the economic agenda was underscored by the mission and to that end MINUSTAH developed a four-pronged plan that a) targeted the leadership of gangs, b) captured territories from gangs, c) provided quick impact projects and d) conducted a community violence reduction programme.[40] However, there was a distinct strategy and implementation gap. The strategy to deal with armed gangs was not an effective part of an overall strategy that included disarmament, demobilisation and reintegration (DDR), security sector reform (SSR), justice development and democratisation. These operations were uncoordinated and segregated. They were in large part driven by the UN military component with less input from police and civilian sections.[41]

Consequently the symptoms of violence were addressed but not its causes. Addressing causes of violence will always take longer, but ensuring that also the short-term stability objectives are viewed within the longer-term security and justice perspectives and programming is critical to sustainability of stability and security. Given that the violence had political, socio-economic and social roots, only tackling the symptoms in isolation did not engender longer-term change. The mission and DPKO clearly saw socio-economic disparity and the inability of the government to deliver services as root causes for the insecurity and development necessary to achieve sustainable stability,[42] but the security operations were not effectively linked to other longer-term programming. No peace operations are mandated to implement economic development, nor should they be. In this case there needed to be more coordination to ensure that the stability dividend was effectively used by development actors. This coordination was attempted by the mission, but it was flawed for three reasons in particular. First, the operations were, as mentioned above, undertaken as security operations and planned accordingly. The coordination aspect could have been more strongly planned for. Second, several development actors were not at the time in favour of this new approach; and were concerned with potential negative outcomes such as civilian casualties and radicalisation.[43] They were thus unwilling to coordinate with the mission to some extent. This meant the stability dividend was not utilised effectively by developmental actors. Third, the gangs' connections to political actors, both inside and outside government, and to the economic elite was not dealt with by the mission. The gang-leaders were arrested, but who paid them to destabilise was not in focus. This would have needed a different mandate and an investigative capacity that the mission did not have at the time. It is also doubtful whether the government would have supported or agreed to MINUSTAH conducting this type of intervention. But it was an issue that undermined the democratisation process.

Even with operational deficits, the ability and willingness to take this 'new approach' did increase, for a time, security and stability. These types of operations were an evolution in peacekeeping. It meant playing an active role in ensuring safety and security of the Haitian people – and was a vast difference to the operations in the 1990s when violence was simply redefined as criminal; and force protection was predominant.

Violence and crime

In most post-conflict contexts, crime increase in the aftermath of war and in a fragile peace. What type of insecurity and why, and what types of crime will inevitably vary. In Haiti after 2004 the types of crime committed were somewhat different to those committed in the 1990s. In particular, kidnapping, which previously had been nearly non-existent in Haiti, plagued the country and decreased stability and security. In addition, homicide rates increased. After the earthquake there was an increase in all major crime, including homicide and kidnapping.[44] Yet as late as 2011 to 2012 there was another dramatic increase in violence.[45] Drug trafficking has for decades permeated Haiti and affected violence levels.

Kidnapping

Initially the reason for kidnappings had its origins in politics, since many Aristide supporters believed that he was kidnapped from Haiti, leading them to kidnap civilians in retaliation. Pro-Aristide gangs also carried out decapitations using similar tactics to Iraqi insurgents, whilst demanding the return of Aristide, calling their campaign 'Operation Baghdad'.[46] Measures taken by the transitional government against Lavalas supporters were brutal and Operation Baghdad was revenge for the repression at the hands of the transitional government.[47] Human rights conditions in general worsened under the transitional government and included summary executions, arbitrary arrests and torture.[48]

Kidnappings considerably affected security, mainly in the capital and urban areas. Verifiable data on kidnappings are difficult to come by, and made more difficult by underreporting. One report states that there were 722 victims of kidnapping in 2006, 293 in 2007 and 162 in the first six months of 2008.[49] A UN report states that from December 2007 to February 2008 there was a significant increase where the monthly kidnappings reached 28 (up from 11 per month the same time the year before).[50] In 2009 the number of kidnappings declined. The fluctuations can be explained largely by the successful UN military and PNH operations to root out armed gangs. Kidnapping yet again increased after the earthquake,[51] as did most other criminal activities. It was not until mid-2014 that there was a 'solid downward trend' in kidnappings with a 74 per cent decrease compared with the year before – a result of dismantling of gangs and kidnapping networks.[52] Yet at the end of 2015 kidnapping in Haiti was still considered 'a high threat'.[53]

Although it originated in politics, from 2007 kidnapping took on an economic perspective in the context of socio-economic under-development; it became a way for gangs to financially sustain themselves. But kidnapping was never one-dimensional and had both political implications and effects – it underscored the inability of the government to ensure the rule of law, especially when targets were high profile, thus affecting good governance and democratisation.

Homicide

There are few statistics on homicide in Haiti. In fact in the period from 1994 until 2007 there are, for example, no UN Office of Drugs and Crime (UNODC) statistics. This is due to a number of factors, including much gang-on-gang violence with revenge attacks and limited reporting to the police; insufficient capacity meant the police did not regularly patrol gang-held areas or collect and store such data. Nonetheless, crime statics collected by the PNH and MINUSTAH showed a substantial increase in homicides in 2012 compared with 2011; this trend continued in 2013.[54] UNODC reported a doubling of homicides in Haiti from 2007 to 2012.[55] The majority of homicides were committed in Port-au-Prince and urban centres; and were recorded in gang territorial disputes in Port-au-Prince.[56] MINUSTAH and PNH noted a reduction in homicides in 2015 compared with 2014.[57]

This rise in homicides can be explained in four ways: an increase in reporting these crimes to the police; an improved police capacity to collect and store this data; an increase in homicides; or a combination of these factors. There was most certainly an increase in reporting as a result of greater trust in the PNH (see Chapter 5), but towards the end of this period armed gangs increased their activities again and many became re-politicised,[58] which could also indicate an increase in the actual number of homicides.

The fluctuations in violence and homicide need to be viewed in the context of political instability and crisis. There were several peaks of political crisis during this period. When governance was weakest the armed gangs and violence increased. For example, as the political impasses and crisis grew during President Martelly's presidency so did violence, particularly after his first year as President. (The political instabilities are discussed in detail in Chapter 8.)

Homicide in Haiti also needs to be put in perspective with the rest of the region. For example, in 2010 the homicide rates were 6.9 per 100,000 population in Haiti compared with 25 per 100,000 population in Dominican Republic, 41.2 in Jamaica and 26.1 in Trinidad and Tobago.[59] UNODC found that in 2012 murder rates in Haiti were 10.2 per 100,000 compared with 22.10 per 100,000 population in the Dominican Republic, 39.30 in Jamaica and 28.30 in Trinidad and Tobago.[60] Yet it must be pointed out that in Port-au-Prince and in certain areas of the city, such as Bel Air and Cite Soleil, the homicide-to-population rate has been much higher, for example in Bel Air in 2011 it was 50 per 100,000 compared with 19 per 100,000 in 2010.[61] This is noteworthy in that in the poorest areas of Port-au-Prince the murder rate was substantially higher than in neighbouring countries and in other areas of Port-au-Prince. Overall the total numbers were still much smaller than in neighbouring countries.

Yet, this violence and crime has destabilised the state and undermined state authority much more profoundly than those of the region. One reason for this arguably lies in the fact that crime and violence often has been political, thus by its very nature designed to undermine state authority and strengthen individual political power, whereas the rule of law has been weak and commonly controlled by political or economic elites. It is therefore arguably not the frequency that matters but the fact that it is conducted for political gain and perceived as such that determines the effect of homicides on instability and democratisation.

Drug trafficking

Haiti has been a transit country for drugs for decades. Prior to 1994 the drug shipments through Haiti were controlled by the army; it was part of how they controlled political and economic life. Yet with the dissolution of the army there was no change in the drug trafficking; 'not even a blip on the screen in relation to the drugs trade was registered with the dissolution of the army'.[62] This is significant in that the armed forces had always controlled drug trafficking in Haiti and although they were dissolved as an institution their networks remained, as did the trafficking. Drug trafficking is an issue throughout the Caribbean, but due to the weaknesses of the Haitian judicial system (see Chapter 7) it has had much more of a destabilising effect.

The lack of control of the land and sea borders by the government was an underlying problem affecting political and economic governance, security and stability through enabling drug trafficking. It has had a corrosive effect on institution and state building, particularly rule-of-law institutions, fuelling corruption among civil servants, judicial officials and the PNH.[63] It also financed armed gangs, increased weapons trafficking and discouraged foreign investment. Efforts were made to tackle drug trafficking by President Préval with some success. For example, in 2007 there was a large seizure of drugs, and a dozen people were arrested, half of them police officers.[64] The shipments of drugs to the US reportedly increased after the earthquake as there was less state authority.[65] The porous borders and unchecked private airstrips have been effectively used by drug traffickers.

The historic involvement of security forces and governments in the drug trade has always undermined governance in Haiti. It continued to corrupt state institutions after 2004, which in turn lent itself to fostering impunity. With the election of Michel Martelly as President, some questioned whether a more permissive era for drug traffickers had begun.[66] Efforts to fight drug trafficking through operations against the armed gangs have not taken a 'bigger picture' approach in understanding the political economy of Haiti, the political actors and the PNH's role in it. It is not only a problem of gangs or organised[67] criminal networks, but also of political actors and security forces. Moreover, most of the drug trafficking has taken place outside Port-au-Prince, whereas 80 per cent of PNH were based, in 2014, in the capital, further making the problem difficult to handle.

Civil unrest and demonstrations

Civil unrest in Haiti increased in the context of socio-economic inequality, high unemployment and high expectations of change which were never met. From the first UN peace operations until the beginning of drawing down of MINUSTAH, there were regular demonstrations and civil unrest. These sometimes undermined security and stability, but more importantly, they underscored the inability of the Haitian state to deal with these activities, the frailty of the PNH, dissatisfaction with the government, and the lack of democratisation and the rule of law. They can broadly be placed in three categories: anti-government demonstrations, anti-UN demonstrations and demonstrations by the former FAd'H.

Governance and justice: Anti-government demonstrations

After 1994 there were regular anti-government demonstrations chiefly in three areas: calling for disarmament, demanding justice, and protesting against the socio-economic policies of the government. The demonstrations calling for the disarmament of the army and the *attachés*[68] were closely related with a demand for justice of the perpetrators during the junta years – the absence of which contributed to insecurity. The demonstrations against the government's privatisation plans, socio-economic inequality and the high cost of living continued throughout 1994–2000.[69] Importantly, none of these anti-government demonstrations had any impact upon security and stability in Haiti during this period, but were rather a reflection of people's increasingly strong dissatisfaction with governance and justice.

During MINUSTAH, anti-government demonstrations had a more substantial impact on security. It was chiefly socio-economic grievances that were a focus. The cost of living had a substantial impact upon the Haitian economy and population – in 2008 Haiti imported 52 per cent of its food (80 per cent of its rice) and all its fuel. Local food production and food aid accounted for 43 per cent and 5 per cent respectively.[70] Food insecurity increased in 2008 and the government estimated that 2.5 million were affected, up from 500,000 to 1,000,000 the previous year.[71] Social remittances relied upon by 70 per cent of Haitian households were affected by the economic crisis in the US and Europe. As the Haitian government was unable to provide basic services most were privatised and also similarly affected. The social and political instability reduced foreign investment.

As a result, demonstrations increased by about 30 per cent in the latter part of 2007 and early 2008.[72] The importance of economic development was underscored by *la vie chère* riots in April 2008. Although other factors played a part in these riots, such as political actors encouraging the riots,[73] there was a clear dissatisfaction with the lack of development and aid coming from the government and international community. As a result of the riots food aid was pledged.

From 2010 onwards, there were frequent anti-government demonstrations throughout the country protesting the high cost of living, the government's failure in dealing with the rule of law and delivering of basic services, as well as frustration with the many political impasses. These types of incidents increased substantially throughout 2015.[74] Some, but not all, of these demonstrations were violent, including destruction of property, road barricades, shootings and attacks on police officers. This was different to the period in the 1990s, when most were peaceful. Critically these demonstrations diverted resources from the PNH in tackling major crimes and gang violence.

The UN and MINUSTAH acknowledged the strong link between socio-economic grievances and the consolidation of stability; the Independent Expert on the situation of human rights in Haiti, Michel Forst, also emphasised the relationship between extreme poverty and instability.[75] But two issues were not sufficiently emphasised: acknowledging the political and historical roots of socio-economic disparity and the use of the discontent with this disparity by political actors to actively contribute to instability. The civil unrest needed to be viewed in the wider contextual and political setting, as these demonstrations were regularly abused for political purposes. Nevertheless, the demonstrations reflected the fundamental frustrations with the limited progress in governance, economic development and the rule of law.

Occupation and cholera: Anti-UN demonstrations

From the very first mandate of the UN in Haiti there were always elements both in Haiti and in the diaspora, as well as among a number of internationals, who severely criticised the UN's role in the country. During the 1990s there were a few demonstrations against what was termed 'the UN occupation'. However these were supported only by a very small group, some of whom were using it for their own political objectives.[76] They got undue attention in certain parts of the Haitian and international press, but never constituted a threat to security and stability.

In many peace operations, the UN has been poor at dealing with public outreach, building trust, and explaining its mandates and their limitations. Haiti was no exception. In the 1990s outreach was infrequent and there were few, if any, effective attempts at explaining the UN's role and activities – thereby inadvertently facilitating a minority discourse on 'the UN's occupation of Haiti'. By 2004 this lesson was learnt, and there was an emphasis on MINUSTAH's public information office (PIO) building trust with the public, predominantly in relation to the operations in gang-held areas. Yet it was not sufficient to ensure transparency of MINUSTAH, what the mission was doing and why. Negative perceptions developed in civil society, partly because of lack of information and transparency, and therefore knowledge, of MINUSTAH's mandate and activities. This meant yet again a vocal minority who spoke in terms of 'the UN occupation'. To rectify this, in 2009 MINUSTAH produced a television programme called *Jwèt Pa Nou* (It's Our Turn), highlighting the work of the UN and the international community; it was broadcast on seven stations in Haiti and eight in the US. The initial positive reaction towards this initiative changed dramatically after the cholera outbreak.

In October 2010 there was an outbreak of cholera, the spread of which was worsened with such a large number of IDPs following the earthquake. In less than three years cholera killed over 8,000; by mid-2015 it had killed over 9,000 and affected an estimated 700,000. The UN was perceived to be the direct source of the outbreak, specifically the camp in Mirebalais. This was based on three facts: location close to the outbreak, newly arrived peacekeepers, and sanitation practices at the camp.[77] As a result, violent demonstrations took place, damaging UN vehicles and premises.[78] The UN immediately denied responsibility, but it set up an independent panel to investigate. However, failing to admit any potential for wrong-doing in relation to the cholera outbreak, prior to the report by the independent panel, had a very negative impact upon the mission. The results of the independent panel indicated that there was a single-source outbreak caused by bacteria that were very similar to a South Asian strain. It concluded that the outbreak was the result of a 'confluence of factors' and 'was not the fault of, or deliberate action of, a group or individual'.[79] The UN's response to the cholera accusations undermined the work the mission had been doing in other areas and what originally had been a small minority who spoke in terms of 'occupation' increased. The UN should have handled the accusations differently and not immediately dismissed the potential for peacekeepers' involvement in the cholera outbreak. It set the mission's work back. Only in August 2016 did the UN acknowledge that it played role in the outbreak of cholera.

Dissatisfaction and malcontents: Former armed forces

There were threats to security by former armed forces during all UN missions in Haiti; they were part of the armed gangs, as discussed above, but they also in periods contributed to civil unrest through public demonstrations.

A large number of former soldiers were dissatisfied with the abolition of the FAd'H. They had lost their profession and income. President Préval refused to recompense the former soldiers, who technically were entitled to back-pay, even when the government of the Netherlands offered to cover it.[80] The soldiers organised pressure groups, such as *Rassemblement des Militaries Révoqués Sans Motif* (RAMIRESM) and *Rassemblement des Militaires Démobilisés* (RAMIDEM), and demanded the reconstruction of the Armed Forces.[81] Their activities increased in 1996 after the Senate had adopted the resolution on the abolishment of the army. In 1996 the former soldiers were deemed a threat to stability and security,[82] but after that time they were not visibly active as a *group*.

With Martelly's electoral promise of reconstituting the armed forces, armed groups of former FAd'H remobilised in several parts of the country in 2012; they recruited new members and conducted training exercises.[83] Their funding and support was not clear. They constituted a threat to security as they rallied outside parliament. Consequently the PNH with MINUSTAH support forced them to vacate ten sites they had occupied in May 2012.[84]

The former armed forces were only a threat to security and stability *as an organised group*, in short specific time periods during UN presence. Their threat was more visible as part of armed gangs. Their ability to organise demonstrations underscores the flaws of the demobilisation, disarmament and reintegration process (discussed in Chapter 4) as well their potential for destabilisation.

Conclusion

When the first UN mission deployed in 1994 the actors of insecurity and destabilisation were clearly identifiable. But without a clear DDR mandate and a focus on police support by the missions, in combination with poverty and extreme economic disparity, political actors actively resisting change or indeed using and creating instability for their own political purposes, insecurity continued throughout UN presence. The country was made much safer but as key areas, which are discussed in subsequent chapters, were not addressed, such as transitional justice, political violence persisted.

By 2004 the environment was different. There were a multiplicity of armed gangs with routinely shifting allegiances, driven by political and non-political objectives, and an overall increase in violence such as kidnapping and homicide. MINUSTAH faced a complex multi-dimensional peacekeeping environment. Lessons had been learnt from previous missions and consequently broader and clearer mandates were set out. More importantly, this period shows that the UN, when willing and provided with adequate resources, in combination with government support, is capable of removing non-traditional peacekeeping threats that undermine security and stability. The 'new experience' in peace operations through robust peacekeeping confronting non-state armed gangs in urban areas shows the possibilities of ensuring a stability dividend. MINUSTAH thus substantially increased security and stability in Haiti, but did not focus on the political linkages of the violence undermining the sustainability of the effort.

These operational and tactical operations were necessary, but not sufficient to deal with the causes of violence, they only removed the symptoms of that violence. Although MINUSTAH from the beginning viewed poverty and disparity as root

48 *(In)security and (in)stability*

causes of the instability, and 'economic reactivation as a major priority of the new government',[85] these operations could only establish the space where these causes of violence could be tackled. Haitians and international development actors, not MINUSTAH, needed to pursue activities in the stability created. However, the absence of an overarching strategy or cohesion meant that the stability dividend was not sufficiently exploited. Continued civil unrest aimed at the government underlined the displeasure with socio-economic disparity, lack of good governance, and inability to provide the rule of law. It was also a reflection of lack of progress in democratisation as a reason for why the demonstrations took place and manipulations of unrest for political purposes.

Notes

1 The term violence here broadly follows the OECD-DAC definition: Armed violence includes the use or threatened use of weapons to inflict injury, death or psychosocial harm, which undermines development, Armed violence reduction enabling development, OECD-DAC, 2009, p.13.
2 For more detailed overview of violence during various periods in Haiti see e.g. Amnesty International, Human Rights Watch, M. Deibert, *Notes from the last testament, the struggle for Haiti*, New York, Seven Stories Press, 2005.
3 'Memorandum for Lawyers Committee for Human Rights', 24 January 1995, p.1
4 Published in Geneva 22 February 1995 cited in, 'Results of UN Human Rights Report Presented', Signal FM Radio, Port-au-Prince, 23 February 1995, as translated in *FBIS-LAT*, 23 February 1995.
5 L. Richardson, 'Disarmament Derailed', *NACLA*, vol.XXIX, no.6, May/June 1996, p.11.
6 Interviews, Port-au-Prince, Jacmel, Gonaives, Cap Haitien, 1997. L. Rochter, 'In Rural Haiti "Section Chief" Rules despite US Presence', *The New York Times*, 31 October 1994.
7 UNMIH ROE, no. 3, 3 March 1995.
8 UNSMIH ROE, no.3, 31 July 1996.
9 Interviews with civil society, political parties and business elites, Port-au-Prince, 1997, 1998.
10 Eric Falt, 'L'Inséurité Banaliseée par des Diplomates', *Le Nouvelliste*, 20 March 1995, p.1.
11 'President Préval Sacks his Security Chief, Reorganises Personal Security Unit', Signal FM Radio, Port-au-Prince, 16 September 1996, as translated in *SWB part 5*, 18 September 1996. Other examples include: US military was brought in to protect President Préval and UNMIH stepped up its military presence at the Palace by 50 per cent to protect the President. 'Washington Sends Troops to Reinforce Préval Security', Signal FM Radio, Port-au-Prince, 16 September 1996, as translated in *FBIS-LAT*, 16 September 1996. 'UN Mission Increases Palace Security to Safeguard President', Signal FM Radio, Port-au-Prince, 17 September 1996, as translated in *FBIS-LAT*, 17 September 1996. 'L'Occupation d'Haiti Renforcée', *Haiti Observateur*, 17–24 September 1996, p.1, 8. The US protection of Préval was still operational at the end of 1998. Other examples of politically motivated violence are: the assassination of J.H. Feuille, a newly elected legislator member of Lavalas, on 7 November 1995. 'Pot Threatens to Boil Over', *Haiti Support Group Briefing*, no.15, December 1995, p.1. Numerous arrests were made due to alleged plots against the state. See e.g. 'Authorities Arrest "Many" over Alleged Destabilisation Plot', Signal FM Radio, Port-au-Prince, 2 March 1995, as translated in *FBIS-LAT*, 2 March 1995. The

mutilated body of a worker of the Prime Minister was found in the house of the Prime Minster. 'Mutilated Body Found in Smarth's Home in Cavaillon', Radio Metropole, Port-au-Prince, 17 May 1996, as translated in *FBIS-LAT*, 17 May 1996. Two leaders of an opposition party (MDN) were assassinated, allegedly by the security guards of the President. 'Mobilisation for Naitonal Development Official Shot, Killed', Radio Metropole, Port-au-Prince, 20 August 1996, as translated in *FBIS-LAT*, 20 August 1996. In six weeks from the beginning of February 1997, 50 people were killed, including the chief of security for the Justice Ministry, a senator's bodyguard and 8 police officers. 'Lavalas Splits, Violence Increases', *Haiti Support Group Briefing*, no.23, April 1997, p.1. A former MP was gunned down in front of UNMIH. 'Former Deputy Gunned Down by 2 Armed Men', Radio Metropole, Port-au-Prince, 24 April 1997, as translated in *FBIS-LAT*, 24 April 1997. A deputy, E. Passé, was shot and later died. 'Un Député Victime d'un Attentat' and 'Le Député Passé est Décédé, *Une Semaine en Haiti*, Collectif Haiti en France, no.382, 9 October, no.384, 21 October 1997. A member of Préval's security staff was killed. 'Member of Préval's Security Staff Killed', Radio Vision 2000 Network, Port-au-Prince, 27 October 1997, as translated in *SWB part 5*, 30 October 1997. The security chief of Aristide's foundation was killed, the target of assassins. 'Aristide Foundation's Security Chief Shot Dead', Radio Nationale, Port-au-Prince, 2 February 1998, as translated in *SWB part 5*, 4 February 1998. Father Jean Pierre-Louis, an advocate for the poor, was assassinated in August 1998. No money was taken from his body. Aristide encouraged the formation of vigilante brigades to counter the actions of anti-change. 'La Fanmi Lavalas Prône le Retour des Brigades de Vigilance', *Le Matin*, 8–10 August 1998, p.1. These are just some of the acts committed in this period.

12 SG report, S/1998/434, 28 May 1998, para.11.
13 This may be a reflection that newspaper media at the time was generally directed to a certain sector of Haitian society and the media, in general, was owned by a few, and that the inefficiency and corruption within the police led to an underreporting of crimes (for elaboration on the latter see Chapter 5).
14 Interviews with civil society, political parties and business representatives, Port-au-Prince, 1997–98. The Platform of Haitian Human Rights Organisations agreed, as did Amnesty International, see 'Protestation Contre l'Actuel Climat de Violence et la Déclaration du Président de la Cour de Cassation', *Le Nouvelliste,* 13 October 1997, p.2, and Amnesty International, 'Haiti: Armed Groups still active', Findings of Amnesty International Delegation, 8 April 2004.
15 SG report, S/1997/244, 24 March 1997.
16 Findings of Amnesty International Delegation, Amnesty, 8 April 2004. Armed Conflicts Report – Haiti, Ploughshares, <http://www.justice.gov/sites/default/files/eoir/legacy/2014/02/25/Haiti.pdf>_(accessed 1 February 2016). For more detail on armed gangs and their behaviour see e.g. M. Dziedzic and R.M. Perito, 'Haiti confronting the gangs of Port-au-Prince', Special report 208, USIP, September 2008. See also A. Kolbe, 'Revisiting Haiti´s Gangs and Organised Violence', HASOW, Discussion Paper, 4 June 2013.
17 E. Lederer,'UN peacekeeping force in Haiti at 40%', Associated Press, 7 August 2004.
18 See R. Muggah, 'Securing Haiti's Transition: Reviewing Human Security and the Prospects for Disarmament, Demobilization, and Reintegration,' Small Arms Survey, Occasional Paper No. 14, October 2005. A much more controversial estimate suggested almost 8,000 murders and 35,000 incidents of sexual assault in the 22 months following the ousting of Aristide. See A. Kolbe and R. Hudson, 'Human Rights Abuse and other Criminal Violations in Port-au-Prince: A Random Survey of Households,' *The Lancet*, 31 August 2006. Cited in G. Hammond, 'Saving Port-au-Prince: United Nations Efforts to Protect Civilians in Haiti in 2006–2007', Stimpson Center, June 2012.

50 *(In)security and (in)stability*

19 Interviews, Port-au-Prince, June 2006.
20 A. Kolbe, Revisiting Haiti's armed gangs and organised violence, Hasow, Discussion Paper 4, June 2013, p.29.
21 Interviews with civil society and political parties, Haiti, June and December 2006.
22 SG report, S/2007/503, 22 August 2007, para.23.
23 UN spokesperson David Wimhurst quoted by S. Jacobs, Associated Press, 10 February 2007. It must be noted that not only MINUSTAH took initiatives to address armed gang violence, but there were several other projects, for example, the US Haiti Stabilisation Initiative (HSI), and bottom-up initiatives such as Viva Rio in Bel Air. The latter type were more disconnected from the top-down model of MINUSTAH; and lacked coordination. For details on these see e.g. T. Donais and G. Burt, 'Vertically integrated peace building and community violence reduction in Haiti', Center for International Governance Innovation Papers, no.25, February 2014, p. 5. R. Muggah, 'The effects of stabilisation on humanitarian action in Haiti', *Disasters*, 2010.
24 SG report, 22 August 2007, S/2007/503, para.22.
25 J. Delva, 'Haiti Residents Enjoy New Peace', Reuters, 18 April 2007. SG report, S/2007/503, 22 August 2007, para.21.
26 The Capstone doctrine defines robust peacekeeping as 'the use of force at the tactical level with the consent of the host authorities and/or main parties to the conflict', 2008, p.19. It is worthwhile noting that the Capstone doctrine was not developed until after these operations; the Haiti operations were part of moving the agenda of 'robust' peacekeeping forward.
27 Estimates vary; MINUSTAH estimated 5,600 escaped prisoners, SG report, S/2011/183, 24 March 2011, para.13.
28 SG report, S/2011/183, 24 March 2011, para.13.
29 SG report, S/2011/183, 24 March 2011, para.13.
30 SG report, S/2011/540, 25 August 2011, para.8.
31 SG report, S/2011/540, 25 August 2011, para. 10. Operation Phoenix was the largest of these operations.
32 M. Dziedzic and R.M. Perito, Haiti, p.8.
33 For details on the various operations and JMACs role see e.g. G. Hammond, 'Saving Port-au-Prince: United Nations Efforts to Protect Civilians in Haiti in 2006–2007', Stimpson Center, June 2012, p.23.
34 Hammond, 'Saving', p.17. See also Dziedzic and Perito, 'Haiti', pp.3–4.
35 M. Dziedzic and R.M. Perito, 'Haiti', p.5.
36 As quoted by Andrew Buncombe, 'Civilians caught in the crossfire during Port-au-Prince raids', *The Independent*, 2 February, 2007.
37 M. Dziedzic and R.M. Perito, 'Haiti', p.5.
38 R. Muggah, 'The effects of stabilisation on humanitarian action in Haiti', *Disasters*, 2010, p.7.
39 Nicolas Lemay-Herbert, 'MINUSTAH', in J.A. Koops, T. Tardy, N. MacQueen, and P.D. Williams (eds), *The Oxford Handbook of United Nations Peacekeeping Operations,* Oxford University Press, 2015, p. 726.
40 See also Hammond, 'Saving', pp.22–23.
41 Interviews, Port-au-Prince, 2008.
42 See e.g. SG report, S/2006/592, 28 July 2006, para. 45; and SG report S/2009/1892, 13 October, 2009.
43 Interviews, Port-au-Prince, 2008.
44 SG report, S/2011/540, 25 August 2011, para.8. All crime statistics in Haiti are notoriously unreliable. This is due to a combination of factors including under-reporting, difficulties in data collection and data storage.
45 A.R. Kolbe and R. Muggah, 'Haiti's urban crime wave?, Results from monthly household surveys, August 2011 – February 2012', Igarape Institute, Strategic note 1, March 2012, p.1.

46 A. Bracken, 'Aristide backers threaten to behead foreigners', Associated Press, 6 October 2004.
47 MINUSTAH representative, Port-au-Prince, June 2006.
48 Human Rights Watch, 'Human Rights Overview: Haiti', 18 January 2006 <http://hrw.org/english/docs/2006/01/18/haiti12210.htm> (accessed 2 February 2006).
49 Crisis Group, 'Reforming Haiti's Security Sector', Latin America/Caribbean Report No.28, 18 September 2008.
50 SG report, S/2008/202, 22 March 2008, para.15.
51 SG report, S/2010/446, 1 September 2010, para. 9.
52 SG report, S/2014/617, 29 August 2014, para. 11.
53 Interview with representative of Control Risks, 5 December 2015.
54 SG reports: S/2012/678, 31 August 2012, para.11, S/2013/139, 8 March 2013, para. 10. Kolbe and Muggah, 'Haiti's', found a dramatic increase between November 2011 and February 2012, p.1.
55 UNODC, <http://knoema.com/UNODCHIS2014/unodc-international-homicide-statistics-2014?location=1000760-haiti> (accessed 22 January 2016).
56 SG report, S/2014/617, 29 August 2014.
57 SG report, S/2015/667, 31 August 2015 para. 16.
58 SG report, S/2013/139, 8 March 2013, para. 10.
59 P. Alpers and M. Wilson, *Armed Violence in Haiti: Conflict prevention, development, peace and security*, Centre for Armed Violence Reduction, London and Sydney, AVRMonitor.org, 22 October 2013. In this chart the data was 2010 for Haiti and 2011 for the other countries.
<http://www.avrmonitor.org/investment/compare/78/rate_of_intentional_homicides_per_100_000_people_any_method/52,90,185> (accessed 22 January 2016)
60 UNODC, <http://knoema.com/UNODCHIS2014/unodc-international-homicide-statistics-2014?location=1000760-haiti> (accessed 22 January 2016).
61 Kolbe and Muggah, 'Haiti's', p.4.
62 US official, interview, Port-au-Prince, 1997.
63 SG report, S/2010/446, 1 September 2010, para.69.
64 SG report, S/2007/503 22 August 2007, para.3.
65 SG report, 2 February 2010 S/2010/200, para.22.
66 W. Kemp, M. Shaw, A. Boutellis, 'The elephant in the room: How can peace operations deal with organised crime?', International Peace Institute, New York, June 2013, p. 35.
67 For details on organised crime in Haiti see e.g. ibid and J. Cockayne, 'Winning Haiti's Protection Competition: Organised Crime and Peace Operations Past, Present and Future', *International Peacekeeping*, Vol. 16, Issue 1, 2009.
68 *1994 au quotidien*, AHP, 24 September, 8 November 1994, pp.117, 140. 'Prime Minister Decries "Gangster-Like" Demonstrators', AFP, Paris, 13 November 1995, as translated in *FBIS-LAT*, 13 November 1995. 'Aristide Declines to Change Call for Disarmament', Signal FM Radio, Port-au-Prince, 14 November 1995, as translated in *FBIS-LAT*, 14 November 1995.
69 See e.g. '"First" Anti-government Demonstration Staged in Cap-Haitien', Radio Metropole, Port-au-Prince, 21 March 1995, as translated in *SWB part 5*, 23 March 1995. 'Anti-government Demonstration Staged in Capital', Signal FM Radio, Port-au-Prince, 24 March 1995, as translated in *FBIS-LAT*, 24 March 1995. 'Anti-government Demonstration Staged in Capital', Signal FM Radio, Port-au-Prince, 24 March 1995, as translated in *FBIS-LAT*, 24 March 1995. 'Port-au-Prince Flooded with Anti-Privatisation Leaflets', Tropic FM, Port-au-Prince, 25 August 1995, as translated in *FBIS-LAT*, 25 August 1995. 'Radio Reports Demonstration against Privatisation', Signal FM Radio, 1 September 1995, as translated in *FBIS-LAT*, 1 September 1995. 'Two Demonstrations Protest Privatisation', Radio Metropole, Port-au-Prince, 19 September 1995, as translated in *FBIS-LAT*, 19 September 1995.

52 *(In)security and (in)stability*

70 SG report, S/2008/586, 27 August 2008, para.50.
71 SG report, S/2008/586, 27 August 2008, para. 52.
72 SG report, S/2008/202, 26 March 2008, para. 16.
73 Interviews with political actors and civil society in Port-au-Prince, April 2008.
74 See e.g. SG reports: 2015 S/2015/667, 31 August, para.17, 2015 S/2015/157, 4 March, para.12.
75 SG report, S/2009/1296 March 2009, para.47.
76 Interviews with civil society, political actors, business representatives, Port-au-Prince, Gonaives, Cap Haitien, 1997, 1998.
77 For detailed overview of the cholera outbreak see e.g. D. Lantagne, G. Balakrish Nair, C.F. Lanata and A. Cravioto, 'The cholera outbreak in Haiti: Where and how did it begin?' *Current Topics in Microbiology and Immunology*, Springer-Verlag, Berlin Heidelberg, 2013.
78 See e.g. SG report, S/2011/183, 24 March 2011, para.9.
79 A. Cravioto, C.F. Lanata, D.S. Lantagne & G. Balakrish Nair, 'Final Report of the Independent Panel of Experts on the Cholera Outbreak in Haiti', 2011, pp.1–2.
80 Interview with Haitian government official, Port-au-Prince, 1997.
81 On e.g. 19 June 1996, former military took to the streets to claim back pay and pensions, *1996 au quotidien*, AHP, 19 June 1996, p.62. 'Fusillade, ce Matin au Grand Quartier Général des Forces Armées d'Haiti', *Le Nouvelliste,* 26 December 1994, p.1.
82 Interview with Haitian government official and UN official, Port-au-Prince, 1997. L. Rohter, 'Haiti's "Little Kings" Again Terrorise its People', *The New York Times,* 25 August 1996.
83 SG report, S/2012/128, 29 February 2012, para.8.
84 SG report, S/2012/678, 31 August 2012, para.3.
85 SG report, S/2006/592, 28 July 2006, para. 45.

Bibliography

Alpers, P. and Wilson, M., 'Armed violence in Haiti: Conflict prevention, development, peace and security', Centre for Armed Violence Reduction, London and Sydney, AVRMonitor. org, 22 October 2013. <http://www.avrmonitor.org/investment/compare/78/rate_of_intentional_homicides_per_100_000_people_any_method/52,90,185> (accessed 22 January 2016).

Armed Conflicts Report, 'Findings of Amnesty International delegation – Haiti', 8 April 2004, Ploughshares, <http://www.justice.gov/sites/default/files/eoir/legacy/2014/02/25/Haiti.pdf> (accessed 1 February 2016).

Cockayne, J. 'Winning Haiti's protection competition: Organised crime and peace operations past, present and future', *International Peacekeeping*, vol. 16, no. 1, 2009.

Collectif Haiti en France, 'Un député victime d'un attentat', no.382, 9 October 1997,

Collectif Haiti en France, 'Le député passé est décédé, une semaine en haiti', no.384, 21 October 1997.

Cravioto, A., Lanata, C.F., Lantagne, D.S. and Balakrish Nair, G., 'Final report of the Independent Panel of Experts on the Cholera Outbreak in Haiti', 2011.

Crisis Group, 'Reforming Haiti's security sector', Latin America/Caribbean Report No.28, 18 September 2008.

Deibert, M. *Notes From the Last Testament, the Struggle for Haiti*, New York, Seven Stories Press, 2005.

Donais, T. and Burt, G. 'Vertically integrated peace building and community violence reduction in Haiti', Center for International Governance Innovation papers, no.25, February 2014.

Dziedzic, M. and Perito, R.M. 'Haiti confronting the gangs of Port-au-Prince', Special report 208, USIP, September 2008.
Haiti Support Group Briefing, 'Working on the ground', no.10, November 1994.
Haiti Support Group Briefing, 'Pot threatens to boil over', no.15, December 1995.
Haiti Support Group Briefing, 'Lavalas splits, violence increases', no.23, April 1997.
Hammond, G. 'Saving Port-au-Prince: United Nations efforts to protect civilians in Haiti in 2006–2007', Stimpson Center, June 2012.
Human Rights Watch, 'Human rights overview: Haiti', 18 January 2006 <http://hrw.org/english/docs/2006/01/18/haiti12210.htm> (accessed 2 February 2006).
Kemp, W., Shaw, M. and Boutellis, A. 'The elephant in the room: How can peace operations deal with organised crime?', International Peace Institute, New York, June 2013.
Kolbe, A., 'Revisiting Haiti's gangs and organised violence', Humanitarian Action in Situations Other than War, Discussion Paper 4, June 2013.
Kolbe, A. and Hudson, R., 'Human rights abuse and other criminal violations in Port-au-Prince: A random survey of households,' *The Lancet*, 31 August 2006.
Kolbe, A.R. and Muggah, R. 'Haiti's urban crime wave? Results from monthly household surveys, August 2011 – February 2012', Igarape Institute, Strategic note 1, March 2012.
Koops, J.A., Tardy, T., MacQueen, N. and Williams, P.D. (eds), *The Oxford Handbook of United Nations Peacekeeping Operations*, Oxford: Oxford University Press, 2015.
Lantagne, D., Balakrish Nair, G., Lanata, C.F. and Cravioto, A. 'The cholera outbreak in Haiti: Where and how did it begin?', Current Topics in Microbiology and Immunology, 379:145–164, 2013.
Muggah, R. 'Securing Haiti's transition: Reviewing human security and the prospects for disarmament, demobilization, and reintegration,' Small Arms Survey, Occasional Paper No. 14, October 2005.
Muggah, R. 'The effects of stabilisation on humanitarian action in Haiti', *Disasters*, vol. 34, no. 3, October 2010.
Richardson, L. 'Disarmament derailed', North American Congress on Latin America, vol. XXIX, no.6, May/June 1996.

UN documents

SG report, S/1997/244, 24 March 1997.
SG report, S/1998/434, 28 May 1998.
SG report, S/2006/592, 28 July 2006.
SG report, S/2007/503, 22 August 2007.
SG report, S/2008/202, 22 March 2008.
SG report, S/2008/586, 27 August 2008.
SG report, S/2009/1296, March 2009.
SG report S/2009/1892, 13 October, 2009.
SG report, S/2010/200, 2 February 2010.
SG report, S/2010/446, 1 September 2010.
SG report, S/2011/183, 24 March 2011.
SG report, S/2011/540, 25 August 2011.
SG report, S/2012/128, 29 February 2012.
SG report, S/2012/678, 31 August 2012.
SG report, S/2013/139, 8 March 2013.
SG report, S/2014/162, 7 March 2014.

SG report, S/2014/617, 29 August 2014.
SG report, S/2015/157, 4 March 2015.
SG report, S/2015/667, 31 August 2015.
UNMIH Rules of Engagement, 3 March 1995.
UNSMIH Rules of Engagement, 31 July 1996.
UNODC, <http://knoema.com/UNODCHIS2014/unodc-international-homicide-statistics-2014?location=1000760-haiti> (accessed 22 January 2016).

Media

AFP (Agence France Presse), 'Prime Minister decries "gangster-like" demonstrators', Paris, 13 November 1995, as translated in Foreign Broadcast Information Service on Latin America (FBIS-LAT), 13 November 1995.
AHP (Agence Haïtienne de Presse), 1994 au quotidien, 24 September, 8 November 1994.
AHP (Agence Haïtienne de Presse), 1996 au quotidien, 19 June 1996.
Bracken, A. 'Aristide backers threaten to behead foreigners', Associated Press, 6 October 2004.
Buncombe, A. 'Civilians caught in the crossfire during Port-au-Prince raids', *The Independent*, 2 February, 2007.
Delva, J. 'Haiti residents enjoy new peace', Reuters, 18 April 2007.
Haiti en Marche, 'Les jours passent, mais se ressemblent trop', 30 November – 6 December 1994.
Haiti Observateur, 'L'ONU préoccupée par le désarmement', 9–16 November 1994.
Haiti Observateur, 'L'occupation d'Haiti renforcée', 17–24 September 1996.
Haiti Progrès, 'Terreur Macoute en complicité avec les occupants', 2–8 November 1994.
Haiti Progrès, 'Des criminels pour combattre l'insécurité', 16–22 November 1994.
Haiti Progrès 'Haiti Commission finds: "the coup continues"', 7–13 December 1994.
Haiti Progrès 'MINUHA: le casque change, les occupants restent', 1–7 February 1995.
Le Matin, 'La Fanmi Lavalas prône le retour des brigades de vigilance', 8–10 August 1998.
Le Nouvelliste, 'Fusillade, ce matin au grand quartier général des forces armées d'Haiti', 26 December 1994, p. 1.
Le Nouvelliste, 'L'insécurité banaliseée par des diplomates', 20 March 1995.
Le Nouvelliste, 'Protestation contre l'actuel climat de violence et la déclaration du Président de la Cour de Cassation', 13 October 1997.
Lederer, E. 'UN peacekeeping force in Haiti at 40 per cent', Associated Press, 7 August 2004.
Radio Metropole, '"First" anti-government demonstration staged in Cap-Haitien', Port-au-Prince, 21 March 1995, as translated in Summary of World Broadcasts part 5, 23 March 1995.
Radio Metropole, 'Two Demonstrations Protest Privatisation', Port-au-Prince, 19 September 1995, as translated in FBIS-LAT, 19 September 1995.
Radio Metropole, 'Mutilated body found in Smarth's home in Cavaillon', Port-au-Prince, 17 May 1996, as translated in FBIS-LAT, 17 May 1996.
Radio Metropole, 'Mobilisation for national development official shot, killed', Port-au-Prince, 20 August 1996, as translated in FBIS-LAT, 20 August 1996.
Radio Metropole, 'Former deputy gunned down by two armed men', Port-au-Prince, 24 April 1997, as translated in FBIS-LAT, 24 April 1997.
Radio Metropole, 'Prison guard reportedly confesses to shooting deputy Passe', Port-au-Prince, 10 October 1997, as translated in SWB part 5, 13 October 1997.

Radio Vision 2000 Network, 'Member of Préval's security staff killed', Port-au-Prince, 27 October 1997, as translated in SWB part 5, 30 October 1997.

Radio Nationale, 'Aristide Foundation's security chief shot dead', Port-au-Prince, 2 February 1998, as translated in SWB part 5, 4 February 1998.

Rohter, L. 'In rural Haiti "Section Chief" rules despite US presence', *The New York Times*, 31 October 1994.

Rohter, L. 'Haiti's "little kings" again terrorise its people', *The New York Times*, 25 August 1996.

Signal FM Radio, 'Results of UN Human Rights Report presented', Signal FM Radio, Port-au-Prince, 23 February 1995, as translated in FBIS-LAT, 23 February 1995.

Signal FM Radio, 'Authorities arrest "many" over alleged destabilisation plot', Signal FM Radio, Port-au-Prince, 2 March 1995, as translated in FBIS-LAT, 2 March 1995.

Signal FM Radio, 'Anti-government demonstration staged in capital', Port-au-Prince, 24 March 1995, as translated in FBIS-LAT, 24 March 1995.

Signal FM Radio, 'Radio reports demonstration against privatisation', 1 September 1995, as translated in FBIS-LAT, 1 September 1995.

Signal FM Radio, 'Aristide declines to change call for disarmament', Port-au-Prince, 14 November 1995, as translated in FBIS-LAT, 14 November 1995.

Signal FM Radio, 'Washington sends troops to reinforce Préval security', Signal FM Radio, Port-au-Prince, 16 September 1996, as translated in FBIS-LAT, 16 September 1996.

Signal FM Radio, 'President Préval sacks his security chief, reorganises personal security unit', Signal FM Radio, Port-au-Prince, 16 September 1996, as translated in SWB part 5, 18 September 1996.

Signal FM Radio, 'UN mission increases palace security to safeguard president', Signal FM Radio, Port-au-Prince, 17 September 1996, as translated in FBIS-LAT, 17 September 1996.

Tropic FM, 'Port-au-Prince flooded with anti-privatisation leaflets', Port-au-Prince, 25 August 1995, as translated in FBIS-LAT, 25 August 1995.

4 Disarmament, demobilisation and reintegration and the defence reform that never was

Disarmament, demobilisation and reintegration (DDR) are core to reducing violence in post-conflict societies, enhancing stability, creating the space for elections to be held and democratisation to take place. It is a vital factor in ensuring sustainable peace and stability after war and conflict, a precursor to development. A complete DDR process has often proved to be difficult however, DDR is a political process that needs the political will of the parties to the conflict, support of local civil society and high-level international political attention to be successful. It is highly context dependent, and DDR responses need to be tailor-made. Moreover, the DD of DDR continues to be more in focus than the R. This is a reflection of the fact that both disarmament and demobilisation are easier tasks than reintegration, resulting in more emphasis and focus as well as donor funding. This has affected outcomes of DDR programmes and this chapter establishes that it considerably affected the DDR programmes in Haiti after both periods of peace operations. How DDR is intimately linked with economic development, justice, reconciliation and security sector reform (SSR) has not been a key consideration when developing DDR programmes. It has been acknowledged that these linkages are important, for example in the Integrated DDR Standards.[1] However, in Haiti this did not effectively translate into programmes.

Two periods dealt with DDR in Haiti: after 1994 and then subsequently after 2004. This chapter analyses the DDR processes in Haiti of both the army and armed groups and establishes the Haitian views on the DDR processes. Defence reform was never conducted in Haiti since the armed forces were dissolved in 1995 (although a new army was established after President Martelly was elected). DDR after 1994 focused on the technical aspects of disarmament and demobilisation, whilst only minimally attempting to address reintegration. In 2004, 'classic' DDR was attempted in a non-traditional peacekeeping setting with limited political will by the transitional government to conduct DDR and insufficient donor coordination. The chapter also explores the mission's reorientation from DDR to a community violence programme (CVR).

Development of DDR

Through the years of UN peace operations definitions of DDR have developed. There has been a steep learning curve, which has helped shape the newer and more developed concepts of DDR. Early on, the focus was primarily on demobilisation of ex-combatants, but this was soon recognised to be flawed. Lessons were identified in several countries where DDR was implemented,[2] criticism of implementation grew[3] and DDR was underscored to be critical for transitioning from war to peace.[4] These helped develop broader definitions of DDR. The problem has particularly been found in reintegration.[5] It has also been recognised that DDR is not a sequential effort and needs to be more firmly placed in the political and social context.[6] These lessons and definitions however, were not identified or learnt in the early and mid-1990s. Moreover, irrespective of the academic discourse on DDR, a gap continues to exist between the developed UN definitions and UN practice; this particularly concerns reintegration and reinsertion.

Disarmament is the collection, control and disposal of small arms, light and heavy weapons, ammunition and explosives within a conflict or post-conflict zone from all parties to the conflict, and sometimes also of the civilian population. It includes the development of arms management programmes, safe storage and destruction of the arms collected. It may entail the assembly and cantonment of combatants.[7] It is frequently described as a confidence-building measure where it aims to increase stability in an insecure environment.[8] The objective is not only to reduce the number of weapons, but also to enhance human security.

Demobilisation is the process in which the combatants of the parties to the conflict disband and begin the transformation into civilian life. There may be an interim stage where some combatants are discharged and others reassembled to create new/restructured armed forces. The aim of the latter process is to improve the efficiency of the armed forces and may be a result of a politically negotiated settlement where each group becomes part of the new armed forces. Each demobilisation process varies, and includes different variables, dependent upon the individual post-conflict situation. Nevertheless, the process broadly involves selection and preparation of assembly areas, planning of logistics, resource mobilisation, selection of those ex-combatants who will be demobilised, cantonment and registration, disarmament, needs assessment, provision of services (health care, basic training), pre-discharge counselling, discharge and transport to home areas.[9]

What is often referred to, particularly by the UN,[10] as the second stage of demobilisation is reinsertion. Reinsertion consists of transitional assistance to help ex-combatants with their immediate needs after having been demobilised from the armed forces or armed groups. This can include food, clothes, shelter, medical services, provision of kits and tools, in some cases short-term education, training, or employment. Reinsertion is short-term focusing on material and/or financial assistance. The term reinsertion has not been used in all UN operations and has been more used in recent operations. It was not used in Haiti where the processes that were attempted were referred to as reintegration after both 1994 and 2004.

Reintegration is the process which allows ex-combatants and their families to re-enter civilian life and adapt economically, through gaining employment and income, and socially through settling into the communities and being accepted by the communities. Reintegration should include both a social and economic process of development. It is a long-term process,[11] which alongside economic and social reintegration includes a substantial psychological adjustment. It needs to be part of the general economic development of the country, and necessitates government will and long-term donor commitment. As discussed below, several of these factors for successful reintegration were not present in Haiti.

Disarmament

There was no UN mandate to disarm in 1994, but UN Security Council Resolution 940 and the Port-au-Prince agreement stated that the aim was to 'foster peace, avoid violence and bloodshed, to promote freedom and democracy'[12] and 'to establish and maintain a secure and stable environment'.[13] It was questionable whether that could have been achieved in Haiti without addressing the issue of disarmament. Therefore, even without a mandate for disarmament several processes were put in place including a buy-back scheme of weapons. Small arms in Haiti, until the early 1990s, were generally limited to the *Forces Armées d'Haiti* (FAd'H) and Duvalier's *Tonton Macoutes*. During the military regime, 1991–94, the FAd'H also distributed weapons to their supporters: *Le Front pour l'Avancement et Progres d'Haiti* (FRAPH) and the *attachées*. Contrary to 1994, in 2004 DDR was a central part of the UN mandate. UN Security Council Resolution 1542 stated that the UN mission was to 'assist the transitional government particularly the Haitian National Police with a comprehensive and sustainable Disarmament, Demobilisation and Reintegration programme for all armed groups'.[14] However, in 2004 the targets for disarmament were no longer only the military and its supporters; it had become more complex.

Multinational Force 1994

The Multination Force (MNF)[15] was unwilling to disarm the Haitian military and the paramilitaries although there were persistent local and international calls for disarmament. This had a significant effect upon UNMIH and is therefore worth looking into in some detail. There were demonstrations calling for the disarmament of the army and the *attachés*, and the Haitian government called for disarmament on several occasions.[16] Still, US Secretary of Defence William Perry stated that disarmament was unlikely.[17] There were four overriding factors that influenced disarmament after 1994: confusion as to the role of the MNF, US fear of body bags, inadequate contextual knowledge and information, and the Haitian constitution.

The first difficulty was the confusion over the nature of the operation among the MNF troops. This concerned the cooperation between the FAd'H and the MNF. One US officer stated that his unit had not disarmed the FAd'H because the operation was meant to be 'a joint, co-op type mission'.[18] This originated in the Port-au-Prince agreement, which emphasised cooperation between the MNF and the FAd'H. It was also claimed that both the paramilitaries and Lavalas had weapons and it would, therefore, be inappropriate to only disarm the paramilitaries.[19] Equating the Lavalas with the paramilitaries revealed a profound lack of contextual knowledge. Moreover, US troops relied on the Haitian army for information, and left the decisions to them about whom to disarm and arrest.[20] Thus the MNF received conflicting and unclear information regarding Lavalas and had to cooperate with the forces they had been deployed to remove from power – this situation obfuscated the disarmament process, which was further complicated by the unwillingness of these forces be disarmed.

The second factor concerned the overriding fear in the US administration that Haiti might turn into another Somalia.[21] US strategies in Haiti were strongly marked by these then-recent events, resulting in risk aversion trying to avoid American body bags.

A third reason for the lack of disarmament, according to the MNF and subsequently the UN, was that there was no reliable information on which to disarm: the number of weapons and paramilitaries were disputed and how to identify the paramilitaries was argued to be difficult.[22] This disregarded the fact that the International Civilian Mission in Haiti (MICIVIH) had been present during the coup era and could identify both FRAPH members and *attachées*. And while the civilian population was willing to cooperate with the MNF in the disarmament process, it was not consulted in any meaningful way.

Lastly, it was also argued that the Haitian constitution (1987) gives the right to civilians to bear arms, and that this could pose complications to a disarmament process.[23] This is however, not strictly correct. The Haitian constitution gives each citizen a right to armed self-defence at home, but a civilian cannot carry weapons outside their home without the authorisation of the Chief of Police.[24] More importantly article 268.3 stipulates that the Armed Forces have the monopoly of fabrication, import, export, use and possession of 'war arms' (*arms de guerre*). These have been defined as larger weapons such as Uzis; only pistols of a small calibre are allowed under article 268.1.[25] The Haitian constitution would, therefore, not have created a problem for disarmament.

Buy-back scheme and raids

Despite having no mandate and a reluctance to disarm, a buy-back scheme of weapons was established by the MNF. This scheme had numerous flaws. First, the MNF paid less than it was possible to obtain on the black market.[26] Selling the weapons on the black market was therefore the preferred option. Second, people who owned guns did not want to part with them because it was more profitable to put their guns to other uses. Third, the majority of the population with weapons had been part of the institutionalised repression during the junta years, and knew that without any guns for protection they could become the targets of vigilante justice. The programme collected some weapons, but many were old and unworkable.

The MNF also carried out a few raids in an effort to disarm. When the MNF first began this form of disarmament in Haiti, it brought about tremendous relief. It was what had been expected from the beginning. People came forward with information on arms and arms caches, because they wanted the MNF to disarm.[27] This was done at great risk to their own personal safety. But the response was limited. A US Army officer explained their position: 'a major problem is determining whether the Haitians are lying or not when reporting arms caches or *attachés*'.[28] The force investigated a few sites, but resisted raiding FRAPH homes and offices.[29] This was a huge disappointment to the population.[30] After receiving criticism for lack of action, the forces raided the FRAPH headquarters in the beginning of October 1994.[31] Weapons collected by the MNF were destroyed or disabled in Haiti by the 8th Ordnance Company US Army. Some modern weapons in good condition were passed on to the US Department of Justice to be reissued to the PNH.[32] The latter was a compelling example of the complete lack of local ownership over these processes.

The disarmament process had very insufficient input from the local stakeholders. This was not due to a lack of political will to conduct disarmament; on the contrary disarmament and demobilisation was viewed as essential for the future security and stability of the country. Yet the process of disarmament itself was entirely controlled externally. There was willingness to cooperate by both government and civil society. But, due to the Port-au-Prince agreement, as discussed above, it became an odd way in which to disarm since the intervening troops cooperated with the main perpetrators of the coup violence, who had the majority of the weapons.

A safe and secure environment: weapons collected

Official disarmament statistics established that about 30,000 weapons were collected.[33] It was maintained that there were not many additional weapons left.[34] In stark contrast, human rights groups estimated the number of weapons in circulation at the time to be between 90,000 and 200,000.[35] It is important to note that estimates on gun ownership vary widely. Normally estimates would be based on registration, experts' estimates, household surveys, proxy indicators or analogous comparisons. In a post-conflict country all of the above become very difficult and only experts' estimates are normally applicable.

Haitians, UN representatives and foreign observers in Haiti at the time, described the disarmament efforts in Haiti as cosmetic.[36] The United States Agency for International Development (USAID) confirmed that vast numbers of weapons were still in circulation, which the MNF had not recovered.[37] As a result the number of weapons in Haiti increased notably.[38] It became a vicious circle. There was no disarmament. Insecurity rose, the police were ineffective, so more people acquired weapons so that they could defend themselves, further increasing the number of weapons.

The UN had wanted the MNF to conduct a more extensive process of disarmament[39] because DDR was not in their mandate. In the Secretary-General's report before the UN Security Council Resolution 940 was adopted, he proposed that the mandate of the intervening force should include the disarmament of paramilitary groups.[40] When disarmament is not in the mandate it is very difficult for the UN to conduct it in any meaningful manner given that the mission will not have the resources to implement it; and their measure of success will be defined and measured by what is outlined in the mandate. However, 'security and stability' is an immense task without the ability to remove the main threats to democracy and stability. As a MICIVIH official emphasised 'it is wrong to say that the mandate was misconstrued, it was supposed to bring a secure environment, it has not'.[41]

The lack of disarmament exacerbated insecurity in the first months after the intervention and continued to play a part in insecurity in Haiti. Violent crime increased significantly in the post-intervention period, political crime was never absent, and the drug trade continued unabated; all of which were aggravated by the prevalence of small arms. The FRAPH were so encouraged by the absence of disarmament that they proclaimed: *Apre nou, se nou* (after us, it is us),[42] indicating that with the withdrawal of the international community they would again reign.

Interim national disarmament efforts

After the UN mission departed in 2001, the Haitian National Police (PNH) conducted some disarmament operations. The PNH initiative was supported by the Organisation of American States (OAS) and the United Nations Development Programme (UNDP).[43] Expecting startling results from this new police force, which already faced immense challenges, was perhaps somewhat optimistic. The PNH's disarmament 'campaign' must also be seen in the context of a police force that had many abusive, corrupt, criminal and politicised elements.[44] This was further complicated by some government officials' support and use of armed gangs for political and security purposes. This meant that there was limited, if any, support for a DDR process in this period.

Hence, in 2002 when the PNH invited people to hand in guns at local police commissariats where they would receive payment, their intentions could be questioned. The results of this buy-back scheme were nominal. In 2002 the PNH also set up numerous roadblocks aimed at disarming drivers. This was highly publicised in the local media, but few weapons were collected.[45] During the whole of 2002 only sixty weapons were seized. A Haitian government report stated that 2,551 arms had been collected, but this included rounds of ammunition.[46] A National Disarmament Committee was established on 31 March 2003, but little progress was made. Incongruously it was not until 20 February 2004 that UNDP organised the first voluntary surrender of weapons by armed gang members;[47] this was in the midst of a revolt which would nine days later see the President in exile.

United Nations Stabilisation Mission in Haiti

The absence of disarmament and increase in weapons were central factors in the continued instability in Haiti in 2000–04. When the new mission deployed it operated with an estimated 210,000 small arms in Haiti, the majority owned by private citizens and private security companies, not armed gangs.[48] This was probably an underestimate, considering this was the number of weapons estimated to have been in circulation in 1995. Assuming that the estimates of the weapons in Haiti at the time of the 1994 intervention of 90,000 to 200,000 were correct, and considering the lack of arms control mechanisms, porous borders, Haiti's status as a transit country for drugs, the increase in armed gangs and civilians accessing weapons to protect themselves, the number is likely to have increased in ten years. This is strengthened by MINUSTAH who noted an increasing number of weapons in circulation in 2010.[49] The number of weapons in civilian hands increased after the earthquake as prison escapees stole weapons from the PNH. MINUSTAH continued to note an increasing number of weapons in circulation,[50] and widespread reports of trafficking in weapons throughout the country remained a concern throughout the mission.[51] Yet it was the original number (210,000) that both the mission and other sources continued to reiterate as of 2015. It is difficult to assess the scale of the problem in 2016 without reliable data; and to predict how it may impact security in the future.

The vast majority of small arms were unregistered and illegal. There were several factors complicating disarmament by the DDR section in MINUSTAH in the first two years: a transitional government that was unwilling and uninterested in supporting DDR, a traditional approach to DDR in the classic peacekeeping sense, a problem in integration,[52] and the fact that the majority of weapons were held by civilians at home. As a result the UN DDR section had, as of August 2006, according to an independent assessment by the United Nations Office at Geneva (UNOG), only disarmed around fifty people.[53]

The National Disarmament Commission (NCD) was created in September 2004, in response to MINUSTAH's demand for a Haitian counterpart in DDR. But due to the transitional government's lack of interest in the issue, the selection of the commission members reflected political connections, and was a random selection of individuals representing different sectors, including civil society, the PNH and the judicial system.[54] In June 2006 there were only three NCD commissioners left. There were many problems of communication and cooperation between the NCD and the DDR unit, which further increased the difficulties of implementing DDR. Because of the non-functioning NCD a new National Commission on DDR (NCDDR), consisting of seven members drawn from different sectors in Haitian society, was established in September 2006. This commission functioned better than the NCD, there was less apparent friction between its members, regular meetings were held, and there was an apparent greater willingness to work on the issues of DDR and much improved cooperation between the DDR unit and the NCDDR. However, there were issues of distrust towards certain members of the NCDDR by the DDR unit, who expressed uncertainty as to the true objectives and agendas of some of the NCDDR members.[55] Even if there were improvements with the establishment of the NCDDR, in 2007 only 200 weapons were collected.[56]

DDR was the activity that was most problematic and criticised by both Haitians and international actors for failing to reach both perceived and mandated objectives. This was also recognised by MINUSTAH staff. The progress of DDR was extremely limited. The initial mandate called for the implementation of traditional DDR, but the situation existing in Haiti upon the deployment of MINUSTAH in 2004 never called for a classic approach to DDR. There were no identifiable factions fighting for power; there was no overview of all the armed groups and their allegiances; a peace agreement did not exist where parties had agreed to a DDR process. Overall it can be questioned whether a post-conflict situation in the common peacekeeping definition of the term existed upon intervention. Nevertheless, due to the mandate, DDR in the classic sense was pursued, and it took far too long to realise that this approach would not work in Haiti, and that it needed to be adapted to better reflect the context. It was not only that the situation was different from a traditional DDR scenario; it was further complicated by the mandate which insisted that MINUSTAH cooperate with the PNH, who were in need of reform and unable to conduct or support DDR.

As dealing with the weapons and the armed gangs through a DDR process met with extremely limited success, the UN adjusted its approach and altered its framework from DDR to Conflict Violence Reduction (CVR).[57]

Demobilisation and reintegration

Demobilisation after 1994 targeted the FAd'H only, although the international community argued for restructuring of the armed forces rather than abolition. Dismantling the FAd'H was successful in that it met the demands of the Haitian population, but the consequences of how it was conducted were felt long after. Reintegration can only be characterised as unsuccessful, as programmes were ill-conceived and excluded the FRAPH and the *attachées*. By 2004 the targets for demobilisation were unclear, and urban gang violence dominated. Demobilisation of armed gangs did not meet with much success until harsher measures were taken in 2007. The reintegration put in place had learnt some of the lessons of the past peace operations, but programmes were implemented which alienated civil society.

The Armed Forces of Haiti

The armed forces were perceived by many Haitians as a repressive symbol and a threat to further democratisation. Hence there was, at the time of intervention, a demand for not only demobilisation but also dissolution. The international community argued for an armed force in Haiti. The Governor's Island agreement stated that the Haitian army was to be 'modernised' with the help of the international community and UN Security Council Resolution 940 reiterated this.[58] There appears to have been three principal reasons for this. First, although the army was responsible for severe human rights abuse and had been throughout its history a very politicised institution, it was functional. It was possible to deal with it as an organisation. Second, it could serve as a counterweight to Aristide, so that he would not return to what had been perceived by the international community as his 'radical' policies. Third, there was a concern that total dissolution would lead to an uprising of the former military.

Throughout the autumn of 1994 Aristide made changes to the army. In November he discharged several officers and in December he reduced the army from 7,000 to 1,500 men.[59] They were demobilised, but not completely disarmed. He promised to rid the nation of its 'cancer' – the armed forces.[60] The changes continued through the beginning of the following year, accompanied by demonstrations, which called for the abolition of the army.[61] There was an insistence on *dechoukaj* (uprooting) of the army.[62] On 28 April 1995 Aristide officially announced the abolition of the army.[63] The following year, on 6 February 1996, Parliament adopted a resolution on the dissolution of the army. Article 1 stated that 'noting the factual disappearance and non-existence of the Armed Forces of Haiti (FAd'H), the Senate of the Republic undertook to present the constitutional amendments establishing their eradication'.[64] Yet, the 1987 constitution was never amended to reflect this. When the constitution was revised in 2012 it did not include a constitutional amendment regarding the armed forces.

Representatives from grassroots and popular organisations, such as peasants' and women's groups, human rights and political organisations, as well as former ministers, did not question that the dissolution of the army was the right action at the time.[65] Sixty-two per cent agreed that disbanding the army would be positive for democracy.[66] The abolition signified that the brutality of the past would finally be dealt with and that the institution, which had been responsible for running Haitian political life since it was created during the American occupation (1915–34), would no longer have that power. It meant that people would be able to elect presidents, rather than having them selected. It was seen as a necessary step for further democratisation and to eliminate the threat of the army again rising as a decisive factor in Haitian politics. It was of great symbolic, as well as practical, significance to the population. The army was so politicised that a democratic process with it still in place would have proved difficult. Few in Haiti discussed or wanted the creation of a new army. It was politically unsound to argue this in Haiti in 1995–99.

Not all of civil society supported the abolition of the army. Some Haitians argued that Haiti needed an army and that reform would have sufficed.[67] A few foreign observers concurred, and reiterated the argument that the army had been the only institution in Haiti which actually functioned.[68] A vetting process could have resulted in a 'new' army, but arguably it would have lacked support in the population. At the time, the force would have been distrusted and stigmatised, due to the history of the army in Haiti.

FAd'H reintegration

The logistical and practical part of the process of demobilisation was reasonably unproblematic; it was the reintegration that created the problems. Furthermore, there was strong political leadership and ownership of the demobilisation of the FAd'H – less so over the reintegration process. The dissolution of the Armed Forces of Haiti was a success in the sense that it removed the threat of institutionalised violence and diminished the possibility of military interference in the democratisation process. It also diminished the possibilities of *organised FRAPH* violence, since they had been closely connected with FAd'H. Critically it was what the majority of the Haitians wanted.

The principal problems with reintegration were that the armed forces did not want to reintegrate, civil society did not want them to reintegrate without parallel processes of justice reconciliation and economic development, and reintegration was politically sensitive for the new government. And as the demobilisation had not included the FRAPH and *attachées*, neither did the reintegration. The number of these supporters was unknown, but the majority kept their weapons.

The army was offered retraining into other professions by the International Organization of Migration (IOM), with a grant by the United States Agency for International Development (USAID) and the Office of Transition Initiatives (OTI). The choices for retraining included: auto mechanics, electrics, computers, welding, carpentry, plumbing, general mechanics, masonry, electronics and refrigeration. Initially, the programme was supposed to provide a public works type of solution to reintegration, although this changed because 'the concept was no longer practical, because the FAd'H found the idea humiliating.'[69] It was a concern that as a result the FAd'H would become a source of instability and also a threat to the MNF.

Half of the force entered into the interim police and 1,500 of them later entered into the new police force, but the majority became unemployed. Unemployment was generally high in Haiti (about 70 per cent), but due to their past as military personnel, although more qualified than many, they had even more difficulty in acquiring jobs. Moreover, the army was a group accustomed to status, income and power. To assimilate such a group back into civil society would take more than retraining them to be carpenters, and expecting them to be satisfied with being a retrained unemployed carpenter. The feeling of having power cannot easily be substituted, or channelled into retraining. It necessitates longer-term training and projects and development, which could ease reintegration into civil society

As a result a number of former soldiers began using their weapons for gain, including drug trafficking. It was only the public institution of the armed forces that dissolved, not its networks. It was emphasised that 'there is still an army working in Haiti today, they are just not wearing uniforms, the whole structure is still there, it is only the visible institutions that are gone'.[70] In a country where the army had run political life for decades it was an illusion to think that its networks would disappear with the removal of uniforms and the use of its buildings for other purposes. The networks were present and used for different ends.

There were two key issues that were not adequately addressed during this process: reintegration's dependency upon socio-economic development, and justice for past crimes. There were no opportunities for free vocational training for ordinary citizens and in the absence of economic development, the reintegration programmes were perceived to be highly beneficial to the armed forces. The projects and retraining the former soldiers received created resentment among Haitians. Ordinary Haitians did not receive paid training programmes, whereas a group of people who had repressed the population did. The former soldiers were also given tool kits, which often was a necessity for obtaining work. The majority of Haitians as well as many foreign observers held the view that the victims of FAd'H oppression had received nothing, but the oppressors reaped the benefits.[71] This was worsened by the lack of criminal justice procedures against any of members of the junta, armed forces or their supporters. This further complicated reintegration into Haitian society. There was little communication with civil society regarding the reintegration process and the need for such programmes. The communities into which the former soldiers were to be reintegrated were more or less ignored.

The Haitian government did not have the political will to support the process of reintegration, because it was politically controversial. Support by the government for the army could have been perceived as a betrayal of the people, who had suffered during the army's regime, and who had worked for the return of the legitimate government. Reintegrating the army back into a society it had been controlling and subduing, without any token of justice, was met with hostility and incomprehension by the population. Nevertheless, what cannot be ignored was the fact that with the dissolution of the armed forces the organised paramilitaries no longer had an institutionalised support base. However, by not disarming or demobilising these groups they continued to be politicised and used as networks and sources of instability (see section below).

The IOM acknowledged that the reintegration into civilian life had not been 'entirely successful', but that this was not necessarily a problem as they constituted only a 'vague' threat.[72] It was flawed in part because people saw the programme as a reward for abusers, there was an unmet demand for justice and the process was never backed up by victim reparation. Long-term reintegration should have been more emphasised, rather than the logistics of removing the uniforms and retraining the force. Retraining meant little when nobody would employ the former soldiers and they felt a considerable loss of power and status. Reintegration could not take place without a parallel process of justice and reconciliation of Haitian society. Demobilising the army was a demand and viewed as a necessity by the Haitian population, but reintegration without justice and reconciliation, as well as economic development, became difficult. As a result former armed forces were part of the overall insecurity in Haiti, and part of the group overthrowing President Aristide in 2004 – so perhaps not such a vague threat after all.

D&R and armed groups

By 2004 the security environment had changed substantially. The violence and its perpetrators had transformed and challenges faced by the UN peace operations were different. There were no armed forces and there was no overview of the number and type of armed gangs and which political affiliations they had, if any. There was no peace agreement, no 'ex-combatants', no political support for DDR and no local counterpart. As mentioned in the previous chapter, in early 2004 the armed gangs included Aristide loyalists, former officials of the Lavalas government, unofficial pro-Aristide armed gangs, gangs who participated in the 1991 coup (including *Le Front pour l'Avancement et Progres d'Haiti* members (FRAPH)), former military officers, former police officers, former rural police (*chefs de section*), and non-political armed groups,[73] none of whom had agreed to demobilise or reintegrate. In this context the processes of reintegration were strikingly similar to the one that had been put in place after 1994: training, education, and few efforts to prepare civil society for reintegration of people they viewed as criminals.

There were several problems with reintegration of these armed gangs. They could earn more in one day through crime than what the DDR programme could offer them in three years.[74] There was at the start of the programme very little incentive for them to reintegrate. The 'incentive' grew once more direct action against the armed gangs was taken by MINUSTAH and the Haitian government.[75] Also, lessons were not learnt from civil society's response to reintegration of the armed forces in the 1990s. It is therefore no surprise that attempts at reintegrating the armed gangs met with even greater difficulty.

The criticisms that followed the reintegration programmes for armed gangs put in place by MINUSTAH's DDR unit after 2004 closely echoed those which followed the 1994 efforts. Chiefly they were severely criticised because they were perceived as supporting the perpetrators of violence.[76] There has consistently been a lack of understanding in Haitian society of why the UN was working with the perpetrators rather than arresting them. This, as earlier, was a reflection of both inadequate information and understanding of what a DDR process entails and the international mandate. Reintegration programmes for armed gangs met resistance because the subjects were viewed as criminals who should be tried in a court of law. Thus initially reintegration was viewed as supporting impunity. Consequently, participants in the programme were harassed by the PNH and local communities.[77] In some cases this resulted in vigilante killings.[78] At times the lack of criminal justice meant that participants of the reintegration programme also used it to further their own ends in the community.[79] Moreover, when participants were let out of the programme at weekends, some used violence against the civilian population.[80]

Political will also played an important part this time. After the 2006 elections there was government support for DDR, however, President Préval's initial handling of the gangs complicated reintegration. At first he seemed not to be dealing with them, and then his new strategy was threatening to kill armed gangs unless they gave up their arms.[81] Neither of these policies had a positive effect on the DDR programme or on a reduction of violence. Given that, the lines between politics and crime were blurred; and because several gangs were perceived to be only criminal gangs the government felt the pressure to hold them accountable and provide and justice, not reintegration, which led to these unclear policies.

The issue of local ownership resurfaced with the DDR process post-2004, and it was one of the criticisms of the process. From the start of the mission a core problem was the vast communications gap between the DDR unit and the local communities. This was acknowledged by the DDR unit.[82] Resolution 1608 emphasised that MINUSTAH should 'urgently develop and implement a proactive communications and public relations strategy, in order to improve the Haitian population's understanding of the mandate of MINUSTAH and its role in Haiti'.[83] Over three years later, the mission had not established this and the DDR unit's work suffered as a result. Although after the elections of the new government and the establishment of the new NCDDR, MINUSTAH had more efficient government counterparts, there is a distinct difference between that type of ownership and engaging Haitians and their perceptions of DDR. DDR was fraught with difficulties due to the negative perceptions which the UN did little to dispel, since it focused its efforts entirely on the government and NCDDR level. There was a need for outreach in Haiti for both increased understanding of what was being attempted as well as ensuring local ownership. The extensive communication gap between MINUSTAH'S DDR unit and Haitian civil society, served to intensify the hostile and critical feelings towards MINUSTAH in this area.

There is a direct link between poverty, lack of development and violence, and the DDR programming should have taken this more into consideration. The timeframe is a critical issue in this context – economic recovery and growth will inevitably take longer than DDR and security sector reform efforts. Nevertheless, for example, when the DDR programme was introduced in Haiti it should not have focused only on the perpetrators of violence, but also on its victims, so that DDR was not seen as a reward for crimes committed. It is not about delaying efforts if the supportive economic conditions are not there, but rather re-thinking specific efforts, for example proper outreach and communication with civil society as well as a reduction of violence approach rather than traditional DDR from the outset would have alleviated a lot of the criticism that the DDR process faced in Haiti. This may have been possible to do from an early stage. Acknowledging the relationship between poverty and violence and beginning to address this does not mean that full economic recovery needs to be achieved for these processes to start. More often than not it is sufficient for civil society to see that changes are happening. It is not an expectation that the economic situation will change overnight, but that changes will begin. Critically although poverty and lack of development feeds violence, violence prohibits development, particularly in terms of foreign investment, which further underlines the need to handle these issues coherently.

Mismanaged UN integration?

The programme was further complicated by a mismanaged integrated approach. The DDR programme functioned as an integrated *programme*. The head of DDR was from MINUSTAH and his deputy from UNDP and they worked together to develop the strategies for DDR. For a time this functioned very well. Nevertheless it was an extremely difficult exercise, so much so that this primary example of UNDP and MINUSTAH *operational* integration split in the summer of 2006. Although maintaining a similar vision of what and where DDR needed to go structurally and practically, the work of DDR UNDP and DDR MINUSTAH was separated, with UNDP focusing on violence reduction and MINUSTAH on DDR. So what was an integrated unit became separated, while remaining integrated in vision.[84] There were several reasons for the split, reflecting budgets and budget cycles, the difficulties the DDR programme had and the necessity to redefine the work. It meant a complex reporting system. As a result, it was felt it would be more cost-effective and would streamline management to split the unit.[85] In many ways, this is an example of the difficulties that integrated field missions face. A unit that had a well-developed strategic vision was complicated through two organisations' very different approaches and structures including management, budget and reporting structures. It highlighted early on the problems of integration. A review of the MINUSTAH and UNDP DDR units was carried out, which argued for better integration and established that DDR should be replaced by CVR. Although the latter was implemented the former never was.

A readjusted approach: from DDR to CVR

Because of the unsuccessful implementation of DDR, MINUSTAH's DDR unit in cooperation with the NCDDR began to restructure its approach to ensure a tailor-made solution to the specific problems of the country. This meant a redefinition of DDR built on five pillars: disarmament and reinsertion of armed gangs, reinsertion of youths, reinsertion of women, a legislative framework for control of arms, and community disarmament. In practice it meant focusing on reduction of violence in the communities, creating Community Development Committees (CDCs) and Committees for the Prevention of Violence and for Development (CPVDs), focusing on women and youths attached to the armed gangs, and putting weapons beyond use.[86] The process was community-focused to ensure a reduction in violence. The changed DDR process was incorporated in the new mandate on 15 August 2006. Security Council Resolution 1702 requested MINUSTAH to redirect the DDR programme to a community violence reduction programme adapted to local conditions. The resolution asked for assistance for initiatives to 'strengthen local governance and the rule of law and to provide employment opportunities to former gang members, and at-risk youth, in close coordination with the Government of Haiti and other relevant actors'.[87] By October 2006, CPVDs had been established in seven of the areas most affected by violence.[88] This restructuring and tailoring the programme closely to the needs to the communities was an exceptional change and is something to be applauded.

CVR

A paper outlined the guiding principles for MINUSTAH's new orientation for CVR.[89] These included, but were not limited to: CVR should be led by the government; credible alternatives to crime needed to be offered; a legal framework for arms control put in place; socio-economic activities closely integrated with local stabilisation priorities; strengthen reform of police and justice; secure storage and destruction facilities for weapons established.

The overall objective was identified as: 'Creat(ing) an enabling environment for the reduction of armed violence and insecurity, through the combination of efforts of community reconciliation, strengthening of State institutions, development of the Haitian National Police, strengthening of the judicial sector and socioeconomic recovery'.[90] This would be achieved through activities such as inter alia: a national CVR strategy; institutional support to the government; improved human security and alternatives to violence-based livelihoods; strengthening of national police capacities, including through community policing; support to authorities for the reinsertion of vetted and decommissioned police officers; and strengthening of the justice system. This strongly underlined all the key links important for a successful outcome of CVR in Haiti.

The strategic approach was also redefined so that all 'intervention dependencies' were identified (GOH, NCDDR, MINUSTAH CVR, UNPOL, Justice, UNDP).

> MINUSTAH and UNDP, in collaboration with key partners, identified the need for a complementary strategy that includes a 'top-down' and a 'bottom-up' approach. The 'top-down' approach, to be carried out by MINUSTAH, consists of reinforcing the State in matters of violence reduction, while the parallel 'bottom-up' approach, to be carried out by UNDP, consists of reinforcing communities and local authorities in matters of violence reduction.[91]

The 'top down' approach was to focus on issues such as law enforcement, reform of the police and justice sectors and disarmament combined with the 'bottom up' approach conflict prevention in the communities and economic development. It thus emphasised the actors and their relationship to each other in this process. It was arguably also an acceptance that UN integration in this area did not work as they simply divided up the tasks, rather than functioning as an integrated whole.

MINUSTAH put in place labour-intensive projects in communities affected by violence; and the projects were identified together with local authorities. Importantly these projects sought to include not only former gang members but also community members. The projects were extensively scaled up after the earthquake.[92]

The changed strategy and mandate was of great significance, it was an acknowledgment that the previous strategy had not worked and that a context-specific solution was necessary and it was developed together with some local counterparts. The strategy was important in that it was community-focused, emphasised reducing violence, focused on victims as well as gang members, aimed to be inclusive, targeted youths, and dealt directly with the issue of women in relation to violence. It underscored that lessons had been learnt from the previous two years in Haiti and showed the ability to change within a relatively short period of time. The significance of this should not be underestimated.

Reoccurring issues

The process after the new mandate was far from problem free. There were principally four factors that reoccurred from earlier processes: poor communication, lack of coordination, limited accountability and lack of socio-economic development.

One factor was that the communication with local communities did not improve much. Even by 2008 some local communities knew very little about this new approach and continued to be critical of the DDR unit's work. Others criticised the way the CPVDs were selected and given legitimacy, because by some the members were viewed as being brought in by MINUSTAH without being real community actors.[93] A problem was that local traditional structures in many areas had disappeared or had been disempowered by the gangs. The choice of community members in the CPVD therefore sometimes did not reflect the traditional senior members of the community.

Another issue was the collaboration between the actors involved in supporting and carrying out the programming, which differed noticeably in practice compared with the vision set out in the strategic documents. The re-constituted NCDDR was the counterpart to CVR strategy.[94] And although the strategy set out a shared vision and a clear division of labour, the operationalisation of the plan continued – as earlier – to be beset by a lack of coordination. As one has commented 'the UNDP, MINUSTAH's Community Violence Reduction (CVR) section and the CNDDR – proved unable to work collaboratively and was characterised by friction, inflexibility and lack of clarity over which organisation should be responsible for setting strategic priorities'.[95] The NCDDR was exceptionally strong in its criticism, stating that from July 2008 the collaboration was derailed and blamed it on MINUSTAH personnel changes.[96] The collaboration with UNDP was even more strained as the NCDDR asked Canada[97] to look into mismanaged funding by UNDP in 2009.[98] This situation led to very limited contact between the actors and parallel interventions, although agreement on the strategic vision remained.[99] The NCDDR closed in 2011, but the collaboration and integration that had been envisioned and set out in the strategic papers had halted long before. Separately the actors contributed to security and stability in the areas of operation for a period of time, but what could have been synergised interventions addressing conflict and violence in urban areas in Haiti was not. The vision that was set out in the strategic papers was bold and different and could potentially have had substantial impact, but fell short in many ways due to lack of effective collaboration. Nevertheless, in the twelve areas that MINUSTAH worked 'quiet headway' was made in 2007–09, despite the lack of coordination and a decrease in MINUSTAH's reputation.[100] By 2013 a report found that in one neighbourhood in Port-au-Prince, MINUSTAH was not viewed by the majority of the population as preventing or resolving conflict in the communities.[101] Importantly, however, as one report states, the decision to shut down NCDDR led to the re-emergence of violence similar to the levels that existed prior to the commission.[102] So arguably even these non-collaborative efforts had a positive impact upon security and stability in some communities.

What was missing in the implementation of these strategic plans was the link to justice. MINUSTAH's CVR strategy specifically mentioned 'Strengthening of the justice system to deal with criminal elements and to stave off impunity'[103] – so it was clearly articulated, however, this was not seen in practice. As will be established in Chapter 6, support for justice reform was limited and beset by a number of problems. But CVR needed to be much more directly linked to criminal prosecutions of the gang leaders to minimise impunity.

Lastly, the training and financial benefits obtained through the CVR programme was not sufficiently tied to broader, longer-term socio-economic development, thus undermining the sustainability of the programme.[104] Again, as before, it became perceived as a reward for armed elements, politicised or not, without a parallel process of economic development and opportunities for education and jobs within the communities they were to be reintegrated back into.

In addition, DDR and CVR must also be put in the context of the actions conducted by the UN peacekeepers with the armed gangs. The 'new experience in UN peacekeeping' had UN peacekeeping troops regularly conducting raids, arresting and ensuring the peace in gang-held areas (see Chapter 3 for more details); although this enhanced considerably security and stability, it was not effectively integrated with the DDR/CVR processes. This would have been a unique opportunity to both ensure that justice, CVR and robust peacekeeping reinforced each other and further increased security and stability.

The strategic vision of CVR was important in that it included all relevant actors as well as processes and factors that both had an impact and were impacted by the CVR processes. The partial failure of the strategy shows the numerous difficulties in a complex environment where cooperation, coordination and compromise to achieve strategies are key. It underlines that understanding each other's organisational context, as well as the field context is imperative for operational coordination, and the need to compromise. It shows that personalities and leadership can derail or abet a process. It is always faster and easier to implement any programme as one section or organisation rather than being part of a process that demands close coordination and coherence in both vision and implementation – however, the results frequently show a diminished return. The structure set out in operationalising the strategic CVR plans may have been too complicated and a more simplified structure for implementing programmes could have facilitated closer integration. The plans may have been too ambitious in the operational context. Nevertheless, it was a great improvement upon the previous DRR process and strategy and in some communities did enhance security and stability.

A new army

Parallel to the DDR and CVR processes more voices were raised for the establishment of a new army, but this was initially predominantly from the economic and political elites. President Préval established the Commission for Reflection on National Security in 2009, which looked at the need for the re-establishment of the armed forces. It continued to be a very sensitive and controversial issue. President Martelly's campaign promise in 2010 was to bring back the armed forces. The international community cautioned that such an army should not be established at the expense of the PNH; that it needed to have oversight and accountability; be framed through a security sector review; and critically that there would be no international financial support for this endeavour.[105] The Ministry of Defense and the post of Minister of Defense were re-established in 2011. Importantly the establishment of the army was outlined in the Poverty Reduction Strategy Paper (PRSP), which stated that 'priority is also given to putting in place a new army'.[106]

President Martelly began to deliver on his promise by having soldiers trained in Ecuador, who returned in September 2013 after completing their training.[107] The Armed Forces had returned to Haiti. It is too early to gauge the consequences of the re-establishment of the army but given the history of the army in Haiti re-establishing it is fraught with problems. Vetting and selection of recruits, training, oversight and accountability would only be a few of the core issues that would need to be tackled from the very beginning.

Conclusion

In 1994 the FAd'H were demobilised but not disarmed. The international community failed to consolidate the intervention by disarming the paramilitaries and the army, which contributed to insecurity and instability and led to problems in the process of democratisation. They no longer had uniforms or an institutional base, but they had the power that weapons give and they used it. This was primarily a reflection of a mandate which did not include DDR. By 2004 lessons had been learnt and DDR was firmly entrenched in the mandate. However, the landscape had changed which demanded a different approach to disarmament, demobilisation and reintegration. The mission adapted the approach as well as the mandate to CVR. This addressed a number of the issues that DDR could not, it did not solve all problems, but was a much more close reflection of the environment.

There was a profound lack of local ownership of the DDR processes during both sets of peace operations – with one significant exception, namely the demobilisation of the armed forces. One result of the largely flawed DDR process with minimal local ownership was an abundance of weapons never collected, groups never demobilised and ex-combatants never reintegrated. This led to continued violence after UN withdrawal in 2001. Lack of ownership also meant fewer tailor-made DDR processes. Civil society had a very negative perception of reintegration in particular, and viewed it as reintegrating criminals back into the communities. This was a result both of not understanding the mandate for DDR due to inadequate communication by the UN missions and limited civil society consultations. The CVR process had much more extensive local ownership.

Two critical connections were never properly tackled. If DDR were to be successful in Haiti, it needed to be conducted in conjunction with some forms of justice and economic development. DDR was not linked to ensuring justice for past crimes, hence reconciliation never occurred. Since former abusers of human rights were allowed to go free, it complicated DDR. This was not the fault of the DDR process or the UN missions as such, as discussed in Chapter 7, transitional justice after the coup era was complicated by many factors. But implementing DDR in its absence contributed to its failure. After 2004 many armed gangs were viewed by many communities as criminals who needed to be held accountable for their crimes. Reintegration in such a context thus was flawed. This is where the CVR approach together with the robust peacekeeping in gang-held areas meant greater stability and change.

Economic development is fundamental to a DDR process to avoid the perception that ex-combatants are rewarded for their violence. The DDR processes were never linked to further economic development of the communities, resulting in negative perceptions of reintegration in Haiti. MINUSTAH rapidly understood and changed their approach, and CVR's approach was in this respect much better in that it also focused on community economic development and job creation. It was a strategy tailored much more closely to the Haitian context.

Notes

1 The Integrated DDR Standards at http://www.unddr.org/iddrs/framework.php
2 See e.g. A. Özerdem, 'Disarmament, demobilisation and reintegration of former combatants in Afghanistan: Lessons learned from a cross-cultural perspective', *Third World Quarterly*, Volume 23, Issue 5, 2002. A. Fitz-Gerald and H. Mason (eds.) *From Conflict to Community: A Combatant's Return to Citizenship*, Shrivenham, GFN-SSR, 2005.
3 R. Muggah, 'No Magic Bullet: A Critical Perspective on Disarmament, Demobilization and Reintegration (DDR) and Weapons Reduction in Post-conflict Contexts', *The Round Table: The Commonwealth Journal of International Affairs*, Volume 94, Issue 379, 2005.
4 M. Knight, 'Guns, camps and cash: Disarmament, demobilization and reinsertion of former combatants in transitions from war to peace', *Journal of Peace Research*, Volume 41, Issue 4, 2004.
5 See e.g. J. Mccullin, *Ex-combatants and the post-conflict state: Challenges of Reintegration (Rethinking Political Violence)*, New York, Palgrave Macmillan, 2013. A. Özerdem, 'A re-conceptualisation of ex-combatant reintegration: "social reintegration" approach', *Conflict, Security & Development*, Volume 12, Issue 1, 2012.
6 See e.g. DDR Forum, *International Peacekeeping*, Volume 20, Issue 3, 2013.
7 This definition of disarmament is broadly based upon the definitions outlined in the Secretary-General's report on the role of UN peacekeeping in DDR, S/2000/101, 11 February 2000, para.6, and the Integrated DDR Standards < http://www.unddr.org/iddrs/framework.php> (accessed 12 October 2008). The EU follows the UN DDR definitions, but uses reintegration mainly not reinsertion. EU Concept for Support of DDR, Approved by the European Commission 14 December 2006 and by the Council of the European Union 11 December 2006 <http://www.eplo.org/documents/EU_Joint_concept_DDR.pdf≥ (accessed 12 October 2008).
8 See e.g. C. Gleichman, M. Odenwald, K. Stenken and A. Wilkinson, *DDR, A Practical Field and Classroom Guide*, Hassmuller Frankfurt, 2004, para. 2.1, p.29.
9 P.J. Croll, 'Voices and Choices of disarmament. Lessons learnt from Bonn International Centre for Conversion's experience in other countries', BICC, 2002.
10 IDDR Standards op.cit.
11 IDDR Standards op.cit.
12 Port-au-Prince agreement para.1, September 1994.
13 Security Council Resolution, S/RES/940, 31 July 1994, para.4.
14 Security Council Resolution, S/RES/1542, 30 April 2004.
15 Although called 'multinational' it was de facto predominantly US forces.
16 See e.g. 'President Aristide Calls for Disarmament of Section Chiefs', Radio Metropole, Port-au-Prince, 31 October (1994), as translated in *SWB part 5*, 2 November 1994 and D. Farah, 'US Urged to Disarm Haiti Thugs', *The Washington Post*, 26 November 1994.
17 D. Williams, 'Perry Indicates US Disarmament of Aristide Opponents Unlikely', *The Washington Post*, 28 November 1994.
18 A. Goodman and L. Richardson taped interviews cited by Regan in *CovertAction*, no.51, winter, 1994–95, p.10.
19 Captain Brower, Second-in-Command, Special Forces, cited in M. Kennedy and C. Tilly, 'Haiti at Aristide's Return: Hope, Fear and US Arrogance', *Crossroads*, December/January (1994/95), p.33.
20 Ibid.
21 In 1993, 18 US service personnel were killed, one helicopter pilot captured, and two helicopters shot down in Mogadishu – called the first battle of Mogadishu. This led to high-risk aversion among US decision-makers.
22 The UN also perpetuated this view, see Eric Falt quoted in L. Richardson, 'Disarmament Derailed', *NACLA*, vol.XXIX, no.6, 1996, p.12.

23 'Operation uphold or something: Haiti', *The Economist*, 22 October 1994, p.84.
24 Haitian constitution, article 268.1.
25 G. Michel, *Le Constitution de 1987. Souvenirs d'un Constituant*, Port-au-Prince: Le Natal, 1992, p.95.
26 Interviews with Haitian officials and civil society, Port-au-Prince, 1997. Five to six months into the programme, prices were increased. M. Mendiburn & S. Meek, *Managing Arms in Peace Processes: Haiti*, Disarmament and conflict resolution project, UN, 1996, p.24. However, it does not state that they were equivalent to marked prices.
27 Interviews with Haitian officials, Port-au-Prince, 1997.
28 T. Robberson, 'US Writ Runs Short of Some Haitian Attachés', *The Washington Post*, 24 October 1994.
29 W. Booth & D. Farah, 'US Raids Haiti Firms for Weapons', *The Washington Post*, 3 October 1994.
30 Interviews civil society, political representatives, Port-au-Prince, 1997.
31 'US Soldiers "Invade" FRAPH Headquarters: Front Leader Emmanuel constant Reacts', Tropic FM Radio, Port-au-Prince, 3 October (1994), as translated in *SWB part 5*, 5 October (1994).
32 BICC, 'Destroying SALW survey of methods and practical guide', Report 13, April 1999, p.17.
33 See e.g. SRSG report, S/1995/183, 6 March 1995, para.7, p.3.
34 D. Williams, 'Perry Indicates US Disarmament of Aristide Opponents Is Unlikely', *The Washington Post*, 28 November 1994. Defence Secretary William Perry stated that it was not clear that there were more weapons in Haiti after 14,000 weapons had been collected.
35 A Haitian newspaper reported that it was closer to 200,000. 'Les Jours Passent, mais se Ressemblent Trop', *Haiti en Marche*, 30 November – 6 December 1994, p.1.
36 Interviews in Port-au-Prince, 1997–98.
37 Memorandum for the Lawyers Committee for Human Rights, 24 January 1995.
38 Interview with MICIVIH representative, Port-au-Prince, 1997. According to the US Support Group (USSG) there were a considerable amount of weapons in the countryside, not only the cities, and grenades had been sold to the group in 1997. Interview senior official USSG, Port-au-Prince 1997.
39 J. Preston, 'US/UN Clash on Disarming Haitians', Washington Post Foreign Service 20 October 1994, referred to by J. Regan in *CovertAction*, no.51, winter 1994–95, p.10.
40 Report of Secretary-General, S/1994/828, 15 July 1994, p.3, para.9 (b, iii). It must be noted, that at the time the SG assumed that the intervention would be taken in a hostile environment, and that the force would 'face hostile actions'. Ibid., 2 para.8.
41 Interview with senior MICHVIH representative, Port-au-Prince, 1998.
42 Memorandum for the Lawyers Committee for Human Rights, 24 January 1995.
43 UNDP, Bureau for crisis prevention and Recovery, 'Support to the National Disarmament Process and to Community Initiatives for the Reduction of Armed Violence in Haiti', 18 February 2003.
44 See Chapter 5.
45 Reportedly only 32 weapons were seized. Agence Haitienne de Presse. 'Haïti/désarmement: la PNH procède à la saisie de 32 armes illégales dans le département de l'Ouest,' 9 July 2002.
46 OAS Secretary-General Report on the Situation in Haiti, CP/doc.3750/03, 20 May 2003.
47 'UNDP successfully tests a strategy for the disarmament and socio-economic reintegration of armed groups in Haiti', ReliefWeb, 26 February 2004.
48 This is an estimate made by R. Muggah, 'Securing Haiti's Transition: Reviewing human insecurity and the prospects for disarmament, demobilisation and reintegration', *Small Arms Survey* Occasional Paper 14, 2005, p. 6. It was argued that this left Haiti very low on the list of guns per capita, ranking 164 out of 178, averaging 0.6 guns per 100

76 *Disarmament, demobilisation and reintegration*

people, as opposed to the US at the top of the list with 88 guns per 100. *Annexe 4. The largest civilian firearms arsenals for 178 countries* <http://www.smallarmssurvey.org/fileadmin/docs/A-Yearbook/2007/en/Small-Arms-Survey-2007-Chapter-02-annexe-4-EN.pdf≥ (accessed 12 November 2015). However, this was based on an estimated 34,255,800 people in 2005, which given that Haiti had a population of less than nine million at the time is clearly a miscalculation; and it would be 2.0 guns per 100 people. Others also used an estimate of around 200,000, e.g. see Aaron Karp, 'Measurement and use of statistical data to analyse small arms in the Caribbean and Latin America', UNODC-INEGI Center of Excellence, Mexico City, 28 April 2012, but acknowledged the vast difficulties with these estimates.

49 SG report, S/2010/446, 1 September 2010.
50 SRSG report, S/2010/446, 1 September 2010, para. 9.
51 See e.g. SRSG reports, S/2009/129, 9 March 2009, para.23, and S/2013/493, 19 August para.26.
52 See subsection 'Mismanaged UN integration' below.
53 D. Miller and J. Mondesir, 'Independent assessment of the DDR programme in Haiti 2004–2006', August 2006, p.3.
54 Interview with NCD member, Port-au-Prince, June 2006.
55 Interview with senior staff member, DDR unit, November/December 2006.
56 SG report, S/2007/503, 22 August 2007, para.33.
57 See subsection 'A readjusted approach: From DDR to CVR' below for detailed discussion.
58 The Governor's Island Agreement was concluded in 1993 between Aristide and the junta, but it was not implemented.
59 'Interim Army Commander-in-Chief Appointed, Officers Discharged', Radio Metropole, Port-au-Prince, 17 November 1994, as translated in *SWB part 5*, 19 November 1994 and 'Aristide Reduces Army, Delivers Ultimatum to FRAPH Leader Constant', Signal FM Radio, Port-au-Prince, 14 December 1994, as translated in *SWB part 5*, 16 December 1994 respectively.
60 'President Aristide Promises to Rid Nation of the "Cancer" of the Armed Forces', Radio Metropole, Port-au-Prince, 1 December 1994, as translated in *SWB part 5*, 3 December 1994.
61 'Demonstrators Call for Army Abolition, Cite Rough Treatment by US Marines', Signal FM Radio, Port-au-Prince, 9 January 1995, as translated in *SWB part 5*, 11 January 1995.
62 'Thousands Greet MPP Leaders', *Haiti Info*, vol.3, no.2, 22 October 1994, p.3.
63 *1995 au quotidien*, AHP, 28 April 1995, p.59.
64 'Haitian Senate Adopts Resolution on Dissolution of Army', Signal FM Radio, Port-au-Prince, 9 February 1996, as translated in *FBIS-LAT*, 9 February 1996.
65 Interviews, Port-au-Prince, Cap Haitien, Gonaives, Jacmel, 1997–98.
66 Arias Foundation, Borge & Associates, *Republic of Haiti National Survey of Public Opinion*, March 1995.
67 Interviews, Port-au-Prince, 1997, and see also, Gérard Gourgue, 'Avoir Remplacé l'Armée d'Haiti par une Police de Cinq Mille Hommes a été une Grande Faute, un Calcul Cynique Tant du Côté National qu'International', *Le Matin*, 30 July 1997, p.6.
68 Interviews, Port-au-Prince, 1997.
69 Multinational Forces Report to the Security Council, S/1994/1208, 24 October 1994, p.13.
70 Interview with senior donor official, Port-au-Prince, 1998.
71 Multinational Forces Report to the Security Council, S/1994/1208, 24 October 1994, p.14.
72 Interview with senior IOM official, Port-au-Prince, 1998.
73 Findings of Amnesty International Delegation, Amnesty, 8 April 2004.
74 Interview with senior staff member, DDR unit, November/December 2006.
75 See Chapter 3 for how MINUSTAH tackled the armed gangs.

76 Interviews with civil society representatives, Port-au-Prince, June and November/December 2006.
77 Moreover, members of UNPOL have also reportedly harassed DDR programme participants. Interview, DDR unit, Port-au-Prince, June 2006.
78 For example, in one week in November 2006, five people who had participated in the programme were killed; it was assumed, but unconfirmed, that this was a result of their participation in the programme. Interview with senior staff member, DDR unit, November/December 2006.
79 Interviews with civil society organisations, Port-au-Prince, June and November/December 2006.
80 Interview with senior staff member, DDR unit, November/December 2006.
81 See also J.G. Delva, 'Haitian gangs agree to give up their weapons', *Reuters*, 17 Aug 2006.
82 Interviews with senior staff of DDR unit, Port-au-Prince, June 2006.
83 Security Council Resolution, S/RES/1608 para. 16.
84 Interviews with UNDP DDR and MINUSTAH DDR, Port-au-Prince, November/December 2006.
85 Interview with senior UNDP staff, Port-au-Prince, November/December 2006.
86 Report on the progress made on the Project Intégré d'appui à la formulation et à la mise en Œuvre de la stratégie national de désarmement, démobilisation et réintégration in Haïti. UNDP / MINUSTAH – DDR section July 2005, p.3.
87 Security Council Resolution S/RES/1702, 15 August 2006, para. 11.
88 Disarmament, Demobilisation and Reinsertion / Community Security Programme Haiti, UNDP, Geneva 2006.
89 MINUSTAH internal paper, 'Re-orienting DDR to Community Violence Reduction (CVR) in Haiti', September 2007, pp.3–4.
90 Ibid.
91 Ibid. p.4.
92 See e.g. SRSG reports: S/2008/586, 27 August 2008 and S/2010/4461, September 2010.
93 Interviews with representatives of international humanitarian organisation and local NGO, Port-au-Prince, December 2006 and 2008.
94 The CNDDR's mandate was to dismantle and reintegrate armed gangs. The reintegration programme included vocational training followed by job placement or business management training and a grant to facilitate a micro-enterprise. They received a US$60 monthly allowance. See also T. Donais and G. Burt, 'Vertically integrated peacebuilding and community violence reduction in Haiti', Center for International Governance Innovation papers, no. 25 February 2014.
95 Donais and Burt, 'Vertically', p.8.
96 CNDDR, Rapport Final 2011, pp.44–45.
97 Canada was the main donor to this programme at the time.
98 CNDDR, Rapport Final, 2011, p.45
99 See also Donais and Burt, 'Vertically', pp. 8–9.
100 R. Muggah, 'The effects of stabilisation on humanitarian action in Haiti', *Disasters*, 34(S3), 2010, p.8.
101 Norwegian Church Aid, 'Haiti: Exploiting inequalities: Conflict and power relations in Bel Air', Annex 3, 2013, p.56.
102 Donais and Burt, 'Vertically', p.9.
103 MINUSTAH'S CVR strategy, 2007, p.3.
104 See also Donais and Burt, 'Vertically', p.9.
105 See e.g. SG report, 2012 S/2012/128, 29 February para.7.
106 IMF Country Report No. 14/154, PSRP Haiti 2014, 6.4, pp.2–3.
107 Kevin Edmonds, 19 September 2013, <https://nacla.org/blog/2013/9/19/restoration-haitian-army-martelly-keeps-one-campaign-promise> (accessed 7 July 2015).

Bibliography

Amnesty International, Amnesty Delegation, Haiti, 8 April 2004.
Arias Foundation, Borge & Associates, *Republic of Haiti National Survey of Public Opinion*, March 1995.
BICC, 'Destroying SALW survey of methods and practical guide', Report 13, April 1999.
CNDDR, *Rapport Final* 2011.
Croll, P.J., 'Voices and choices of disarmament. Lessons learnt from BICC's experience in other countries', BICC, 2002.
DDR Forum, *International Peacekeeping*, vol. 20, no. 3, 2013.
Donais, T. and Burt, G., 'Vertically integrated peacebuilding and community violence reduction in Haiti', Center for International Governance Innovation papers, no. 25 February 2014.
Edmonds, K., 'Restoration of the Haitian Army: Martelly keeps one campaign promise', NACLA, 19 September 2013 <https://nacla.org/blog/2013/9/19/restoration-haitian-army-martelly-keeps-one-campaign-promise> (accessed 7 July 2015).
EU Concept for Support of DDR, Approved by the European Commission 14 December 2006 and by the Council of the European Union 11 December 2006 <http://www.eplo.org/documents/EU_Joint_concept_DDR.pdf> (accessed at 12 October 2008).
Fitz-Gerald, A. and Mason, H. (eds) *From Conflict to Community: A Combatant's Return to Citizenship*, Shrivenham: Global Facilitation Network for Security Sector Reform, 2005.
Gleichman, C., Odenwald, M., Stenken, K. and Wilkinson, A. *DDR, A Practical Field and Classroom Guide*, Frankfurt: Hassmuller, 2004.
Haitian Constitution, 1987.
IMF Country Report No. 14/154, Poverty Reduction Strategy Paper Haiti 2014.
Karp, A., 'Measurement and use of statistical data to analyze small arms in the Caribbean and Latin America', UNODC-INEGI Center of Excellence, Mexico City, 28 April 2012.
Kennedy, M. and Tilly, C., 'Haiti at Aristide's return: hope, fear and US arrogance', *Crossroads*, December/January 1994–95.
Knight, M. 'Guns, camps and cash: Disarmament, demobilization and reinsertion of former combatants in transitions from war to peace', *Journal of Peace Research*, vol. 41, no. 4, 2004.
Lawyers Committee for Human Rights, 'Memorandum', 24 January 1995.
Mccullin, J., *Ex-combatants and the Post-Conflict State: Challenges of Reintegration (Rethinking Political Violence)*, New York: Palgrave Macmillan, 2013.
Mendiburn, M. and Meek, S., *Managing Arms in Peace Processes: Haiti*, Disarmament and conflict resolution project, UN, 1996.
Michel, G., *Le Constitution de 1987. Souvenirs d'un Constituant*, Port-au-Prince: Le Natal, 1992.
Miller, D. and Mondesir, J., 'Independent assessment of the DDR programme in Haiti 2004–2006', United Nations Institute for Disarmament Research (UNDIR) August 2006.
Muggah, R., 'Securing Haiti's transition: Reviewing human insecurity and the prospects for disarmament, demobilisation and reintegration', *Small Arms Survey* Occasional Paper 14, 2005.
Muggah, R. 'No magic bullet: A critical perspective on disarmament, demobilization and reintegration (DDR) and weapons reduction in post-conflict contexts', *The Round Table: The Commonwealth Journal of International Affairs*, vol. 94, no. 379, 2005.
Muggah, R., 'The effects of stabilisation on humanitarian action in Haiti', *Disasters*, vol. 34, no. S3, 2010.

Norwegian Church Aid, 'Haiti: Exploiting inequalities: Conflict and power relations in Bel Air', 2013.
OAS Secretary-General Report on the Situation in Haiti, CP/doc.3750/03, 20 May 2003.
Özerdem, A., 'A re-conceptualisation of ex-combatant reintegration: "social reintegration"approach', *Conflict, Security & Development*, vol. 12, no. 1, 2012.
Özerdem, A., 'Disarmament, demobilisation and reintegration of former combatants in Afghanistan: Lessons learned from a cross-cultural perspective', *Third World Quarterly*, vol. 23, no. 5, 2002.
Port-au-Prince agreement, September 1994.
Regan J., *CovertAction,* no.51, Winter, 1994–95.
Richardson, L., 'Disarmament derailed', *NACLA,* vol. XXIX, no.6, 1996.
Small Arms Survey, 'Annexe 4. The largest civilian firearms arsenals for 178 countries' *Yearbook*, <http://www.smallarmssurvey.org/fileadmin/docs/A-Yearbook/2007/en/Small-Arms-Survey-2007-Chapter-02-annexe-4-EN.pdf> (accessed 12 November 2015).

UN documents

Integrated UN DDR Standards <http://www.unddr.org/iddrs/framework.php> (accessed 12 October 2008).
MINUSTAH internal paper, 'Re-orienting DDR to Community Violence Reduction (CVR) in Haiti', September 2007.
MINUSTAH'S CVR strategy, 2007.
Multinational Forces Report to the Security Council, S/1994/1208, 24 October 1994.
Security Council Resolution, S/RES/940, 31 July 1994.
Security Council Resolution, S/RES/ 1542, 30 April 2004.
Security Council Resolution, S/RES/1702, 15 August 2006.
Security Council Resolution, S/RES/1608, 22 June 2008.
SG report, S/1994/828, 15 July 1994.
SG report, S/1995/183, 6 March 1995.
SG report, S/2000/101, 11 February 2000.
SG report, S/2007/503, 22 August 2007.
SG report, S/2008/586, 27 August 2008.
SG report, S/2009/129, 9 March 2009.
SG report, S/2010/446, 1 September 2010.
SG report, S/2012/128, 29 February 2012.
SG report, S/2013/493, 19 August 2013.
UNDP, Bureau for crisis prevention and Recovery, 'Support to the National Disarmament Process and to Community Initiatives for the Reduction of Armed Violence in Haiti', 18 February 2003.
UNDP, Disarmament, 'Demobilisation and Reinsertion / Community Security Programme Haiti', Geneva 2006.
UNDP / MINUSTAH – DDR section, 'Report on the progress made on the Project Intégré d'appui à la formulation et à la mise en Œuvre de la stratégie national de désarmement, démobilisation et réintégration in Haïti', July 2005.

Media

Agence Haitienne de Presse AHP, *1994 au quotidien,* 1994.
Agence Haitienne de Presse AHP, *1995 au quotidien*, 1995.

Agence Haitienne de Presse, 'Haïti/désarmement: la PNH procède à la saisie de 32 armes illégales dans le département de l'Ouest,' 9 July 2002.
Boot, W., and Farah, D., 'US Raids Haiti Firms for Weapons', *The Washington Post*, 3 October 1994.
Delva, J.G., 'Haitian gangs agree to give up their weapons', *Reuters*, 17 August 2006.
Farah, D., 'US Urged to Disarm Haiti Thugs', *The Washington Post,* 26 November 1994.
Gourgue, G., 'Avoir Remplacé l'Armée d'Haiti par une Police de Cinq Mille Hommes a été une Grande Faute, un Calcul Cynique Tant du Côté National qu'International', *Le Matin*, 30 July 1997.
Haiti en Marche, 'Les Jours Passent, mais se Ressemblent Trop', 30 November – 6 December 1994.
Haiti Info, 'Thousands Greet MPP Leaders', vol.3, no.2, 22 October 1994.
Radio Metropole, 'President Aristide Calls for Disarmament of Section Chiefs', Port-au-Prince, 31 October (1994), as translated in *SWB part 5*, 2 November 1994.
Radio Metropole, 'Interim Army Commander-in-Chief Appointed, Officers Discharged', Port-au-Prince, 17 November 1994, as translated in *SWB part 5*, 19 November 1994.
Radio Metropole, 'President Aristide Promises to Rid Nation of the "Cancer" of the Armed Forces', Port-au-Prince, 1 December 1994, as translated in *SWB part 5*, 3 December 1994.
ReliefWeb, 'UNDP successfully tests a strategy for the disarmament and socio-economic reintegration of armed groups in Haiti', 26 February 2004.
Robberson, T., 'US Writ Runs Short of Some Haitian Attachés', *The Washington Post,* 24 October 1994.
Signal FM Radio, 'Aristide Reduces Army, Delivers Ultimatum to FRAPH Leader Constant', Port-au-Prince, 14 December 1994, as translated in *SWB part 5,* 16 December 1994.
Signal FM Radio, 'Demonstrators Call for Army Abolition, Cite Rough Treatment by US Marines', Port-au-Prince, 9 January 1995, as translated in *SWB part 5,* 11 January 1995.
Signal FM Radio, 'Haitian Senate Adopts Resolution on Dissolution of Army', Port-au-Prince, 9 February 1996, as translated in *FBIS-LAT,* 9 February 1996.
The Economist, 'Operation uphold or something: Haiti', 22 October 1994.
Tropic FM Radio, 'US Soldiers "Invade" FRAPH Headquarters: Front Leader Emmanuel constant Reacts, Port-au-Prince, 3 October (1994), as translated in *SWB part 5*, 5 October 1994.
Williams, D., 'Perry Indicates US Disarmament of Aristide Opponents Unlikely', *The Washington Post*, 28 November 1994.

5 Police reform

The next two chapters deal with police, justice and prison reform, as these are critical to sustainable peace and development, and moreover, have been established as core in most peace operations. The importance of police reform and how it can profoundly affect the stability or indeed reoccurrence of conflict is underlined by Haiti. The way that police reform was conducted was a principal contributing factor in increasing destabilisation and insecurity and to the police force's gradual unravelling after 1994. The fact that police, justice and prison reform were not approached concurrently or recognised for the way in which they interact and are interdependent also added to the volatility. After 2004 lessons were learnt from the previous experience, but it took over two years of UN presence before a more effective police reform process could begin. This was a result of numerous factors, including an unwilling transitional government, donors with different agendas and lack of international cooperation and coordination.

The police reform process underwent three distinct phases from 1994 to 2016: the establishment of an interim police force immediately after the first intervention; the creation of a new civilian Haitian police force; and after its demise, the re-establishment of the Haitian National Police (PNH)[1] after 2004. The latter phase incorporated the new and enormous challenges faced by the PNH and the UN in the aftermath of the earthquake. This chapter discusses the failure of the interim police force; the difficulties of establishing the PNH in a politically changing and charged environment with decreasing democratisation; and the re-establishment of the PNH during transitional government, political stalemates and inadequate resources, whilst highlighting issues such as local ownership, coordination and insufficient justice support.

Reforming police forces: Building police services

The success of reform in the security sector is closely tied to the other issues discussed in this book such as economic development, justice and DDR. Due to its very political nature and the large number of actors involved in police reform, results have often been mixed. The discourse on both police and security sector reform (SSR) has been incredibly rich and varied and served to develop improved approaches in these sectors.[2] UN support for police reform and implementation however, has nonetheless continued to be beleaguered by a host of problems. The actors involved in police reform range from individual states, regional organisations, international organisations, non-governmental organisations and private enterprises. These have diverging strategies and programmes frequently reflecting donors' own agendas and not that of the recipient country. Frequently training programmes, capacity-building and provision of equipment and infrastructure have been viewed as blueprints for police reform. However, capacity-building needs to be synchronised with organisational and institutional change; without it capacity-building means nothing. In times of conflict and under authoritarian regimes the security sector lack legitimacy and there is profound distrust of the system among the civilian population, in particular because these systems are often used as part of the systematic abuse of the population. Engendering trust in security sector institutions through changing norms and values of the security sector services is therefore at the core of police reform. A major problem lies in changing norms and values. It is therefore crucial to focus on the mind-set shift. This is by far the most difficult task in any reform process. It is also what will take the longest time – changing minds towards an acceptance that reform will leave all actors better off is not achieved overnight, nor can this be enforced from the outside. There is an often un-stated understanding that this is the goal of the reform processes. In the context of a UN peace operation with short-term mandates this is especially difficult.

Policing peace operations: UNPOL

International policing is a core part of peacebuilding and plays a crucial role in establishing stability in post-conflict societies. Irrespective of the breadth of the mandate, a successful police operation is necessary to ensure long-term peace in the mission country since the police forces oversee the development of the public security forces – which often determines whether there will be peace or the resumption of conflict. International policing was for a long time undervalued and its role not sufficiently understood or investigated. This changed considerably during the period in discussion, but a number of challenges remain in order to have successful policing operations.

Civilian police have been a part of UN peace operations since the United Nations operation in the Congo (ONUC) in 1960–64, although their role has undergone substantial change. The number of civilian police officers participating in peace operations has risen considerably. In 1994 the average number of UN police officers (UNPOL) deployed in peace operations per month was 1,677; by September 2005 this number had increased to 6,167; in March 2016 13,251 UNPOL officers were deployed in peace operations around the globe.[3] It is not only the number of officers that has changed, but also the mandates. They regularly include monitoring, mentoring, assisting and training of local police forces, as well as direct law enforcement.

In 1997, the important role played by international police officers was underlined by the President of the Security Council who stated that 'the civilian police perform indispensable functions in monitoring and training national police forces and can play a major role, through assistance to local police forces, in restoring civil order, supporting the rule of law and fostering civil reconciliation' and that the Security Council 'sees an increasingly important role for civilian police…'. The Brahimi report reflected the increasing value of international civilian policing in peace operations and contained an analysis of the role of UNPOL and outlined recommendations for change. Importantly, it emphasised that 'the modern role of civilian police needs to be better understood and developed. … [A] doctrinal shift is required in how the Organisation conceives of and utilises civilian police in peace operations…'. The Hippo report underscored that a change in approach is needed as 'the UN's model of short-term police deployments is supply-driven and unsuited for capacity development'.[4]

UNPOL is currently an integral part of all peacebuilding operations. The success of an international policing operation should not only be defined in terms of reaching a predetermined set of mandated objectives, it must also be viewed in terms of long-term stability and operability of the local public security forces. Although the increasing value attached to international policing since the mid-1990s has been reflected by expanded mandates and growing numbers of deployed police officers, it has not led to sufficient resources, donor commitment or adequate understanding of what support is necessary for international police officers in the field. While crucial lessons have been learned, there is still substantial progress to be made in ensuring high-quality efficient international policing and subsequently successful local police reform. In particular, the gap between policy and operations remains significant.[5]

Providing support to national police forces by UNPOL is complex. National police forces are workers and managers with their own interests, values and goals; they are always a very political institution, even more so in a post-conflict, post-authoritarian state; they as an institution are shaped by the context. They are influenced by their government, the international community and the public. In addition, insecurity, judicial and penal reform all affect police reform. These factors were all highly visible in Haiti.

Haiti had never had a separate civilian police force. It had been part of the armed forces of Haiti. Establishing the police force therefore was of great importance. UN Security Council Resolution 940 authorised the UN mission to assist the Haitian government with establishing a secure and safe environment, and the creation of a separate police force.[6] The subsequent UN resolutions all referred to assisting in the professionalisation of the police.[7]

UN Security Council Resolution 1542 adopted on 30 April 2004 established MINUSTAH and stipulated that the mission should 'assist the transitional government in monitoring, restructuring and reforming the Haitian National Police…' and to 'assist with the restoration and maintenance of the rule of law'.[8] MINUSTAH's mandate was renewed on the 15 August 2006 and reinforced and expanded the existing mandate. It increased the number of police officers.[9] The UN mission was renewed each year thereafter, each mandate emphasising the importance of support for the police. After the earthquake in 2010 the number

84 *Police reform*

of UNPOL officers was increased from 2,211 in 2009 to 3,711; this was further increased in June 2010 to 4,391.[10] It was gradually decreased from 2012 and in 2015 there were 2,239 UNPOL officers (including formed police units).

As all the UN missions in Haiti had a strong mandate to support the PNH, UNPOL became central to the successful outcome of the mandates. Unfortunately the varying quality of UNPOL officers is an issue repeatedly found in peace operations. UNPOL has suffered from deficient pre-planning, narrow knowledge of context due to lack of pre-deployment and in-mission training, frequent rotations thus decreasing institutional memory, and non-targeted skills, to mention only a few problems. The quality control and selection of UNPOL officers across peace operations have increased significantly in the past decade, as is also exemplified by Haiti, but many issues remain.[11]

In Haiti, criticisms were at times directed at the poor quality of certain UNPOL officers and the lack of French-speaking officers. Specific skills among UNPOL was needed to support the national police with tackling such crimes as gang violence, kidnapping, drugs and weapons trafficking, sexual and gender-based violence, and transnational crimes. Other issues included the need for co-location and a greater number of UNPOL officers to support the reform process. These issues were acknowledged and addressed by increasing the number of officers throughout the mandates and extensive co-location as well as deployment of specialised teams to deal with, for example, sexual and gender-based violence.

Box 5.1 Haitian National Police[12]

The PNH was established in 1995. The PNH falls under the responsibility of the Haitian Ministry of Justice and Public Security (Ministère de la Justice et de la Sécurité Publique d'Haïti). It is a civilian institution under the authority of a single director general, the mission of which is 'to ensure law and order and protect the life and property of citizens'.[13]

It has the following structure:

- Headquarters (Direction générale): security policy and strategic development for the institution;
- Inspectorate General (Inspection générale): enforcement monitoring;
- Three central directorates (Directions centrales):
  ○ Central Directorate of Administrative Police (Direction centrale de la Police administrative), which ensures public security;
  ○ Central Directorate of the Judicial Police (Direction centrale de la Police judiciaire, DCPJ), which combats crime;
  ○ Central Directorate of Administrative and General Services (Direction centrale de l'Administration et des Services généraux), which handles administrative management.

Ten departmental directorates, one in each of the ten jurisdictions of Haiti (Directions départementales).

- The Central Directorate of Administrative Police is responsible for crime prevention and intervenes through specialised units:
- Special intervention and law enforcement unit (Corps d'intervention et du maintien de l'ordre);
- National police intervention unit (Groupe d'intervention de la police nationale);
- General security unit of the national palace (Groupe d'intervention de la police nationale);
- Presidential security unit (Unité de sécurité générale du palais national);
- Coastguard (Garde-côtes);
- Motorised intervention brigade (Corps des Brigades d'intervention motorisées);
- Roads and traffic police unit (Direction de la circulation et de la police routière);
- Fire brigade (Corps des sapeurs-pompiers);
- Airport commission (Commissariat de l'aéroport);
- Diplomatic security unit (Unité de sécurité diplomatique).

The Direction centrale de la Police judiciaire (DCPJ) is charged with combating crime in close collaboration with the judicial authorities. It operates through:

- The Office of Scientific and Technical Police (Bureau de la Police scientifique et technique);
- The Office of Financial and Economic Affairs (Bureau des Affaires financières et économiques);
- The Bureau of Forensic Intelligence (Bureau de Renseignements judiciaires, BRJ);
- The Bureau of Criminal Affairs (Bureau des Affaires criminelles);
- The Drug Trafficking Investigation Bureau (Bureau de lutte contre le trafic des stupéfiants);
- The Auto Theft Brigade (Brigade de lutte contre le vol de véhicules);
- The Bureau for the Protection of Minors (Le Bureau de protection des mineurs);
- The Research and Intervention Brigade (La Brigade de recherches et d'intervention);
- The Kidnapping Unit (Cellule contre l'enlèvement).

This structure was not established in 1995, it evolved through the years, but was current in 2015. The components/units were not all operational at all times, and some were still not operational in 2015.

continued...

Box 5.1 continued...

The number of police officers in the PNH has varied. It tripled from 2004 to approximately 10,000 officers in 2014. The 2006 reform plan set the PNH at 14,000 officers, not including administrative staff, but acknowledged that additional security personnel in some form were required (18,000–20,000 in total including the police). The new police reform plan adopted in 2012 aimed to have 15,000 officers by 2016. In 2015 the total strength of the PNH was 11,900 officers. In 2016 the force still had only half of the recommended police to population ratio.

In 2015 approximately 80 per cent of PNH officers were stationed in Port-au-Prince and the West department, where the capital is located. This had not changed since 1994. Thus the PNH continuously had a limited presence in the country's rural areas.

The Haitian Interim Police Force

Prior to the full deployment of United Nations Mission in Haiti (UNMIH) the Multinational Force (MNF) oversaw the establishment of the interim police force, which was established and operational while the new Haitian police force was being formed and trained. This force consisted of 'recycled' former soldiers, who received six days of retraining by the International Criminal Investigation, Training and Assistance Programme (ICITAP).[14] The US insisted that the interim police force should consist of former FAd'Hs, because they had public security experience.[15] The objective of the establishment of the interim police force was to hinder mission creep and avoid the MNF exercising policing duties.[16]

There were two main problems in relation to using former soldiers as an interim force: the population was extremely opposed to it, which made the force ineffective, and the former soldiers were abusive and contributed to lawlessness.

The population was strongly against the interim police force with its 'recycled' former soldiers. The uniforms were new, but the men were not and there were several demonstrations against the force.[17] The change in uniform did not constitute a change of mentality, and six days of retraining could not achieve that objective.[18] Approximately half of the former FAd'H participated in this force and 200 entered the Palace Guards. Paradoxically they were protecting the legally elected government that they ousted three years earlier.

There was a form of vetting[19] of the interim force, but it lacked transparency and accountability. The selection had a clear political dimension. From a US perspective the selection was based on a strategy to ensure a 'balance' of supporters and opponents of Aristide in the force,[20] whereas the Aristide government wanted to ensure as few former coup supporters as possible in the force. As a result the US demanded a purge of the interim police force, when some were hired without their approval.[21] They argued that there had been Haitian political bias in the selection of the interim force and people who had not undergone the vetting process had been included.[22] A proper vetting procedure in Haiti at the time was close to impossible, particularly considering the short timeframe. Overall it was a much politicised procedure where people that were supported by the MNF were selected and the government tried to get their own supporters in. This was a concerning example of bilateral political influence and a complete lack of local ownership of any parts of the process of establishing the interim force. 'Vetting' or not, the force cannot be characterised as anything but a failure.

The force was inadequate in dealing with the increasing insecurity in Haiti and did not have the means to assure stability. Because of the intense dislike and distrust it faced, it was often too frightened to go out on patrols and would insist on International Police Monitors (IPMs) accompanying them, or would simply not respond to calls.[23] They were terrified of the people and, therefore, not very effective.[24] Human rights organisations reported that the interim police force was contributing to the increased lawlessness, and did not have the confidence of Haitians.[25] It was a body that has been described as demoralised, fearful, incompetent and abusive.[26] Contrary to this were the reports sent by the MNF to the Security Council, which stated that the force was 'confident and competent' in their duties. The MNF highlighted 'the success and acceptance' of it and referred to the 'integration' of the interim force.[27] These reports were arguably affected by the MNF's exit strategy, since it wanted to demonstrate that a secure and stable environment had been established, so it could transfer control to the UN. However, the interim police was never a stabilising factor in Haiti. The force was dissolved on 6 December 1995.

The interim force was established to limit the MNF's role in policing, it ignored the demands of both the government and the population in that they did not want former soldiers conducting policing duties. It did not serve as a force for stability but rather increased insecurity. It laid the foundations for the new police force and the UN had to contend with the fall-out from the interim police force. This served to complicate rather than facilitate the establishment of a democratic civilian police force – making the UN's tasks even more complex.

The Haitian National Police (PNH)

The Haitian Police Force was established in 1995. The largest bilateral donors during this phase were the US, followed by Canada and France. From 1994 to 2000 the US provided nearly US$70 million to support the establishment of the PNH, Canada provided US$30 million in the same period, and France – a much smaller donor – delivered technical assistance to the judicial police in 1997–2000 costing US$834,000.[28] These countries also contributed through the UN mission and UNPOL. Because of the US' and Canada's reductions in their bilateral policing assistance towards the end of the period the UN emerged as the largest donor. Owing to the multiple actors involved in police reform this section addresses the effects of the combination of efforts.

Despite the support described above the PNH began its descent and fragmentation early after its establishment. Human rights abuse became a problem within the newly-established force as early as 1996, as well as crime, mainly drug-related, and corruption, and the PNH carried out torture, ill-treatment and extra-judicial executions.[29] From 1997 the PNH was politically active in some rural areas.[30] This expanded into urban areas soon thereafter. The director of the judicial police resigned in protest on 18 August 1998, against what he called 'the arbitrary practices of a political militia in this institution'.[31] Parts of the police force became increasingly politicised. The UN stated in spring 1995 that they (UN, MNF) 'must leave a heritage, a police force that is capable of ensuring the security of the Haitian people'.[32] They did not. Several factors were involved in the failure of the PNH, including lack of donor coordination; lack of ownership; Haitian political will to reform; a changing political context; and strong bilateral influences, which at times complicated the UN's role.

Selection, capacity-building and training

The establishment of a new police force was viewed very positively by civil society in Haiti and queues for recruitment were long. But the former soldiers had experience, education and weapons training, and therefore 1,500 former army troops were included in the new force.[33] According to a former prime minister they were also included because the US wanted the army in the PNH as a counterweight to Lavalas supporters, as they had insisted upon in the interim police force.[34] The Haitian government had not wanted 1,500 'recycled' soldiers in the new police force.

There are major difficulties with establishing new police forces in post-conflict societies. In any context where the population traditionally is sceptical and opposed to security forces, establishing trust becomes a difficult task. Haiti had experienced 200 years of brutality by security forces; to change the population's perception of them would take a long time. However, the training and capacity-building was formed by the need to get the police on to the street as quickly as possible. What should have been taken into consideration was the fact that the force was created in an institutional vacuum where no real tradition of civilian policing existed.

The training was short, with courses lasting only four months,[35] which was further reduced because approximately half the courses were given by internationals who needed an interpreter.[36] Moreover, because of the lack of facilities in Haiti the force was trained half of the time on US military bases. This was a sensitive issue since a large part of the officer corps of the former Haitian army had previously been trained at US army bases. The training of the civilian police force in the US was, therefore, strongly objected to by the Haitian government. Their main concern was that the force would lose credibility with the public.[37] Ordinary Haitians also objected to the fact that so much of the training of the civilian police force was left in US military control.[38] This was also an issue raised by other international actors involved with police training. But the US administration showed a serious lack of concern for Haitian objections.

The different donors followed different approaches to the training. There was no unified strategy or approach to supporting the establishment of a new Haitian police force by international donors. This was reflected in the bilateral support to the PNH, as well as among UNPOL within the various UN missions. For example, Canada was trying to create a community based force,[39] whilst the US, reflective of their own policing practices, focused less on community outreach and more on crowd control, stop and search, use of firearms and police procedure, as well as provision of equipment and supplies. In any police support programme, differences in approach are a common feature of bilateral support – and Haiti was no exception. This was further complicated by the lack of local ownership of these processes and different, albeit unclear, visions of what policing in Haiti should look like. There was enormous political support for the establishment of a civilian police force, however what the Haitian government and civil society wanted that police force to look like was sidelined.

Vetting of the new force was problematic. No human rights violator was to be included in the PNH. Candidates were checked for criminal records, but in Haiti this was very difficult as a complete list of human rights abusers did not exist.[40] ICITAP demanded proof of the violations, which was difficult to obtain since it was only the outcry of the people who identified them.[41] Verifying that they were telling the truth about abuses was a complicated process, and tracing the past of each recruit impossible. The vetting process could therefore be considered flawed, as evidenced by the human rights abuse conducted by the force. Inadequate vetting of former FAd'H was a particular problem creating a 'small group culture of contempt and impunity' similar to what existed in the FAd'H.[42]

There was too little emphasis on human rights in the training. Out of the four months of training, there were nine hours of human rights instruction and a sixteen-hour human dignity course.[43] In a society where for 200 years weapons and uniforms have meant power and money, it would be necessary to provide a different role model. The new members of the police grew up thinking that weapons equalled power and money, and some went into the academy with the thought of obtaining just that.[44] Training them in the use of firearms, crowd control and police procedures was simply not sufficient. The international community acknowledged that the first graduates from the police academy had received too little training. The situation did not improve with the graduates who received longer training, in part because human rights and community policing continued to be insufficiently included.

Human rights, oversight and accountability

Human rights abuse rapidly became a problem within the new force. Between July 1995 and January 1997 the PNH was responsible for at least 46 killings, wounding numerous others, scores of human rights abuses and other abuses of authority.[45] Reports emphasised that the special police units *Compagnie d'Intervention et de Maintien d'Ordre* (CIMO) and its regional equivalent *Unités Départmentales de Maintien d'Ordre* (UDMO) were especially heavy-handed.[46] It was found that police with former FAd'H commanders committed many abuses.[47] The types of abuse committed were in addition often suggestive of the modus operandi of the former army.[48] But the problem of human rights violations cannot be blamed exclusively on the former FAd'H officers. There were two commissariats, which consisted only of former army personnel. They were disliked because of this, but there were no human rights abuses in these departments; since they were distrusted this served as a control mechanism and they conformed more to the rules.[49]

One of the major problems with the force was the lack of internal prosecution. Corruption and crime were rampant, but the office dealing with internal prosecution was deemed 'not sufficiently active'.[50] Not one police officer had been convicted of killing as of January 1997.[51] One attempt to eradicate the undesirable elements of the force was undertaken in 1996 and a number of police officers were fired from the force due to involvement in drugs, human rights abuse, robberies and arms trafficking. After eleven people were killed by the police in Carrefour Feuilles in Port-au-Prince in May 1999, police officers were for the first time tried and convicted of killing. They were however only sentenced to three years imprisonment. This was one small step in ensuring accountability of the police, but with numerous crimes committed by police officers, it was simply not enough. There was no efficient control system for the force. Nor did it seem that there was political will to consolidate oversight and accountability by the government. For example, the head of the internal prosecution unit was removed in April 2000 and a permanent replacement had not been appointed by the end of that year.

Bilateral and UN support was predominantly focused on training and capacity-building; internal and external accountability was more marginalised, in part a result of the need to ensure that Haitian police officers were quickly deployed. The UN had at the time capacity to support the development of internal and external accountability mechanisms (this has only increased with time); in a context where there was no history of civilian policing and no accountability of security forces it should have been a priority. It was a missing element in the support for the creation of the PNH and facilitated the police returning to tactics similar to earlier security forces.

Public expectations and attitudes

The expectations of the new police force and how it would serve the community were high; people expected a community based civilian police force that would serve the people's needs. Initially the population was very positive about the new force, but this progressively changed. Trust was never achieved between civil society and the police. There was agreement across the political spectrum and class that by 1997 the majority of the police were thugs, criminals and could not be expected to uphold the law.[52] There was no respect for the police, but rather a deep mistrust. This was a result of inexperienced, young police officers with inadequate training, who were under-equipped, some of whom committed human rights violations, crimes and corruption.

A rural–urban divide was evident in 1997–98 in relation to attitudes towards the police. At the end of 1997 some areas still did not have police officers in their village and were asking for police presence. In other areas the police had been removed due to conflict with the local population or they had abandoned their posts.[53] In some cases where the population had removed the police, they asked them to return due to unchecked crime.[54] Fewer police officers were stationed in

Police reform 91

the rural areas, and they were assessed for their individual acts, rather than the acts of the whole PNH. This encouraged a rather more positive attitude in the rural areas towards the force. In Port-au-Prince and the other major cities, on the other hand, the whole police frequently became tainted by the acts of the criminal and corrupt elements of the force.

In the context of a deteriorating democratisation process,[55] armed gangs, increasing insecurity and political maneuvering, the police became a disappointment in the eyes of the Haitian population. They were not protected by the police and they were sometimes abused by them. The police would rather stay in the police station than go out into the slums and fight the *zenglendos*[56] because they were overpowered and under-equipped. They could only carry handguns (apart from the CIMO) when most of the criminals they faced were carrying semi-automatic weapons.[57] One of the major problems with the police force was that they did not have a monopoly on power. There were too many groups with weapons in Haiti.[58] There were limits to what the PNH would and could do for the community. The force did not seem capable of dealing with the real and potential violence by anti-democratic elements, some of which were contained within the force itself.[59]

Shortcomings of international support

There are several reasons why police reform did not meet with greater success: the US played a strong role, which occasionally ran contrary to support provided by the UN; lack of strategic vision and coordination among all the donors supporting police reform; a focus on police to the detriment of judicial sector; decreasing Haitian political will combined with a derailing democratisation process towards the latter parts of the missions (1998–2001).

As established above the US, Haiti's largest donor, economic trading partner and with a history of influencing Haiti's political processes, followed their own strategic goals in support of policing, which sometimes impeded UNPOL's role. This also meant that there was more limited local ownership. This was combined with a lack of strategic vision and coordination between all actors and donors supporting police reform in Haiti. Individual bilateral states provided what they saw as best policing practice without any effective coordination mechanism.

Judicial reform, discussed in Chapter 6, was marginalised by all actors. The UN had no mandate for it and for example, 70 per cent of all financial assistance by the US was given to the police and not the judiciary.[60] An effective police force needs a functional judiciary and penal system. The police, as well as the population, will become disillusioned when the non-functioning judicial system reduces the benefits of the police force's work, which happened in Haiti. There was no functioning justice system to support the PNH; arrested alleged perpetrators were regularly released due to corruption and inefficiency in the judicial system. This could be a factor in explaining some of violations conducted by the police, such as the abuse and extrajudicial killings. When an arrest was made the police knew they would have to face the person(s) on the street again shortly, because of the inadequacies of the judicial system. Consequently it was easier to punish the offenders than to arrest them. Equal support for the police and the judiciary was a necessity, but this was not provided and problems ensued.

Although Haitian political will to establish a civilian police force was very strong early on, this was reduced in the latter years. This was a result of two factors in particular. First, there was a lack of local ownership of the police reform processes. No Haitian visions of Haitian policing were taken into consideration and the police were selected and trained according to international decisions. Second, a gradual unravelling of the democratisation process, discussed in Chapter 8, led to increasing politicisation of the police.

In addition, several other mistakes could have been avoided. First, the force should not have been trained part-time at US military bases, other solutions should have been sought; lessons from history should have been drawn and sensitivity shown. Second, irrespective of the urgency in getting the force onto the streets fast, the training should have been longer. The only objective that was achieved with the short training was that the international community, more or less, escaped policing duties. Third, extensive community and human rights training needed to be provided, together with more thorough screening for human rights abusers. Fourth, support to developing internal and external oversight and accountability mechanisms should have been more of a priority in this context.

The Haitian National Police revisited

In the period 2001–04, when there was no UN mission in Haiti, the PNH regularly violated human rights, corruption was prevalent and the force was involved in drugs trafficking. The politicisation of the PNH was extensive, where many operated as bodyguards for politicians. The government and other political actors in Haiti were complicit in the politicisation of the police. The force lacked legitimacy, was feared by the population and the non-corrupt, non-abusive elements within it were unable to change the situation. Therefore, at the time of UN deployment in 2004 the PNH was a force with corrupt, politicised, criminal and abusive elements; it was an integral part of the problem of insecurity in Haiti and in desperate need of reform and restructuring. The scale of the task that faced the international community and the UN mission in supporting police reform should not be underestimated.

During the conflict in 2004 most of the infrastructure of the PNH was destroyed or vandalised. It was established that 125 commissariats needed to be rehabilitated and 75 needed rebuilding; the police lacked equipment, infrastructure and personnel. A year after the deployment of MINUSTAH, Mario Andrésol, PNH's Police Chief at the time, stated that a quarter of the force was corrupt, involved in kidnappings and arms trafficking.[61]

Assistance to the PNH was from the beginning an essential part of MINUSTAH's mandate as well as a priority for international donors. MINUSTAH and the US and Canada were the most prominent in supporting reform. Other bilaterals also supported the PNH including Spain, France, Japan, Mexico, Colombia, Chile, the Bahamas and Germany – with infrastructure, non-lethal equipment, training, IT and other resources. UNDP and IOM similarly supported reform efforts. Yet progress was extremely slow and many agreed that two years were lost in police reform, which only began in December 2006.[62] This was a result of a combination of factors: predominantly an unwillingness by the transitional government to focus on police reform, insufficient MINUSTAH capacity early on, and an absence of donor and MINUSTAH coordination and coherency.

Albeit slow, police capacity, effectiveness, leadership and infrastructure had been considerably strengthened by early 2010 when the earthquake provided a major setback. Before the earthquake the PNH had a new headquarters and 253 stations and substations, but 55 of these were destroyed or damaged in the earthquake, including police headquarters.[63] This dramatically reduced PNH's capacity to provide rule of law. In response MINUSTAH supported the operational capacity of the police to ensure public order. But MINUSTAH's support role was also temporarily interrupted due to the damage the mission itself suffered.

Will to reform

The primary reason for the delays in police reform after 2004–06 was the transitional government. It actively opposed any security sector reform (SSR) activities attempted by MINUSTAH, and it was violent and continued to breach the rule of law and human rights by for example illegally arresting and detaining political prisoners. The transitional government's use of violence and opposition to reform and democratisation was part of their pursuit of their own political agenda: to limit *Famni Lavalas*' support. In this sense they were a spoiler which slowed down the democratisation process and establishment of the rule of law. The majority of the transitional government had been firmly against Aristide's government and many had supported the armed groups and violence that led to his exile. They wanted to eradicate Lavalas' support and in many ways used their time in office to obtain that goal. But armed pro-Aristide supporters were also spoilers who impeded the democratisation process and the rule of law. The PNH was part of the conflict since both Aristide and non-Aristide supporters were in the force. Moreover, they were powerless to tackle the situation since at the time they were under-equipped, under-staffed, needed reform and most critically lacked legitimacy and credibility.

With the election of the Préval government in February 2006 the political will to support police reform and other security sector reform efforts changed. It was not until the inauguration of President Préval that local government counterparts could be found. An indicator of this political will was the re-appointment of Andrésol as Police Chief by President Préval and statements by both the President and Prime Minister Jacques Alexis that police reform would be a focus of the new government, whilst acknowledging the need for MINUSTAH support.[64] In the early months of the Préval administration there was a lack of clarity in terms of what the new government would commit to. This gradually became clearer, and the Haitian government's commitment to reform appreciably strengthened.

Political contexts are commonly a constraining factor in SSR overall and it was a key problem in the implementation of police reform in Haiti. Although the Préval government was positive to reform, the political environment continued to be sensitive in its early days and affected police reform. When Prime Minister Jacques Alexis was forced to leave after a vote of no-confidence, after the April 2008 riots, a new prime minister was not confirmed until September that year. This placed strain on all support efforts as the country was without a prime minister, a reflection of the fluctuating political environment and the weak democratisation process.[65] The support for democratisation was never closely enough linked with reform of the police. Leaders at different levels at different times sought to influence the police and use them accordingly, which continued to varying degrees until 2016. This has been a historically repetitive pattern in Haiti. Training the police in the rule of law matters little if the political system and governance of the rule of law does not change or want to change. If local and national political authorities seek to consolidate power through support of the police and use them to intimidate or harass political opponents, then this ultimately leads to disillusionment and a disrespect for the rule of law by security services and civil society alike. Police reform programming should have been more firmly placed in the wider political and historical context and more closely connected with support provided for the democratisation process. In post-conflict countries, emphasising police institution-building and ensuring the police's ability to provide effective services is all for naught unless similar efforts are made in the political system.

Importantly after Andrésol's appointment, there was a will in the PNH leadership to reform and broader acceptance of international involvement. For the first time there was ample PNH support for reform. The Ministry of Justice and Public Security (MOJPS) were also very supportive of police reform and strongly engaged in the process, although the MOJPS did not provide a proper oversight role. After the end of Andrésol's term in mid-2012, police reform continued to be hampered by the political infighting, for example, through the inability to appoint a prime minister and an inspector general, both whom are members of the Superior Council of the PNH.[66] This, for example, delayed the endorsement of the new police development plan. Thus the slow and intermittent progress in democratisation fundamentally affected police reform.

Planning for reform

Central to police reform is creating a viable police reform plan. One was written by MINUSTAH without Haitian input and signed by transitional Prime Minister Gerard Latortue in February 2006, giving MINUSTAH broad powers over the police reform process.[67] The police commissioner indicated he had not been consulted. There was outrage that this document had been signed by the transitional government immediately prior to the inauguration of an elected president, at the lack of consultation, and at what were perceived to be far too extensive powers given to MINUSTAH. As a result the agreement was annulled. This disregard for local ownership of reform processes by MINUSTAH was surprising and unfortunate – it increased distrust towards the mission by the government and civil society.

A new reform plan was scripted in the summer of 2006 and adopted by the government of Haiti on 8 August 2006.[68] This plan set the PNH at 14,000 officers (by 2011), not including administrative staff, but acknowledged that additional security personnel in some form would be required (18,000–20,000 in total including the police). It also outlined a budget, standards and a sequence for implementation of the reforms. The financial constraints of Haiti were a consideration when creating the PNH plan, but it was recognised that the development of the PNH would be heavily reliant upon external donors.[69]

A new development plan for 2012–16 was drafted in 2011, but due to the political stalemates there was at the time limited political engagement.[70] This cast doubts over local ownership of the initial parts of this process. The plan was adopted in August 2012 and a new Director General, Godson Orélus, was appointed. Key objectives included a minimum of 15,000 serving officers by 2016. In January 2015 the strength of the PNH was 11,900.[71] There were also vast budgetary restraints on implementation of this plan and insufficient funding for targets to be met even with bilateral support.[72] The Haitian government had not allocated sufficient funds for the larger force, not even in order to cover salaries. For example, the Ministry of Justice and Public Security only received 5.76 per cent of the total budget in 2013, and although 83 per cent was earmarked for the national police[73] this would not be sufficient for what the new police plan outlined. This presented a problem: it had the potential of increasing corruption and politicisation of the police force as they would look to other means of income. In turn this could undermine democratisation, the rule of law and stability.

This points to the important link with economic development. Implementation of any security sector reform programme will be hampered if conducted in a vacuum of economic development.[74] The state budget will not be able to pay for the required changes in the security structures, and more than likely corruption and politicisation result. Therefore, any planning process of police reform should be more closely coordinated with efforts in the economic development sector. This by no means indicates that UN missions should conduct economic development programmes, only that when planning for police reform together with national counterparts, these plans need to be sustainable within the current economy and state budgets. And moreover economic development programmes and international financial institutions need to understand the needs of the rule of law better and ensure that some of their efforts are tailored accordingly. This was lacking in Haiti.

Census and vetting

MINUSTAH put into place a census to establish the number of police officers because the exact number of PNH officers was unknown. Many officers left the force during the first months of 2004, others had joined claiming to be PNH and there were many 'ghost' officers appearing only on the payroll. The census was a necessary step towards establishing an accountable PNH. But because of the chaos in the PNH after 2004 and the lack of records, which led to difficulties in verification, it took a long time to complete.

Lessons were learnt from the previous police reform efforts that vetting to remove corrupt and abusive officers was a necessity for an accountable PNH and achieving sustainable reform. Vetting began in January 2007 and was conducted region by region. It started in the Jéremie region.[75] By May 2008 three departments were remaining: Artibonite, North-West and West. By this stage 930 officers had been removed, some that only existed on payrolls, others left fearing what the vetting would result in.[76] Port-au-Prince was the last region to go through the vetting process as it was expected to be the most difficult. The vetting used UNPOL and PNH vetting teams, which increased in numbers as PNH officers went through vetting. This ensured local ownership and was aimed to speed up the process. A confidential phone line was established to report officers.[77] The vetting was slow and difficult because obtaining information about the officers was problematic as there were few records; people were reluctant to provide information about the officers; and UNPOL officers' frequent rotations.[78] Vetting stalled after the earthquake and restarted in September 2011, when some argued that it had not cleared the force of 'its rogue elements'.[79] Only 130 officers had at that stage been recommended for dismissal, many for falsifying educational backgrounds, which was incongruent with the public perceptions of abuse and corruption.[80] By August 2012 not one officer had been dismissed as a result of the vetting. This changed when later in the year the Minister for Justice and Public Security for the first time dismissed 79 vetted officers.[81] Nonetheless since then there were regular reports of human rights abuse, arbitrary arrests, torture, kidnappings, violence and even killings by police officers.[82] However, there was nothing to indicate it had turned systemic. It is worth noting that over 800 former FAd'H were included in the PNH, in high-ranking positions. This was concerning given FAd'H's previous history of abuse and in undermining the rule of law. But there was no evidence that these officers were, in 2016, more involved in or the cause of human rights abuse, than other officers. Nonetheless, given the history of the FAd'H this inclusion gave cause for concern.

Albeit delayed, the vetting process was well planned and well set out to ensure local ownership. It would not have happened without UN support and was a critical part of ensuring a more effective and less corrupt police force. But vetting is connected to democratisation; if political leaders want a politicised force and want specific officers in the force it is very difficult for any police reform support programme to succeed.

Capacity-building and training

UNPOL conducted training both at the academy and 'in-service'. The 'in-service' training was taught by UNPOL, but funded bilaterally by the US. This was a 40-hour course, which included human rights, crime scene investigation, handcuffing, use of force, report-writing, traffic control and weapons training.[83] Furthermore, MINUSTAH supported the development of a revised curriculum. The majority of training was provided at the *L'Ecole National de Police* (ENP).[84] UNPOL also provided specialised training including border control, gender, close protection, crowd control and judicial policing.[85] A number of specialist courses were taught by bilaterals including Chile, US, Mexico and Canada – this included anti-kidnapping, forensics and investigations. Critically, UNPOL provided training in police stations on how to respond to sexual abuse and rape complaints. Basic training was transferred to PNH from UNPOL in 2008, which was positive for local ownership, whilst UNPOL still continued to provide support for preparation and audited courses.[86] UNPOL also tested a new approach to increase police capacity to deal with sexual and gender-based violence (SGBV). They deployed a team of Norwegian police SGBV experts who trained the PNH in investigations and prevention. This team model had not previously been used by missions, but 'has since been recognised as a potentially useful model for UN missions'.[87] Using specialised teams such as this in UNPOL can be a rapid way of closing the capacity gaps that UNPOL habitually face. It can increase skill levels in the national police forces faster and help build specialised units to tackle these crimes.

In the last UN missions to Haiti, prior to 2004, UNPOL was co-located with Haitian police both in police stations and on patrol. Co-location has repeatedly proven to significantly strengthen the capacity-building aspects of any mission. This was not possible from the start of MINUSTAH, because of the slow deployment of UNPOL officers, for example, Resolution 1608 authorised 1,897 UNPOL yet by summer 2006 only approximately 700 civilian police officers had reached Haiti.[88] Both PNH leadership and civil society stated that having *more* UNPOL officers co-located assisting and mentoring the PNH in their daily duties would be an advantage.[89] From 2007 there were more rapid deployment of UNPOL officers and increasing numbers of officers in the mandates. Consequently UNPOL was co-located in commissariats throughout the country; this was also extended to the strategic planning unit and central intelligence,[90] and thus PNH's capacities grew. Successful co-location depends on several factors, not only sufficient number of UNPOL officers, but critically the right expertise needed for supporting police development. As late as 2013 the SRSG pointed out that there was a lack of qualified UNPOL to support the PNH in all the areas they needed, referring to 'budget and finance, procurement and supply, legal affairs, logistics management, monitoring and evaluation, project management, registry and archives, forensics and information technology.'[91] So although there was progress with PNH capacity-building, several areas remained weak.

Nonetheless 2006–10 saw increased police presence on the streets of Port-au-Prince, both on foot and in vehicles (although in certain gang-held areas they were absent, because they would be targeted), and an anti-kidnapping unit was established. However many did not report kidnappings to the PNH because of the force's prior (and perceived current) involvement in kidnapping.[92] Salaries grew by 35 per cent in this period, aimed at reducing corruption.[93] The PNH were still not capable of ensuring security and stability without the support of the UN when the earthquake struck. Their ability to provide security diminished substantially in the aftermath of the earthquake when the police headquarters were destroyed along with several other police stations and facilities; many officers were killed and hundreds injured; this was combined with thousands of prisoners escaping and new security challenges facing the police. It was chiefly the security within IDP camps which created these new challenges. This meant that MINUSTAH had to support the PNH extensively with patrolling and providing security and PNH regularly asked for UN assistance especially with demonstrations and crowd control.[94] As a result in 2014 more than 80 per cent of the joint UN-PNH operations against the armed gangs were conducted only by peacekeepers, as the PNH neither had the capacity nor the equipment to carry out these operations.[95] In the latter part of 2014 / early 2015 only 9 per cent were joint patrols.[96] It proved difficult to recoup previous progress after the earthquake and capacity remained weak.

Even if there was a shortage of police personnel after the earthquake trust in the police increased, for example a survey showed that nearly 28 per cent more of the respondents would turn to the police if they felt threatened in 2010 than in 2009, and they felt the police should be in charge of security (63.7 per cent).[97] But this changed soon thereafter; complaints of police misconduct, corruption and sexual harassment began to increase in 2011, and there were doubts about the ability and willingness of the police to protect people against crime and violence.[98] This was more in line with results prior to the earthquake when UN Rule of Law Indicator Project (ROLIP) data showed that 51 per cent believed it possible to avoid arrest through bribes and 52 per cent thought the police were unconcerned about people in the communities.[99] More concerning were persisting reports of officers being involved with drug trafficking, kidnapping and crime,[100] as well as reports of use of excessive force and abuse.[101] This seems in part have been a consequence of poorly functioning oversight systems.

Oversight of the security sector

One missing element in UN support for police reform was establishment of effective civilian oversight critical in a context where security forces have a history of politicisation. However, internal and external oversight was not explicitly outlined in the mandates and subsequently only addressed in a more marginalised form – during all UN presence – by some support to the Inspector General's Office by MINUSTAH and civil society oversight support mainly through UNDP projects.

Due to a lack of capacity and resources, MINUSTAH began to effectively strengthen the Inspector General's Office only at a later stage. This was unfortunate given that there was an opportunity to urge the government to prioritise and support the oversight agenda. The frailty of oversight was underscored in January 2013 when the MOJPS dismissed the Inspector General (IG). This was arguably a consequence of the IG conducting investigations and recommending the dismissal of several PNH officers. These recommendations were not acted upon by the MOJPS or the Director General of the PNH. The IG was replaced three times in 12 months.[102] This raised questions regarding the independence of the Inspector General at the time, as they seemingly were replaced if they attempted to do their job. By the end of 2015 the situation had improved and 76 police officers had been dismissed as a result of the IG's recommendations, and overall 989 investigations were opened in 2015.[103] Yet the office continued to be slow in investigating allegations of human rights abuse and excessive use of force by the PNH.[104]

MINUSTAH was not involved in support to external civil society oversight of the security sector. In 2008 UNPOL leadership expressed the view that it was too early to build external civil society oversight of the PNH and that it was not possible to do so because there was not enough mutual respect between civil society and the police. Yet, it is critical that civil society oversight starts to be encouraged from an early stage, police–civil society relations will always be tense early on in a reform process but that does not mean that oversight should be postponed indefinitely. In Haiti however, MINUSTAH and UNPOL would not have been able to play an effective role in supporting civil society oversight. The relationship between MINUSTAH and civil society was not of the character that would suggest that the mission would have been able to undertake such a process.[105]

Coordination, cooperation and communication

Coordination, cooperation and communication of SSR activities, and in this case police reform activities, with other UN agencies and with other donors is critical to ensure that resources are placed where they are needed most, for effective implementation and to avoid duplication. Cooperation and coordination of police support met with severe problems early on in Haiti. This adversely affected implementation and in some cases extensively delayed reform. Although in several cases there were structures in place to guarantee coordination and cooperation, in practice they did not functioned adequately.

Donors

The lack of cooperation and coordination between donors and MINUSTAH in a couple of instances contributed to delaying reform, or made it more ineffective. One example was the duplication of efforts in creating a police reform plan. The Canadian International Development Agency (CIDA) had designed a police reform plan and MINUSTAH created its own reform plan (*Plan strategique de la police nationale*) without involving CIDA.[106] There was a feeling that MINUSTAH co-opted the plan and the work of Canada.[107] Subsequent actions by CIDA were viewed by many as contributing to the delay of police reform in Haiti.[108] This situation also affected the relationship with the Haitian authorities who cancelled meetings due to the existing tension. This was only one among numerous reasons for the delay of the first PNH reform plan, but it did play a part, and it would have been beneficial if both parties had cooperated and coordinated their responses to police reform to avoid delaying the process. Another example of absent cooperation can to be found in vetting PNH participants on police training courses. The US was in charge of vetting but refused, in the first two years, to share any information with the PNH or UNPOL, except for stating who could not be included in the training courses without providing any further explanation,[109] limiting both UNPOL oversight, as well as Haitian ownership.

Representatives of a number of donor countries, who attended coordination meetings with MINUSTAH, complained about the reluctance of the UN mission to coordinate with donors and other actors involved in police reform, and felt that at times MINUSTAH had a tendency of dictating policy and that the donors' input was not wanted. In 2006–08 coordination between MINUSTAH and donors was virtually no more than information sharing at best.[110] Not until February 2009 did the Organisation of American States (OAS) and DPKO agree to establish a working group to coordinate Latin American support to PNH, but it was interrupted by the earthquake.[111] By 2011 the US Embassy hosted a monthly working group which brought together national and international actors.[112] This was a step in the right direction in terms of coordination of initiatives and support, however, this should not have been led by a bilateral donor. The government should always lead, if possible, on coordination to ensure ownership of the processes. If that is not possible due to lack of capacity then a multilateral organisation, in this case the UN, should lead but the coordination forum should be co-chaired by national stakeholders – leading such fora both increases capacity and ensures ownership.

What must also be recognised is that actors within the government and the institutions that were undergoing reform in this period, had different views on police reform and the level of international involvement needed or wanted. This was an additional reason for the often contradictory responses of donors, because they communicated with Haitian actors receiving different responses to police reform without coordinating with each other.

UN Country Team coordination

UNDP had initially very little to do with UNPOL's work and police reform, and integration was lacking. This began to change in July 2006 on the initiative of the new deputy police commissioner who worked in partnership with the UNDP to both parties' satisfaction. The first aim was to transform the PNH plan into an operational plan, and the areas of responsibility between MINUSTAH and UNDP was clearly established from the start. The initiation of this cooperation was reliant upon certain key people in both UNPOL and UNDP, rather than systemic integration and cooperation. This was an integrated mission from the beginning, but lacked in parts simple cooperation. In 2012, to ensure greater integration and collaboration in the rule of law sector, the Global Focal Point (GFP) for Police, Justice and Corrections Areas in the Rule of Law in Post-Conflict and other Crisis Situations was established in New York. It intends to 'provide a united front for overall UN assistance in these areas'. This mechanism had not fully been operationalised in all mission areas by autumn 2016. It has led to is increasingly more joint work plans and collaboration as it did in Haiti, so as to avoid duplication of activities.

Government and civil society: local ownership

By 2004 it had been recognised that for security sector reform processes to succeed local ownership was key. Local ownership was defined very differently in practice versus in UN policy documents. For example, both staff at DPKO and several MINUSTAH staff involved with the police reform plan process stated that the new plan had buy-in and local ownership. Yet, it was acknowledged that 'we have not sat down with the Haitians and asked them what kind of police force they want'.[113] The locals were defined narrowly as the government and the PNH leadership and only they were consulted in any meaningful way.

In the first four years of the mission MINUSTAH continued to be criticised by civil society, the diplomatic community and other UN agencies for not ensuring local ownership and because it had a tendency to tell Haitians what to do.[114] In many ways this was the pot calling the kettle black as bilateral donors and other UN agencies had similar failings in ownership. MINUSTAH improved in ensuring local ownership in the latter years, but there remained a tendency to define local ownership too narrowly, focusing predominantly on either government or the institutions to be reformed; civil society in particular was left out of the process. There was a lack of communication and cooperation between MINUSTAH and civil society and other non-governmental actors in Haiti. Civil society objected to this absence of cooperation and felt left out of the processes. Parts of civil society have been extremely critical of MINUSTAH's presence and even when invited to meetings refused to participate because they would not cooperate with the 'enemy' or 'occupiers', which naturally excluded them from the opportunity to influence and own the process. As discussed in Chapter 3, communication improved through establishing outreach mechanisms, informing civil society about what the mission was doing and achieving. However, this did not mean a more inclusive approach to civil society in relation to police reform.

Conclusion

The results of police support post-1994 in Haiti can at best be described as mixed. The interim police force was a failure and set a problematic precedent of lack of ownership of these processes. Establishing the PNH suffered from minimal donor and agencies coordination, poor ownership, at times insufficient UN capacities, and a political context where the democratisation process was unravelling having a substantial impact upon the police – eventually culminating in a politicised police force. After 2004 the transitional government hindered any meaningful progress for two years. After 2006 however, considerable progress was made. For example, a vetting process was initiated, training was delivered and mentoring was ensured through co-location. But there were several issues that were not addressed and lessons not learnt from previous efforts.

There was insufficient and ineffectual coordination with other donors, actors as well as the government. This created an environment undermining a more strategic approach to police support. None of the actors supporting police reform coordinated effectively and in some cases they did not want to coordinate. UNPOL not having a close working relationship with civil society constrained reform efforts. It may have been difficult for UNPOL to work with civil society due to problems outside of their control, but there should from the start have been much more of an outreach to civil society, to include them as owners of the process. After all they were the beneficiaries of what supposedly was a service.

The mission's aims in police reform also suffered from the under-development of Haiti. Although development was not in the UN mission's mandate – it is here the cooperation and coordination with UNDP and the international financial institutions becomes critical. For any sustainable police reform there needs to be economic development, and although this was acknowledged by all actors involved with police reform in Haiti, not enough was done to ensure that the economic conditions in Haiti did not hinder progress or sustainability of reform.

The process was also not initially sufficiently placed in the broader political context. In 2012 the SRSG to Haiti stressed the need to increase the capacities of the PNH despite progress achieved after 2004; he acknowledged that progress had been slow in police training and he highlighted a certain lack of political will. He linked police reform directly with peace and stability as he did the political situation.[115] The relationship between police reform and security is an obvious one, but the political aspect of this in a context of a tradition of authoritarianism was not sufficiently considered. The focus was on training of the police, but not in the framework of the political leadership ensuring good governance or that the leaders in fact wanted a non-politicised police force. This may in part be tied to contextual knowledge as well as a broader process of democratisation efforts. What was not confronted was that security forces in Haiti have been politically controlled and influenced since their inception as far back as independence; and the security forces post-1994 continued to be extremely susceptible to politicisation. The failure to do so had negative consequences for reform initiatives. The susceptibility to politicisation is linked to two issues: first, the belief in certain sectors of Haitian society that the security forces can and should be politicised and controlled for their own gain, and second, the fact that being a member of the security forces has always meant power and money. The latter was tackled through the vetting and dismissal of corrupt and criminal police officers. But both issues needed to be addressed for police reform to be successful.

Significant strides were made in police reform in Haiti in the past ten years in particular, but they were as of autumn 2016 still unable to provide security and stability and ensure the rule of law. In the context of the drawing down of MINUSTAH and the re-establishment of the armed forces of Haiti this was unsettling.

Notes

1 The term 'police force' as opposed to 'police service' is purposefully used throughout – the aim was to establish a police service in Haiti, but although improved, at the time of writing, the Haitian police still constituted a force rather than a service.
2 There are far too many to mention; examples include: N. Ball, 'The Security Sector Reform Strategy', Department for International Development (DFID), Evaluation Report 647, London, March 2004. M. Sedra (ed.) *The Future of SSR*, Center for International Governance Innovation (CIGI), 2010; A. Bryden and F. Olonisakin, *Security Sector Transformation in Africa*, Geneva, DCAF, 2010; Eric Scheye, Realism and Pragmatism in Security Sector Development, USIP Special Report, 2010; A. Hills, 'Somalia works: Police development as state-building', *African Affairs* Vol.113 no.450, 2014; A. Goldsmith, 'Police reform and the problem of trust', *Theoretical Criminology* November 2005 vol. 9 no. 4. In addition, think tanks, particularly since

the late 1990s, have devoted considerable efforts in building thought leadership on the issues, for example, Democratic Control of Armed Forces (DCAF); Global Facilitation Network for SSR; Centre for International Governance Innovation among others.
3 UN peacekeeping, 'Troop and police contributors,' <http://www.un.org/en/peacekeeping/documents/Yearly.pdf>, (accessed 3 May 2016).
4 'Uniting our strengths for peace – politics, partnership and people' Report of the high-level independent panel on UN peace operations, 16 June 2015, para.156.
5 There has been a significant development in UN policing in the last decade. Core areas that were previously unaddressed have firmer frameworks put in place by the UN Police Division. Where there was a dearth of policy frameworks and guidance there now is, for example, the *Policy on UN Police in Peacekeeping Operations and Special Political Missions* and *Guidelines on Police Capacity Building and Development* both part of the strategic guidance framework developed by DPKO, in addition to Security Council Resolution 2185, S/RES/2185, 20 November 2014, which was dedicated to policing.
6 UN Security Council Resolution, S/RES/940, 31 July 1994, paras. 9 (a) (b).
7 UN Security Council Resolutions: S/RES/1063, S/RES/1123, S/RES/1141; and General Assembly Resolution A/54/193.
8 UN Security Council Resolution, S/RES/1542, 30 April 2004, paras. 7, I, (b), (c), (d).
9 UN Security Council Resolution, S/RES/1702, 15 August 2006, paras. 2, 3, 11, 14.
10 UN Security Council Resolutions, S/RES/1908 19 January 2010 and S/RES/1927 4 June 2010.
11 For more detailed analysis regarding UNPOL and key problems they face, see e.g. E. Mobekk, 'Identifying lessons in UN international policing missions', DCAF Policy paper 9, 2005; W.J. Durch and M. Ker, 'Police in UN Peacekeeping: Improving Selection, Recruitment, and Deployment,' Providing for peacekeeping no.6, IPI, November 2013; 'Uniting our strengths for peace – politics, partnership and people' Report of the high-level independent panel on UN peace operations, 16 June 2015 and the forthcoming External Review of UN Police Division.
12 See Immigration and Refugee Board of Canada: Haiti: The Haitian National Police (Police nationale d'Haïti, PNH), including its effectiveness, reform, and the reliability of reports issued by the police and justices of the peace; whether there is an authority that handles complaints about the police 13 June 2013 <http://www.ecoi.net/local_link/252500/363655_en.html> (accessed 10 July 2015).
13 Haitian constitution 1987, article 269(1).
14 C. Arthur, *After the Dance the Drum is Heavy, Haiti: One Year after the Invasion*, London: Haiti Support Group, 1995, p.18.
15 Interview with senior Haitian government official, Port-au-Prince, 1997.
16 J. Dworken, J. Moore and A. Siegel, *Haiti Demobilisation and Reintegration Programme. An Evaluation Prepared for USAID*, Institute for Public Research, March 1997, p.13.
17 J.F. Harris, 'Haitians Jeer US Sponsored Policemen: Military Past Held Against First Officers Picked for New Cap-Haitien Force', *The Washington Post*, 10 October 1994. 'US, Haitian Military Thrown on the Defensive', *Haiti Progrès* 23–29 November 1994, p.9.
18 S. Castor, *La Formation de la Police. Un Enjeu de la Transition* Port-au-Prince: CRESFED, 1994, p.24.
19 'Vetting refers to the processes of assessing the integrity of individuals—including adherence to relevant human rights standards—to determine their suitability for public employment. Countries undergoing transitions to democracy and peace frequently use such processes to exclude abusive or incompetent public employees from public service'.< https://www.ictj.org/our-work/research/vetting> (accessed 12 July 2015).
20 Interviews, Haitian officials, US official, Port-au-Prince, 1997.

104 Police reform

21 D. Farah, 'US Exercises its Influence on Aristide: Security Force Purge Escalates Tensions', *The Washington Post,* 22 February 1995.
22 Ibid.
23 R. Neild, *Policing Haiti: Preliminary Assessment of the Civilian Police Force*, 1995, p.15.
24 R. Neild, *Police Reform in Haiti*, conference paper presented at Fondation canadienne pour les Amérique, November 7–8, 1996, p.2.
25 Human Rights Watch for the Americas and the National Coalition of Haitian Refugees, *FBIS-LAT*, 11 April 1995.
26 Neild, *Policing Haiti*, p.15.
27 S/1994/1258, 7 November 1994, p.3. S/1994/1430, 19 December 1994, p.4. S/1995/108, 6 February 1995, p.2.
28 US General Accounting Office, Report to Congressional Requesters, Foreign Assistance, 'Any further aid to Haitian justice system should be linked to performance related conditions', October 2000, Appendix 1, pp. 22–25.
29 See e.g. Human Rights Watch/Americas, NCHR, WOLA, 'The Human Rights Record of the Haitian National Police', January 1997, p.1; L. Aucoin, J. Exumé, I. Lowenthal, H. Rishikof, *Assessment of the Justice Sector in Haiti*, prepared for USAID/HAITI, 6 November 1997, pp.31–32; Amnesty International, *Haiti: Still Crying Out for Justice*, July 1998, summary.
30 Interview with MICIVIH official in Haiti, October 1998.
31 *Le Nouvelliste*, 18 August 1998, p.1.
32 Eric Falt, 'La Mission des Nations Unies en Haiti', *Haiti En Marche*, 12 April 1995, p.9.
33 Interviews with US State Department officials, Washington DC and Haitian government officials, Port-au-Prince, 1997.
34 Interview with former Haitian Prime Minister, 1997.
35 R. Neild, *Police Reform*, p.3.
36 R. Neild, *The Haitian National Police*, WOLA Brief, 18 March 1996, p.11.
37 R. Neild, *Policing Haiti*, p.20.
38 S. Castor, *La Formation de la Police. Un enjeu de la Transition*, Port-au-Prince: CRESFED, 1994, p.25.
39 Interview with Canadian police trainer, Port-au-Prince, 1998. There are many difficulties with a multinational force attempting to implement different types of community policing models in an international operation; but this discussion is outside the scope of this book.
40 Neild, *Policing Haiti*, p.22.
41 Ibid.
42 Aucoin, Exumé, Lowenthal, Rishikof, *Assessment*, pp.31–32.
43 Ibid. p.23.
44 Interviews with civil society, Port-au-Prince, Gonaives, Cap-Haitien, Jacmel, 1997–98.
45 Human Rights Watch/Americas, NCHR, WOLA, *The Human Rights Record of the Haitian National Police*, January 1997, p.1.
46 Amnesty International, *Haiti: Still Crying Out for Justice*, July 1998, pp.27–29. CIMO was the Haitian equivalent of a SWAT team.
47 Human Rights Watch/Americas, NCHR, WOLA, *The Human Rights Record*, p.3.
48 Interviews with Haitian officials and civil society, Port-au-Prince, Gonaives, Cap Haitien, 1997–1998.
49 Interview with National Coalition for Haitian Rights (NCHR) representative and MICIVIH representative, Port-au-Prince, 1998.
50 Neild, *The Haitian National Police*, p.5.
51 Human Rights Watch/Americas, NCHR, WOLA, *The Human Rights Record*, pp.1, 2.
52 Interviews with politicians, officials and civil society, Port-au-Prince, 1997.

Police reform 105

53 Aucoin, Exumé, Lowenthal, Rishikof, *Assessment,* p.34.
54 Interviews with PNH officials and UNPOL, 1997.
55 See Chapter 8 for more on the democratisation process.
56 Term used to describe criminals, but also used interchangeably with Tonton Macoutes.
57 Later they were authorised to carry heavier weapons, which created concern among some Haitians that it might be used against the population. 'Des Armes Lourdes pour la Police!', *Haiti Progrès*, 16–22 April 1997, p.6.
58 See Chapter 4 for details on weapons and disarmament in Haiti.
59 Human Rights Watch/Americas, NCHR, WOLA, *The Human Rights*, p.4.
60 GAO (the US General Accounting Office), 2000, pp.1–3.
61 See e.g. *Associated Press*, 'In notoriously troubled Haiti, 15 officers to face the bar of justice for brutal murders', 11 October 2005.
62 Interviews with UNPOL, New York and MINUSTAH senior staff, Port-au-Prince, November/December 2006.
63 Crisis Group, 'Keeping Haiti safe: Police reform', 2011, p.4.
64 See e.g. AlterPresse, 'Haiti-Preval: Le noveau president prone le dialogue et la paix', 14 May 2006.
65 See Chapter 8 for more on democratic developments.
66 SG report, S/2012/678, 31 August 2012, para.19.
67 'Accord concerning the control, the reconstruction and the reform of the Haitian National Police and the rule of law and public security in Haiti complementary to the accord between the UN and the Haitian government on the MINUSTAH', signed by Juan Gabriel Valdes, Special Representative for the Secretary-General to Haiti and Prime Minister Gerard Latortue, 22 February 2006.
68 Haitian National Police Reform Plan, S/2006/726, 12 September 2006.
69 Ibid. Interviews, UN Police Division officers, DPKO, New York, November, 2006.
70 See also SG report, S/2011/540, 25 August 2011, para.23.
71 SG report, S/2015/157, 4 March 2015, para.18.
72 SG report, S/2013/139, 8 March 2013.
73 SG report, S/2013/139, 8 March 2013.
74 For example, at the most basic level the situation was such that many of the PNH officers were unable to do the physical requirement test because of malnourishment. Interview with senior UNPOL officer, Port-au-Prince, November/December 2006.
75 Interview with Police Division officers, UN DPKO, New York, June 2007.
76 Crisis Group, 'Reforming Haiti's security sector', 2008, p.9.
77 Crisis Group, 'Reforming', 2008, p.9.
78 Procedures were put in place to minimise the effects of UNPOL rotations, interview with UNPOL leadership, MINUSTAH, April 2008.
79 Crisis Group Latin America/Caribbean Briefing, 26, 'Keeping Haiti safe: Police reform', 8 September 2011, p. 6.
80 Crisis Group, 'Keeping', 2011, p. 8.
81 SG report, S/2013/139, 8 March 2013, para.25. This was described as a milestone.
82 See e.g. Amnesty International, Haiti: Open letter, 2 February 2015, <http://www.amnesty.org.uk/press-releases/haiti-open-letter-prompts-new-prime-minister-take-human-rights-challenge> (accessed 21 July 2015); Amnesty International, Haiti: Protestor beaten to death, <http://www.amnesty.org.uk/press-releases/haiti-protestor-beaten-death-following-attack-camp> (accessed 21 July 2015); Human Rights Watch, Haiti Country Summary, January 2010.
83 Interviews with senior UNPOL officers, Port-au-Prince, November/December 2006.
84 Crisis group, 'Reforming', 2008, p. 10.
85 See e.g. SG report, S/2011/540, 25 August 2011, para.21.
86 Crisis group, 'Keeping', 2011, p.9. See list of detailed courses provided.
87 W. Kemp, M. Shaw, A. Boutellis, 'The elephant in the room: how can peace operations deal with organised crime?' IPI, June 2013, p.43, footnote 26. Yet it was not received

106 *Police reform*

  very positively by other UNPOL contingents. Interview with donor representative, 22 February 2016
88 Interview with senior UNPOL officer, Port-au-Prince, June 2006.
89 Interviews, Port-au-Prince, June and November/December 2006.
90 SG report, S/2015/157, 4 March 2015, para.27.
91 SG report, S/2013/493, 19 August 2013, para.29.
92 For more on kidnapping see Chapter 3; Crisis Group, 'Reforming', 2008, p.4.
93 Crisis Group, 'Reforming', 2008, p. 7.
94 See e.g. SG report, S/2014/617, 29 August 2014, para.14.
95 SG report, S/2014/617, 29 August 2014, para. 25.
96 SG report, S/2015/157, 4 March 2015, para.15.
97 R. Muggah, 'Security and safety in Haiti: What is the role and impact of perception surveys?', Igarape Institute, June 2012. < http://www.odi.org/sites/odi.org.uk/files/odi-assets/events-presentations/1274.pdf> (accessed 11 January 2016).
98 A. Kolbe and R. Muggah,'Haiti's urban crime wave – results from monthly household surveys August 2011 – February 2012', Igarape, Strategic Note, March 2012, pp.1, 6, 7.
99 C. Stone, 'A new era for justice sector reform in Haiti, p.5.
100 SG report, S/2011/183, 24 March 2011, para.12.
101 SG report, S/2014/162, 7 March 2014 para.38. ROLIP is a standard system for measuring change in the rule of law in post-conflict societies. It was tested in Haiti in 2009.
102 SG report, S/2013/139, 8 March 2013, para.29.
103 Haiti Libre, 'Haiti – Security: 989 investigations of police officers in 2015', 8 January 2016, <http://www.haitilibre.com/en/news-16269-haiti-security-989-investigations-of-police-officers-in-2015.html> (accessed 1 March 2016).
104 SG report, S/2014/162, 7 March 2014, para.38.
105 This is linked to issues discussed in Chapter 3 as well as in Chapter 4.
106 Interview with Canadian Embassy official, Port-au-Prince, November/December 2006.
107 Interview with Canadian Embassy official, Port-au-Prince, November/December 2006.
108 Interviews with MINUSTAH officials Port-au-Prince, November/December 2006 and UNDPKO officials New York, November 2006.
109 Interview with senior US police officer, Port-au-Prince, June 2006.
110 Interviews with donors and diplomats, Port-au-Prince, November/December 2006, April 2008.
111 Crisis Group, 'Keeping', 2011, p. 13.
112 Crisis Group, 'Keeping', 2011, p.13.
113 Interview with senior MINUSTAH official, Port-au-Prince, November/December 2006.
114 Interviews, Port-au-Prince, 2008.
115 Police reform vital to improve security situation in Haiti – UN envoy, 8 March 2012, <http://www.un.org/apps/news/story.asp?NewsID=41487#.VZ53pflViko> (accessed 10 February 2016).

Bibliography

'Accord concerning the control, the reconstruction and the reform of the Haitian National Police and the rule of law and public security in Haiti complementary to the accord between the UN and the Haitian government on the MINUSTAH', signed by Juan Gabriel Valdes, Special Representative for the Secretary-General to Haiti and Prime Minister Gerard Latortue, 22 February 2006.

Amnesty International, *Haiti: Still Crying Out for Justice*, July 1998.

Amnesty International, 'Haiti: Open letter', 2 February 2015 <http://www.amnesty.org.uk/press-releases/haiti-open-letter-prompts-new-prime-minister-take-human-rights-challenge> (accessed 21 July 2015).

Amnesty International, 'Haiti: Protestor beaten to death', <http://www.amnesty.org.uk/press-releases/haiti-protestor-beaten-death-following-attack-camp> (accessed 21 July 2015).

Arthur, C., *After the Dance the Drum is Heavy, Haiti: One Year after the Invasion*, London: Haiti Support Group, 1995.

Aucoin, L., Exumé, J., Lowenthal, I. and Rishikof, H. *Assessment of the Justice Sector in Haiti*, prepared for USAID/HAITI, 6 November 1997.

Ball, N. 'The security sector reform strategy', Evaluation Report 647, London: Department for International Development (DFID), March 2004.

Bryden, A. and Olonisakin, F. *Security Sector Transformation in Africa*, Geneva: Democratic Control of Armed Forces, 2010.

Castor, S., *La Formation de la Police: Un Enjeu de la Transition* Port-au-Prince: Le Centre de recherche et de formation économique et sociale pour le développement (CRESFED), 1994.

Crisis Group, Latin America/Caribbean Briefing 'Reforming Haiti's security sector', 2008.

Crisis Group, Latin America/Caribbean Briefing, 26, 'Keeping Haiti safe: Police reform', 8 September 2011.

Durch W.J. and Ker, M., 'Police in UN peacekeeping: Improving selection, recruitment, and deployment', Providing for peacekeeping no.6, IPI, November 2013.

Dworken, J., Moore, J.and Siegel, A. *Haiti Demobilisation and Reintegration Programme. An Evaluation Prepared for USAID*, London: Institute for Public Research, March 1997.

Forum Citoyen pour la Réforme de la Justice, 'Pacte pour la réforme de la justice', June 2006.

Goldsmith, A. 'Police reform and the problem of trust', *Theoretical Criminology* November 2005 vol. 9 no. 4.

Haitian constitution, 1987.

Haitian National Police Reform Plan, S/2006/726, 12 September 2006.

Hills, A. 'Somalia works: Police development as state-building'. *African Affairs* vol. 113 no. 450, 2014.

Human Rights Watch/Americas, NCHR, Washington Office on Latin America, WOLA, 'The human rights record of the Haitian National Police', January 1997.

Human Rights Watch, Haiti Country Summary, January 2010.

Immigration and Refugee Board of Canada, 'Haiti: The Haitian National Police (Police nationale d'Haïti, PNH), including its effectiveness, reform, and the reliability of reports issued by the police and justices of the peace; whether there is an authority that handles complaints about the police' (2010–May 2013) [HTI104397.FE], 13 June 2013, <http://www.ecoi.net/local_link/252500/363655_en.html> (accessed 10 July 2015).

International Centre for Transitional Justice, 'Vetting' <https://www.ictj.org/our-work/research/vetting> (accessed 12 July 2015).

Kemp, W., Shaw, M. and Boutellis, A. 'The elephant in the room: how can peace operations deal with organised crime?' IPI, June 2013 <https://www.ipinst.org/2013/06/the-elephant-in-the-room-how-can-peace-operations-deal-with-organized-crime> (accessed 30 September 2016).

Kolbe, A. and Muggah, R. 'Haiti's urban crime wave – results from monthly household surveys August 2011 – February 2012', Igarape, Strategic Note, March 2012.

Mobekk, E., 'Identifying lessons in UN international policing missions', Democratic Control of Armed Forces Policy paper 9, 2005.

Muggah, R., 'Security and safety in Haiti: What is the role and impact of perception surveys?', Igarape Institute, June 2012, < http://www.odi.org/sites/odi.org.uk/files/odi-assets/events-presentations/1274.pdf> (accessed 11 January 2016).
Neild, R. *Policing Haiti: Preliminary Assessment of the Civilian Police Force*, Washington, DC: WOLA 1995.
Neild, R., *The Haitian National Police*, WOLA Brief, 18 March 1996.
Neild, R., 'Police reform in Haiti', conference paper presented at Fondation canadienne pour les Amérique, November 7–8, 1996.
Scheye, E. 'Realism and pragmatism in security sector development', USIP Special Report, 2010.
Sedra M. (ed.) *The Future of SSR*, Waterloo, ON: Center for International Governance Innovation (CIGI), 2010.
US General Accounting Office, Report to Congressional Requesters, Foreign Assistance, 'Any further aid to Haitian justice system should be linked to performance related conditions', October 2000.

UN documents

General Assembly Resolution A/54/193, 17 December 1999.
Police reform vital to improve security situation in Haiti – UN envoy, 8 March 2012, <http://www.un.org/apps/news/story.asp?NewsID=41487#.VZ53pflViko> (accessed 10 February 2016).
Report of the high-level independent panel on UN peace operations, 'Uniting our strengths for peace – politics, partnership and people' 16 June 2015.
SG report, S/1994/1258, 7 November 1994.
SG report, S/1994/1430, 19 December 1994.
SG report, S/1995/108, 6 February 1995.
SG report, S/2009/129, 6 March 2009.
SG report, S/2011/183, 24 March 2011.
SG report, S/2011/540, 25 August 2011.
SG report, S/2012/128, 29 February 2012.
SG report, S/2012/678, 31 August 2012.
SG report, S/2013/139, 8 March 2013.
SG report, S/2013/493, 19 August 2013.
SG report, S/2014/162, 7 March 2014.
SG report, S/2014/617, 29 August 2014.
SG report, S/2015/157, 4 March 2015.
UN peacekeeping, 'Troop and police contributors,' <http://www.un.org/en/peacekeeping/documents/Yearly.pdf>, (accessed 14 March 2016).
UN Security Council Resolution, S/RES/940, 31 July 1994.
UN Security Council Resolution, S/RES/1063, 28 June 1996.
UN Security Council Resolution, S/RES/1123, 30 July 1997.
UN Security Council Resolution, S/RES/1141, 28 November 1997.
UN Security Council Resolution, S/RES/1542, 30 April 2004.
UN Security Council Resolution, S/RES/1702, 15 August 2006.
UN Security Council Resolutions, S/RES/1908, 19 January 2010.
UN Security Council Resolution, S/RES/1927, 4 June 2010.
UN Security Council Resolution S/RES/2185, 20 November 2014.

UNDP, 'Latin American experiences in strengthening the role of civil society organisations in political processes', January 2004.
UNDPKO, 'Policy on UN Police in Peacekeeping Operations and Special Political Missions', 1 February 2014.
UNDPKO, 'Guidelines on Police Capacity Building and Development', 1 April 2015.

Media

AlterPresse, 'Haiti-Preval: Le noveau president prone le dialogue et la paix', 14 May 2006.
Associated Press, 'In notoriously troubled Haiti, 15 officers to face the bar of justice for brutal murders', 11 October 2005.
Farah, D., 'US exercises its influence on Aristide: Security force purge escalates tensions', *The Washington Post,* 22 February 1995.
Haiti En Marche, 'La mission des Nations Unies en Haiti', 12 April 1995.
Haiti Libre, 'Haiti – security : 989 investigations of police officers in 2015', 08 January 2016, <http://www.haitilibre.com/en/news-16269-haiti-security-989-investigations-of-police-officers-in-2015.html > (accessed 1 March 2016).
Haiti Progrès, Des armes lourdes pour la police!', 16–22 April 1997.
Haiti Progrès 'US, Haitian military thrown on the defensive', 23–29 November 1994.
Harris, J.F. 'Haitians jeer US Sponsored policemen: Military past held against first officers picked for new Cap-Haitien force', *The Washington Post*, 10 October 1994.

6 Judicial and prison reform

The rule of law is critical to ensure security and stability in a post-conflict society, and essential for democracy. It is 'a principle of governance in which all persons, institutions and entities, public and private, including the State itself, are accountable to laws that are publicly promulgated, equally enforced and independently adjudicated, and which are consistent with international human rights norms and standards'.[1] It refers to equality, accountability and transparency, and separation of powers. As Carothers points out 'the relationship between the rule of law and liberal democracy is profound'.[2] There has been an imbalance however, in focusing on support for police development by UN missions and other international actors and not the tripod of the rule of law: police, justice and prisons. Rule of law in Haiti suffered from a multitude of problems and in many areas continues to do so to this day, which undermined stability, and facilitated impunity and political manipulation.

The judicial system in Haiti was in considerable disarray from 1994 through to 2016 and could only be described as dysfunctional. Access to justice was hindered by socio-economic divides furthered by the structure of the justice system: lack of human and financial resources; language barriers where the language of the courts is French, but the vast majority speak Haitian Creole (10 per cent or less speak French); and where illiteracy rates were at an estimated 60 per cent (improved to 51 per cent by 2008–12). Moreover, equality under the law was hampered by political appointees, corruption and, to a smaller extent, laws that had not been updated and changed. The prison system was in an equally poor state, suffering from dilapidated buildings with regular mass outbreaks; huge numbers of pre-trial detainees, which meant extremely limited space and resources; low numbers of prison officers; and human rights abuse.

There have been numerous judicial reform projects since 1994 in Haiti, none of which has as yet achieved the objective of an independent functioning judiciary. Several rounds of penal reform were conducted after 1994 and again after 2004, which increased numbers of prison officers and rebuilt facilities, yet during this period there were multiple escapes and the prison service continued to be beset by problems. This chapter discusses the support for judicial and prison reform, the obstacles to this support, and the results of it. It focuses predominately on post-2004 efforts when the UN mission had a clear mandate to support judicial and penal reform.[3] It establishes that Haitian will to conduct reform in the judicial sector was limited and undermined results achieved with the police, and that penal reform remained weak at best. Crucially it seeks to emphasise that the downward spiral of the criminal justice system should have been placed in the context of previous authoritarianism and a collapsing democratisation process. It argues that years of authoritarianism still affected the justice system and the flaws of the judicial system were firmly rooted in the political system, where it had yet to transition from authoritarianism to a democracy.

Reforming a judicial system – a lesson in context

There are three main types of judicial reform: reform of laws, strengthening of institutions and 'increasing government's compliance with law'[4] – the latter the most difficult and often the least focused on. In many ways judicial reform is more complex[5] than police reform in that it needs to address a larger number of different actors including judges, prosecution services, lawyers, courts and clerical staff, probation services, internal and external oversight institutions and bar associations. It also means supporting different types of law systems and within a peace operation context it can be a challenge to get the staff with knowledge of that system. Ultimately judicial reform needs a long-term perspective. Factors influencing judicial reform include the political context, economic realities, international law and traditional mechanisms. In post-conflict and post-authoritarian states such as Haiti where the judicial system has not been independent, for years or at all, this is the critical factor influencing judicial reform. Changing a largely government controlled judicial system to an independent one, without connecting the support of the democratisation process to interventions in the judicial system can have a very negative effect. It means that judicial reform is not rooted in an understanding of the incentives for political control by the political elites and thus resistance to reform. The judicial system must be viewed within the political system which frequently has, and had in Haiti, more benefits from keeping it compliant with government wishes.

Marginalising judicial reform – take one

The justice system in Haiti was beleaguered with immense problems from the start, which was an inheritance of the dictatorship eras – as a former minister explained: 'justice has never been a free institution in Haiti'.[6] There were a multitude of problems: lack of an independent judiciary, lack of personnel, outdated legal codes, and inadequate infrastructure. There were two predominant problems: corruption and Duvalierists. Corruption could partially be explained by the fact that judges were paid less than police officers, which created grave problems.[7] A greater problem was that many within this judicial system were, during the 1990s, partisans of the old regime.[8] This led to inequality, as those who could afford to paid to have their cases dismissed; and partiality, as judges would favour certain perpetrators. It could at best be described as semi-functioning.

Box 6.1 The Haitian judicial system

The court structure in Haiti has four levels: Peace Courts (Tribunal de paix), first instance courts, courts of appeal and the Supreme Court. There were in the period of discussion over 180 Peace Courts. These are the courts that are most accessible to citizens and are the primary point of entry to the judicial system, consequently they hear a large number of cases. There is one first instance court in each jurisdiction (15). There are five courts of appeal (appellate courts) dealing with 2–4 of the first instance courts. The Supreme Court (Cour de Cassation) sits in Port-au-Prince. Judges of the Supreme Court are appointed by the president from candidate lists submitted by the Senate of the National Assembly. Article 174 of the Haitian Constitution states 'Judges of the Supreme Court…are appointed for ten years', whereas Article 177 states 'Judges of the Supreme Court…are appointed for life'.[9] Article 175 states that: 'Supreme Court justices are appointed by the President of the Republic from a list submitted by the Senate of three (3) persons per court seat. Judges of the Courts of Appeal and Courts of First Instance are appointed from a list submitted by the Departmental Assembly concerned; Justices of the Peace are appointed from a list draw up by the Communal Assemblies'. There are also specialised courts with national remit including the labour court and the superior court of accounts and administrative disputes.

Haiti's judicial sector applies the Napoleonic Codes; the Code Penal was promulgated on 11 August 1835; the Code d'Instruction Criminelle was promulgated on 31 July 1835. There have been several amendments to these over the years, the latest in 1988. In March 2015 a new draft Penal Code was submitted to the President. Several recent legal texts set out the Haitian administration of justice and court structure including the Haitian constitution 1987 and the new revised Haitian constitution 2012.

The virtually missing element

UN Security Council Resolution 940 did not provide a mandate for judicial reform. It stated that the mission should assist the Haitian government in sustaining a secure and stable environment, the professionalisation of the Haitian armed forces and the creation of a separate police force, and holding free and fair elections.[10] Subsequent mandates of the UN Support Mission in Haiti (UNSMIH), the UN Transition Mission in Haiti (UNTMIH) and the United Nations Civilian Police Mission in Haiti (MIPONUH) made no reference to the justice sector and focused only on police. It was not until the International Civilian Mission in Haiti (MICAH) of March 2000 that justice became one of three pillars: justice, police and human rights, but its mandate expired in February 2001. The International Civilian Mission in Haiti (MICHIVIH) supported efforts in judicial reform through, for example, support to public prosecutors.

This was a regrettable omission for two reasons: the negative impact this had on the ability of the mission to support justice transformation and the imbalance this engendered by focusing on establishing and supporting a national police service. Despite the lack of mandate, the missions did provide some assistance and support to judicial reform, for example through the École de la Magistrature and training to judges, but were curtailed in their effectiveness due to the absence of a mandate, because it meant there were inadequate to no resources. It is noteworthy that the missions supported justice sector transformation even in the absence of a mandate. Overall the problem with the assistance offered by the international community to the rule of law was that the majority of resources were given to the police and not to the judicial sector. This slowed down the pace of judicial reform.

The UN mission cannot be critiqued for not addressing what was not in their mandate. They could not have effected changes that they were not mandated to do. Judicial reform (as well as penal reform) should have been in the mandate from Resolution 940 onwards. It negatively affected each sector because it was not tackled coherently and as part of an overall intervention. This had unfortunate consequences.

Reform efforts

The main donor in judicial reform in this period was the US. From 1995 to July 2000 they spent US$27 million[11] on reforming the justice sector in Haiti. This support focused pre-dominantly on training of judges and prosecutors, management practices of judicial institutions and ensuring greater access to justice.[12] Other bilateral donors included Canada who provided US$5.5 million, the European Union US$1.9 million and France US$0.9 million. They focused their efforts on specific projects within the justice sector. Canada primarily reconstructed and rehabilitated first instance courts and helped design a case registration and tracking system for these courts. The EU supported the work of the judicial reform commission, and France assisted with developing long-term training at the magistrate school.[13] UNDP in this period provided technical assistance to the Ministry of Justice to a total of US$1 million, and finally MICAH's budget was US$7 million to be spent within less than a year of the mission's operation. A government-initiated process of purging the system of judges supporting former regimes was begun in 1995, but had by 1999 met with limited success. This was not only based on resistance to change, but also there were practical obstacles such as the fact that educating judges takes time and therefore, it would be impossible to purge the system, replacing the Duvalierist elements quickly.

The Haitian authorities established the Preparatory Commission on Legal and Justice Reform (*Commission préparatoire à la réforme du droit et de la justice*), which convened from 1997 to 1999 and issued a report calling for major systemic reforms. A law on judicial reform was also adopted in 1998. There was little follow-up or implementation of these plans. Therefore the actual will of the government to change the judicial system can be questioned. A report on the justice sector concluded that the support for judicial reform among Haitian politicians was weak, the legal system structures were not in place, the legal system itself was inaccessible and inequitable, and the institutional capacity within the Haitian government for justice was simply insufficient.[14] In many parts of the country jury trials had not been held for years. The judiciary was described as incompetent and politicised,[15] and it was impossible to talk about justice within the existing system.[16] It was characterised as corrupt and rotten and stated that judicial reform was necessary for justice to be served.[17]

Some important changes were implemented during this period, for example, the École de la Magistrature was established in 1996. In 1997, it provided 60 judges with six months of training. In 1999, 39 judges received six months classroom training and six months interning in the courts. This was supported by the international community including the UN mission. But although there had been efforts to improve the system the Common Country Assessment noted there had been a decrease in justice and a growth in insecurity.[18] After eight years of justice interventions, it was found that the causes of the problems in the justice sector still included:

> a general lack of accountability within the Ministry of Justice; a judicial inspection unit that is small, frail, and ill-defined; arbitrary judicial fees and endemic corruption; poor communication among actors in the criminal process; over-formal, outdated, and unnecessary criminal justice procedures; a judiciary that is not independent; all-but absent legal assistance for most defendants; insufficient training of judges and clerks; and missing mid-level management.[19]

Weakening the rule of law

There were four critical factors that hindered effective support to the justice sector in Haiti in this time period. First, there was deep resistance in the justice sector to receiving any type of support. The government recognised the importance of reform, and for example, established a coordination group on judicial reform and a 32-point implementation plan.[20] But although the government had pledged to remove Duvalierist elements and reform the sector, it did very little to implement any changes. This was a significant hindrance to achieving change. Second, the justice sector was viewed as key to the sovereignty of the country, therefore having international support in 'reforming' this sector was met with hesitancy by the government, civil society and the justice sector itself. In view of Haiti's history and external involvement in its affairs of government this attitude may be to some extent understandable, but it meant that providing support became difficult. Third, there was less support for judicial reform by international actors because donors and the Haitian government agreed that the priority was to establish an effective police service. Fourth, the lack of mandate effectively hindered the UN missions in offering support, even though the UN emphasised the importance of justice reform.

The implications were several. It meant that frequently, as mentioned in Chapter 5, the Haitian National Police (PNH) resorted to what in effect was vigilante or summary 'justice', as they knew the cases would stagnate in the judicial system. The police had through international support increased their capacity to investigate. But the judicial system did not change at the same pace, undermining efforts in the police. This was further exacerbated by poor, if any, institutionalisation of links between justice professionals and the PNH. In addition, as the public 'face' of the rule of law, which communities most regularly encountered, the police were accused of incompetency, even when it was the dysfunctional justice system that was at fault.

Another consequence was a staggering number of accused in pre-trial detention. By 2002 there were twice as many inmates as in 1995, and over 80 per cent of these were in pre-trial detention.[21] This was a reflection of judges' reluctance to release accused on bail, scant access to legal representation, lack of personnel and corruption. This in turn led to huge problems in the prisons. They needed to deal with large numbers of pre-trail detainees with insufficient facilities and resources. This meant riots and escapes, further increasing instability.

It also had an effect on justice for past crimes, as exemplified by the Constant case.[22] Emanuel 'Toto' Constant was the leader of *Le Front pour l'Avancement et Progres d'Haiti* (FRAPH), a paramilitary group which had committed human rights abuses and political killings. He escaped to the US after the arrival of the Multinational Force and was demanded to be extradited by the Haitian government on several occasions. This was denied on the grounds that Constant would not get a free and fair trial in Haiti.[23] This was a valid argument, as the Haitian courts were not able to conduct trials such as Constant's, given the problems in the judicial sector. Therefore, the inability of the judicial system to hold free and fair trials affected the process of transitional justice for the perpetrators of the coup and contributed to establishing a sense of impunity.[24]

Democracy and the rule of law are interdependent variables where democracy rests on the rule of law, but where the judicial system needs a functioning democracy to be transparent, non-corrupt and independent. Thus the judicial system was also affected by the slowly unravelling democratisation process. The more the democratisation process unravelled the less incentive was there for judicial sector to transform, leading to a further politicisation of parts of the judicial system. When the UN mission returned in 2004 the judicial system had continued to deteriorate in the absence of the UN and there was an ever greater need for transformation.

Marginalising judicial reform – take two

With the onset of 2004 and the new intervention there was an overwhelming need for reform of the judicial system in Haiti. The system suffered from corruption, political appointments and poor or destroyed facilities. Many judges were unwilling or too intimidated to deal with certain types of cases. This was particularly related to political and gang violence. There was also uncertainty regarding the educational background of some of the judiciary. Criminal and penal codes needed reform and no national judicial record was in existence, which meant that it was impossible to know whether the accused had a conviction for prior crimes or were accused of other crimes in other jurisdictions. Pre-trial detention continued to be exceptionally high. The court infrastructure was poor in many parts of the country, since several courts were ruined during the 2004 conflict, and basic supplies were few including office supplies and furniture.[25] Access to justice was exceptionally poor, caused predominately by four issues: the cost of accessing the criminal justice system was prohibitive in a context where nearly 70 per cent were unemployed and the vast majority was living below the poverty line; inadequate justice system presence in rural areas; laws and the language of the courts were in French, yet the vast majority speak Haitian Creole and no interpreters were provided; and lack of identity documents needed to proceed in court. However, it was the lack of judicial independence that was the predominant issue. Support for judicial reform faced huge challenges.

Introducing reform

Lessons were learnt from the previous UN operations in Haiti and support for judicial reform was included in the new mandates for MINUSTAH. This was an important change, providing the mission with human and financial resources to support judicial transformation.

The first MINUSTAH mandate for judicial reform was established by Resolution 1542 and referred to assisting and providing advice to the transitional government regarding the development of a reform plan and institutional strengthening of the judiciary.[26] Resolution 1608 referred to the Secretary-General's call for making an assessment of the Haitian judiciary and exploring possibilities for further international community support.[27] Resolution 1702 emphasised that MINUSTAH would provide 'assistance and advice to Haitian authorities ... including through technical assistance to review all relevant legislation, the provision of experts to serve as professional resources'.[28] Subsequent resolutions referenced support for the judicial sector, although in much less detail than police support and encouraged the Haitian government to take advantage of the support. The US continued to be the largest bilateral donor, followed by Canada. For example, the US had a US$20 million five-year programme (2009–14) to strengthen justice sector institutions, increase access to justice, and improve service delivery.[29] Other actors included the UNDP, the OAS, the EU, France and organisations such as the United States Institute for Peace (USIP) and International Institute for Democracy and Electoral Assistance (IDEA). The majority of attention was focused on legal codes and the organisational structure of the judiciary.[30]

MINUSTAH provided technical support and advice to the Ministry of Justice and Public Security (MOJPS) throughout the period; supported the School of Magistrates; trained justices of the peace, prosecutors, judges and court clerks; and improved access to justice. These efforts were much more consolidated after 2008 when MINUSTAH had greater capacity and resources to provide support. The earthquake halted the work in the justice sector for a period of time, given the significant damage to infrastructure suffered by the judicial system including the destruction of the Ministry of Justice and the Supreme Court. Although progress after the earthquake was slow, particularly in strengthening capacity, nonetheless, with the support of MINUSTAH and other international partners three legal aid offices were opened in 2010.[31] An additional eight offices were opened within the next year.

Support for judicial reform was a very difficult and controversial task for MINUSTAH. Since the deployment of the mission, there was extremely limited progress in the area of judicial reform. There were three critical factors influencing this: political and judicial unwillingness to transform, the issue of sovereignty, and too little UN and bilateral donor resources compared with the assistance provided to the police. Unwillingness was at first a reflection of the transitional government and its abuse of the justice system for its own ends, combined with the opposition within the judiciary to conduct a reform process. This was exacerbated by sensitivities surrounding external involvement in judicial reform.[32]

Collaboration

Further complicating judicial support was the fact that UNDP and MINUSTAH worked on separate tracks concerning judicial reform. It was not only an absence of integration, but even an absence of communication. For example, a judicial reform plan was drafted by the MOJPS with assistance from the justice section at MINUSTAH. It was an action plan detailing what needed to be done in both the short term (2006–07) and in the longer term (2007–09).[33] The UNDP also drafted a judicial reform project document, which duplicated some of the efforts outlined in the MOJPS document,[34] but this was not done in collaboration with the Ministry or MINUSTAH. Although these efforts did not necessarily conflict with one another, there was no combined single strategic objective for support to the Haitian government by UNDP and MINUSTAH.

Collaboration between MINUSTAH and the UNDP improved in the subsequent years when, for example, they provided support to the Superior Council of the Judiciary and the MOJPS.[35] Yet it was not an integrated approach and more of a division of labour, lacking a strategic vision of support. A closer working relationship with all actors involved in the justice sector would have acted as a force multiplier, given that considerably fewer resources were aimed at this sector by all donors involved.

Political will and the issue of sovereignty

Although all security sector reform is political, judicial reform in many ways touches the core of sovereignty, above all through law reform. Judicial reform is therefore repeatedly resisted by national stakeholders, especially within the justice system.

As discussed in previous chapters, the transitional government was not in support of any type of reform in the rule of law sector, including judicial reform. In the first two years this was therefore a substantial obstruction in MINUSTAH's and other donors' ability to support judicial reform. With the election of President Préval there was more will to focus on judicial reform and the need for external assistance to achieve this. For example, the Préval government asked the UN to adapt its support with an increased focus on judicial reform and institutional support.[36] But there was no significant commitment to *implementing* judicial reform by the new government. Political will for change only increased incrementally with subsequent governments. For example, several senior judicial posts were vacant for years, casting doubts over the veracity of the claims that the governments wanted real changes implemented in the judicial system. The president and vice-president of the Supreme Court were not appointed until 2011. This was ostensibly because of a concern that the Senate would name corrupt or politically partial candidates.[37] The president's post had been vacant since 2004 – further underscoring a lack of will to address the extensive problems in the judicial system. In January 2012, President Martelly established a Working Group on Justice Reform with a mandate to propose appropriate measures for justice reform; it was given 24 months to carry out its mandate.[38] There had been several commissions looking into this, as well as international assessments; the problems in the judicial sector were well documented, but implementation of reform was lacking. The President regularly declared the need for an independent justice system, but practice did not follow intent. Again there seemed to be a lack of political will to change the judicial system.

A principal reason for this absence of will to external support was the issue of sovereignty. The government acknowledged the need for reform, and that there was no capacity or will within the judicial system to conduct such reform of its own institutions. But there was an inherent opposition to what was perceived as 'too much' international involvement because it is so strongly interconnected with the issue of sovereignty. The Préval government needed to take a strong position on this issue and decide what assistance it would be willing to ask for and accept. But this only partially happened and consequently the judicial system suffered. Subsequent governments had the same reticence about international involvement in the justice sector. Civil society was similarly concerned about the issue of sovereignty and judicial reform – pointing to Haiti's history and as a result not wanting extensive involvement of foreign donors. Many were quite vocal against any external involvement in support of a reform of the judicial system.[39] It seems that this concern albeit very legitimate, was also promoted by political leaders to avoid actual judicial reform.

Corruption and lack of judicial independence

Although the Haitian 1987 (and the revised 2012) constitution guarantees an independent judiciary the primary concern in Haiti's judicial system has been a complete lack of judicial independence. The judicial system has historically been politically manipulated and controlled. It has functioned at the behest of the ruling class or regime, which has not had an incentive to safeguard its independence as it has been used to persecute political opponents. The international support provided to the judicial system did not adequately take into consideration the historic abuse of a co-dependent judicial system and the poor progress in the democratisation process with negligible improvements in the judicial sector.

This can be exemplified through three laws central to judicial reform which were promulgated in December 2007. These established the Superior Council for the Judiciary (*Conseil Superieur du Pouvoir Judiciaire* CSPJ) with authority to select, appoint and discipline judges and administer resources and tasked with ensuring the integrity and independence of the judiciary; the *Statute de la Magistrature* ensuring judicial career management, adjustment of wages and working conditions of magistrates;[40] and the School for Magistrates (*Ecole de la Magistrature*[41] EMA) (re-)establishing the training academy for judges and prosecutors. Although these laws were a positive step they did not translate into a more effective justice system. The School of Magistrates was not established until 2009, the CSPJ was not sworn in until 2012, wages continued to be low, facilitating corruption, but more importantly the independence of the judiciary continued to be in question. In sum, these failed (thus far) in providing a basis for meaningful change.

The Préval government never filled the positions of the Supreme Court, which meant that the CSPJ could not be convened. One of President Martelly's electoral promises was to ensure the CSPJ was established. Yet it was only established in 2012 over a year after his inauguration. This was a welcome development to ensure greater oversight and to ensure that judges were not politically appointed. But the CSPJ from the start had difficulties in rectifying political appointments and interference in proceedings. For example, in 2014 the mandate of 81 judges was not renewed because authorities forwarded other candidates, and in one month the government removed three judges, promoted one and nominated another although this was the purview of the CSPJ.[42] The judicial system was also used against political opponents and human rights defenders.[43] The apparent will to change the prerequisite laws for reform mattered little when implementation was lacking and political manipulation persisted.

The Haitian judicial system also suffered from extensive corruption, and whether or not a case progressed in court was often a result of political and economic pressures placed on the judges. For example, in 2006 Haiti ranked last on Transparency International's list of corrupt countries; by 2010 it had improved and was at 146. Yet, by 2014 it had dropped again to 161. Because of corruption there was limited predictability or efficiency of rulings. Corruption was not only restricted to judges, but also prosecutors and other judicial officials. Inadequate training, low salaries, negligible supervision and job security left judges, prosecutors and judicial personnel vulnerable to corruption.[44] It also meant that they often took additional jobs, resulting in not showing up in their court functions. This was also linked to political issues where judges' susceptibility to corruption led to increased opportunities for political leaders to shield their supporters from prosecution. For example, the Raboteau landmark judgement of 2000 was overturned in 2005, which was viewed as politically motivated.[45]

As a result of extensive corruption, political appointments, and questionable educational background[46] there was an urgent need to vet judges. There was however, a significant resistance to a MINUSTAH-led vetting process from civil society, the judiciary and politicians, even if these acknowledged the need for external assistance. It was suggested that vetting could be undertaken by a revised *Conseil Supérieur de la Magistrature*.[47] MINUSTAH and other donors were keen to support a vetting process, but it was never a priority of any government. To facilitate a process of vetting the UN Special Representative of the Secretary-General to Haiti, Edmond Mulet, suggested in 2006 using international judges in Haitian courts as an interim measure during reform of the judicial system. This was rejected by all fronts of Haitian society, ostensibly out of a concern for sovereignty. Given the subsequent action by the governments, as discussed above, it can be questioned whether sovereignty was the real concern or whether an unwillingness to implement change was the root cause. As a result vetting of judges did not start until the end of 2014.

Change in the rule of law must be based on a national will to transform; if the benefits of keeping the status quo are perceived to be greater, change will not come about. The flaws in the democratisation process (discussed in Chapter 8) consolidated a dysfunctional justice system.

Law reform

Law reform is an area where there have been consistent international efforts to provide support in post-conflict societies. Models have also been established to facilitate law reform.[48] In Haiti part of the dysfunctional judicial system rested on the outdated criminal and penal codes. Thus reform of the criminal and penal codes was a focus of international support efforts from early on, as they were woefully outdated. These codes were both written in 1835. Revisions had been made regularly but, at the time of MINUSTAH's deployment in 2004, the latest revision had occurred in 1988.[49] The codes did not reflect international human rights standards, inadequately addressed issues affecting women and children, included outdated penalties, and in some cases contradicted the 1987 constitution. In addition, they did not reflect all the different types of 'new' crimes, particularly in relation to armed gang violence, kidnapping, drugs and weapons trafficking. These laws were supplemented by a number of laws and presidential decrees seeking to rectify in parts the gaps in the criminal and penal codes. But these in many ways served to further complicate the criminal justice system as they were unknown by many in the legal community. It also provided further opportunities for manipulation as the laws became unclear. The MOJPS requested assistance from MINUSTAH's justice section for law reform as early as 2006, but the mission suffered from a lack of capacity and resources and was unable at the time to handle these requests.[50] Given the sensitivities surrounding external assistance to judicial reform, this was a window of opportunity for MINUSTAH to engage. MINUSTAH should have been able to respond positively to these approaches by the MOJPS, but it needed the capacities and resources to do so. It was not until later that MINUSTAH was able to provide this type of support.

Draft revisions of the Criminal Procedure Code and Penal Code[51] were conducted by the Presidential Commission for the Reform of Justice. Work on this had started under President Préval with support from MINUSTAH and other international donors, but was halted. President Martelly reconstituted the commissions in 2012, but the draft revision of the penal code was not completed until March 2015 when it was presented to the President.[52] Although the process of revising the Haitian Criminal Procedure Code was begun at the same time as that of the penal code, it had yet to be presented by early 2016. Revision of the penal code signified an important step in law reform, but must be viewed in the light of over twenty years of international support for judicial reform.

Pre-trial detention

A severe consequence of the dysfunctional, corrupt and politicised justice system was the extent of pre-trial detention. Under Haitian law, defendants are entitled to a trial within four months of being arrested, yet pre-trial detention increased from an average of 76 days in 2004 to an average of 408 days in 2006.[53] In December 2006 approximately 85 per cent of all people in prisons were in pre-trial detention, many exceeding the maximum allowable sentence for their offence.[54] By 2010 this had been reduced to 67.7 per cent.[55] It increased again in 2015 to 72.8 per cent. In addition many were also regularly held for long periods in cells at police stations – where according to the law they could only be held for 48 hours.[56] UN peace operations elsewhere have effectively supported a reduction of pre-trial detention and it was also an important focus for MINUSTAH. But in the main due to the lack of independence of the judicial system results were scarce in Haiti.

The pre-trial detention problem was exacerbated by the fact that the police became much more efficient in their duties and arrested and detained more alleged perpetrators, whilst similar progress was not made in the judicial system. There were also not enough justice officials, and cases took a long time to go through the system, if they did at all. Moreover, the Code of Criminal Procedure required the convening of only two jury trial sessions in each jurisdiction per year, but in reality there was rarely more than one session per jurisdiction per year.[57] It was possible to hear about ten cases at each session, so the total capacity of the system was in this time period about 160 to 320 jury trials per year.[58] This increased radically the number of people in pre-trial detention. Other factors that affected the numbers of pre-trial detainees included judges unwilling to release defendants on bail, fearing they would be accused of corruption if bail were to be granted. There was inadequate legal representation for the majority of defendants who had few, if any, resources to pay for such representation, and therefore had 'no effective way of challenging their detention'.[59] Importantly MINUSTAH supported the establishment of legal aid centres.[60] This was incredibly important to increase access to justice, ensure representation for defendants and ensure greater equality under the law, and to reduce pre-trial detention.[61]

Further complicating the issue of pre-trial detention was the fact that no case management system in the individual jurisdictions or at the national level was in place to show the number of cases pending trial, the number of cases heard, and their disposition (although courts maintained a number of manual ledgers). Without it, it was impossible to know whether the accused had a conviction for prior crimes or were accused of other crimes in other jurisdictions.[62] This made it nearly impossible to measure judges' performance, to hold them accountable, or to assess the performance of the judicial system as a whole.

In May 2008 the Inter-American Court of Human Rights ordered the government to reform the system so as to reduce prolonged pre-trial detention by 2010.[63] In 2011 the United Nations Human Rights Council reiterated the Court's decision as it had yet to be acted upon by the government. It urged the Haitian Government to 'take the necessary steps to respect the Haitian Constitution's articles concerning prolonged pre-trial detention and prioritise the improvement of prison facilities'.[64] Yet there was no effective response from the government, further underscoring the unwillingness to reform the criminal justice system. The ineffectual justice system and inability to reduce pre-trial detention led to overcrowding which increased prison insecurity and exacerbated already inhuman conditions, discussed below.

Prison reform

Prisons have tended to receive less attention and funding by bilateral donors and the UN than police and judicial reform in post-conflict societies. It is very difficult for bilateral donor agencies to politically justify to their constituents why their tax money should be spent on incarcerating individuals in a country that has suffered war for years or decades, and where there may be famine, IDPs, and a lack of health care and education. Furthermore, throughout the 1990s and long into the 2000s the relationship between police, justice and penal reform was underestimated, not in policy, but in practice and operationally. Haiti was no exception. There has been much progress in this area since the mid-2000s. For example, there has been a steady increase in providing corrections officers to UN missions.

Governments in post-conflict countries rarely tend to prioritise support for improving prison conditions. This is understandable given the inadequate budgets of countries rebuilding after conflict and competing priorities. Politically it is also difficult for national governments to justify spending on prisons, including food, water and medical care when their populations are starving. They tend to be less opposed to external involvement in support for prisons as it is less complex and touches less on issues of sovereignty.

From an international perspective support for prison reform is couched in human rights language and the need to treat perpetrators and alleged perpetrators as we would others. A much-cited quote by Dostoevsky is 'the degree of civilisation in a society can be judged by entering its prisons'.[65] However, there are also many more pragmatic reasons for prison reform – instability and insecurity. Overcrowded and under-resourced prisons rife with abuse tend to lead to riots and escapes. In Haiti there were several and regular large-scale prison escapes, which had a destabilising effect and contributed to insecurity. They undermined the efforts conducted in support of police and justice sectors. Additionally, if there are continuous problems within a country's prison system it could undermine belief in the government's ability to ensure the rule of law.

Box 6.2 The Haitian prison system

Haitian prisons were previously administered by the Haitian Armed Forces (Forces Armées d'Haïti). In this period Haiti's prisons were in extreme disrepair. During the Duvalier governments illegal detention with no records was common.

The National Penitentiary Administration (Administration Pénitentiaire Nationale, APENA) was established in 1995. In 1997 APENA was integrated into the Haitian National Police (Police Nationale d'Haïti, PNH), as the Penitentiary Administration Department (Direction de l'administration pénitentiaire, DAP). This reflected the 1987 Constitution, which placed the penitentiary administration as a unit of the police.

The number of prisons have fluctuated. Prior to the destruction of several prisons in 2004 there were 24 prisons. By 2015 only 17 had been rebuilt and/or reopened.

Interventions to improve prison conditions[66]

Security Council Resolution 940 did not make any reference to the mission supporting penal reform, neither did the subsequent resolutions. Nevertheless, there were several international interventions to support prison reform in Haiti post-1994; this included the MICIVIH, UNDP, a number of INGOs and NGOs, and the US Armed Forces.

Early on the US Armed Forces (1994 to February 1996) conducted interventions to improve prison conditions. International experts were deployed and recommendations were provided to APENA/DAP. None of these were longer term support.[67] The International Committee of the Red Cross (ICRC) carried out rehabilitation work in Haitian prisons including rebuilding dispensaries, providing sources of clean water and building septic tanks.[68] Several NGOs provided food for the prisoners because the Haitian national budget had limited funds for prisons. The lack of food was worsened by corruption, as it tended to disappear on its way to the prison population and when it reached the prisons there was little left.[69] This was hardly surprising in a context where the vast majority of Haitians lived on less than US$1 per day.

The MICIVIH monitored human rights abuses in prisons, conducted human rights training with staff, delivered technical assistance to prison administration and built civil society capacity for human rights monitoring of prisons.[70] From 1995 to 2000 UNDP was the primary donor supporting prison reform in Haiti through its project Assistance to Penitentiary Reform (*Assistance a la reforme pénitentiaire*). This support included improving prison management, record-keeping, internal policies, modernising and codifying procedures and regulations, training of personnel and improving physical facilities. UNDP had international advisers co-located with the DAP to enhance capacity-building. It was the first time a civilian administration had been established in the prison service and professional training had been provided.[71] A critical achievement in this time period was the establishment of a separate prison for women and minors in Port-au-Prince in 1995. Across the country men and women shared prisons, as did minors, it was only in Port-au-Prince that men and women were separate in prisons.

There was also a connection between the democratisation process and progress in the prison system. Early on Aristide's return resulted in an improvement in the prison system because he ensured that they were placed under the MOJP and therefore became civilian. The slow process of naming a successor to Aristide and putting in place a government undermined progress since decisions on critical issues were not taken.[72] Subsequently when Préval became president there was a gradual unravelling of the democratisation process when parliament was dissolved and he began to rule by decree. Consequently, the situation in the prisons began to deteriorate.[73]

Overall the results of international and national efforts were few. DAP personnel were better trained, had a greater degree of professionalism, and a record-keeping system for prisoners was put in place.[74] But there were reports of abuses regularly committed by DAP prison staff.[75] The prison population nearly tripled between 1995 and August 2000. Yet the prison budget remained fixed at 1995 levels because of the economic crisis.[76] The daily food budget per prisoner was reduced from US$2.67 in 1996 to US$0.40 in 2001.[77] This was a result of the reduction in international support, combined with an economic crisis in Haiti and an unwillingness by the government to focus on prison reform. In a frail post-conflict economy where a vast majority live below the poverty line, prisons will not be prioritised. In Haiti it led to malnutrition and disease among prisoners. In March 2000, Amnesty International reported that 'overcrowding coupled with outdated facilities and lack of resources has created conditions that are far below the level required by the Standard Minimum Rules for the Treatment of Prisoners and in some instances constitute cruel, inhuman and degrading treatment.'[78] Conditions were by 2001 extremely poor, and did not meet either national or international standards. These deteriorated further in the next three years.

Prison reform post-2004

At the time of UN deployment in 2004 the Haitian prison system was in extreme need of reform. It was in an even worse condition than in 1994 since during the conflict in 2004 several prisons were destroyed. Importantly, although much of the infrastructure was destroyed in the prisons during the conflict in 2004, the structure of the DAP which had been established in the 1990s survived.

The Corrections Advisory Unit and the UNDP

The mandate in Resolution 1542 stated that the mission was to 'assist with the restoration and maintenance of the rule of law…including the re-establishment of the correction system'.[79] However, MINUSTAH's corrections unit suffered from under-funding and under-staffing from the start. Although the DAP, UNDP and MINUSTAH's Corrections Advisory Unit (CAU) early on recognised the needs, they worked under severe restraints since prison reform was given inadequate support by the UN system, by the government and by international donors. For example, the budget for refurbishing some of the prisons had to come out of the budget for police reform. Accordingly, prison reform saw progress in only a few areas. The mandate in 2006 authorised the deployment of sixteen correctional officers,[80] but by June 2007 only nine had been deployed.[81] Recruiting and deploying a sufficient number of correctional officers to any mission is difficult and often takes a long time as it is difficult to get them released from their duties at home. No country has readily available correctional officers that can be deployed to a UN peace operation. The number of correctional officers in MINUSTAH was not increased in subsequent mandates, although the importance of correctional reform was underscored in all. In 2013 the resolution called on the mission to align UNPOL skills with the support for capacity-building needs of prison officers.[82] This was also reiterated in the subsequent resolution.[83] The need for further mentoring and training was thus identified but not matched with resources. Correctional officers have a very specific set of skills which cannot easily be substituted by police officers with scant knowledge of the subject. And, as discussed in Chapter 5, it is challenging enough to find police officers with adequate skills for policing duties let alone with the added skills in corrections. Also, if someone having a corrections skillset was hired as an UNPOL officer rather than a CAU officer, once deployed the need for UNPOL officers was so great in Haiti that co-location to a prison would be very difficult. Human resources therefore remained poor.

UNDP, since 1995, provided consistent support to prison reform in Haiti. MINUSTAH's very insufficient human and financial resources in supporting prison reform and UNDP's long-standing involvement in prison reform, combined with MINUSTAH being an integrated mission should have encouraged greater collaboration between the two agencies in this area. There was a day-to-day working relationship on the ground between MINUSTAH and UNDP on prison reform, but there was little coordinated planning or integration of efforts.[84] Integration was not only lacking in implementation, but also in vision of prison reform in Haiti. UNDP had the longer-term involvement; MINUSTAH had a declared intention of providing support and an identified need, but lacked sufficient personnel. MINUSTAH should have consolidated and enhanced UNDP's efforts in this area as they lacked the ability to lead on it. The lack of integration did not obstruct or delay support, as it did in other areas, but it did reduce the potential multiplier effect the support could have had.

Aid and will to change

Although the CAU was under-resourced and under-staffed it provided support in several areas. For example, it assisted the DAP with drawing up their Strategic Development Plans for prison reform ('*Plan de développement stratégique de*

126 *Judicial and prison reform*

la Direction de l'Administration Pénitentiaire'), mobilised donors to support refurbishment projects in prisons, built senior and middle management capacity, trained prison personnel and supported the development of standard operation procedures. In addition, MINUSTAH had a number of quick impact projects, but the impact of the first QIPs were questioned because of conception and implementation.[85] Support was particularly focused on implementation of the Strategic Development Plans (2007–12 and 2013–16). After the earthquake (2010) priorities shifted to ensuring security of prisons and prisoner well-being.

There was a positive development among donors to support prison infrastructure from 2006 onwards, when prison reform was placed somewhat more firmly on the agenda.[86] For example, throughout this period Canada was a principal donor in prison reform, and in 2006–13 spent US$11.5 million. This included infrastructure and renovation as well as deployment of correctional officers through MINUSTAH.[87]

The DAP welcomed assistance and involvement from MINUSTAH and the UNDP, since they did not have sufficient capacity or resources to carry out reform. However, MINUSTAH was frequently unable to respond due to under-staffing, for example, human rights training for correctional officers did not start until more than two years after deployment. Co-location of MINUSTAH corrections officers in prisons meant improved capacity-building, mentoring and training. But the CAU only had sixteen officers, which meant they were not in all prisons and they were not present at all times due to the cycle of rotations and leave. This had an impact upon the mentoring and sustainability.

There was always a will to reform by the DAP leadership, but what this external support should focus on fluctuated several times throughout the mission. For example, initially the DAP leadership supported the deployment of international correctional officers in Haitian prisons to mentor and support Haitian prison officers.[88] But this shifted and the DAP no longer supported this and only wanted resources. This change in priorities can perhaps be explained primarily by the change in leadership of the DAP during this period. The new leadership emphasised infrastructure and equipment as their key priority and stressed that advisers and mentors should not be the first priority, although acknowledging the need for training.[89] It is often the case that recipients of reform only want resources and not mentoring and monitoring, but more than 'bricks and mortar' is needed if reform is to be successful. Similarly, only advice and mentoring without sufficient aid to repair infrastructure and provide equipment will also be of limited use. Training, capacity-building, mentoring and monitoring, in combination with infrastructure refurbishment and rebuilding based on needs[90] and cultural understanding to ensure a high-quality prison service is critical to reform. Over the years international support provided to DAP was a combination of infrastructure support, mentoring and training, but it lacked sufficient resources.

Even if there was the will to reform by DAP, prisons was low on the agenda of the Haitian government. If referred to, it was in the broader context of the rule of law or the criminal justice system. This meant cursory support and engagement, and very reduced budgets for prisons. The capacity and resources to undertake reform were considerably reduced after the earthquake. The international community continued to pressure the government to reform the prisons.[91] But there was what can only be described as disinterest. Overall there has been a lack of resources and leadership to conduct reform. This lack of interest also meant that it was a more or less uncontested area for international support.

Much remained the same

The result of primarily focusing assistance and attention on the police, and to a lesser extent the judicial system, was an abysmal situation in the prisons. The incarceration rate increased due to a more efficient PNH and UNPOL, in combination with a still ineffective judicial system, leading to the vast majority being in pre-trial detention and severe over-crowding. This led the United Nations Independent Expert on the Situation of Human Rights in Haiti to conclude that 'the efforts to improve the criminal justice system in Haiti have been insufficient, resulting in no viable improvements'.[92]

Thus results were meagre. Staffing in prions was increased by about 50 per cent by mid-2007.[93] This was a huge improvement although still notably below international standards. The structure and administration of DAP was much enhanced, and strategic plans and standard operation procedures were in place. Even so, as of 2015 all prisons were still overcrowded; the prisoners had minimal to no medical care; abuse continued to be rife within a number of prisons;[94] there was deficient management, excessive pre-trial detention, food and water shortages; and infrastructure and funding were inadequate. For example, there was a steep rise in prison deaths in the first six months of 2012, reflecting poor healthcare in particular.[95] Malnutrition was endemic as food budgets were inadequate and the prisoners relied on family members to bring them food.[96] Seventy per cent of prisoners suffered from a lack of basic hygiene, malnutrition, poor quality health care, and water-borne illnesses.[97] The conditions in the prisons were so poor that in 2014 a report found that 'they are tantamount to cruel, inhumane and degrading (CID) treatment'.[98]

There were approximately 4,600 prisoners in 2,500 square metres of prisons in October 2006.[99] This meant there was 0.54 square metres per prisoner. The ICRC has established 3.4 m^2 per prisoner as the minimum. Due to the conditions there were several prison riots and in December 2006 there was a multiple escape from the National Penitentiary. In October 2007 prisoner numbers, as a result of the more effective police, had risen to 6,370 prisoners.[100] In many prisons the detainees took turns sleeping. They were often not let out at all because the perimeter walls were not solid enough.[101] MINUSTAH and donors worked to reduce overcrowding, and some progress was made, for example, by 2011 the overall size of prisons had increased by 11 per cent. Yet in 2013 overcrowding was at 335.7 per cent.[102] This meant Haitian prisoners had roughly 40 cm^2 per prisoner.[103] In January 2015 there were 10,266 prisoners; it was then declared that the official capacity of Haitian prisons was 5,958 and the occupancy level had been reduced from previous years to 172 per cent.[104] However, the official occupancy level was in all probability exaggerated given that the number of prisons had not increased since 2011. With a prison population of 11,046 as of the end of 2015 this would indicate an occupancy level of 454.4 per cent.[105]

A consequence of the dilapidated state of the prison system was frequent mass escapes, some seemingly facilitated, albeit unconfirmed, by prison officers. Prisons have also been emptied several times in Haiti, starting after the fall of Baby Doc. In September 1994, there were multiple escapes from prisons, and some were emptied. This was repeated in 2004 prior to UN deployment. After the earthquake an estimated 5,000–6,000 prisoners escaped. This has had multiple effects, for example, leaving record maintenance and judicial checks near impossible. It also posed a serious risk to overall security in Haiti. MINUSTAH and PNH operations against armed gangs (Chapter 3) led to many armed gang leaders and gang members being in prison. The regular escapes added to the volatility in gang-held areas when these escapees returned. For example, in 2014, approximately 329 prisoners escaped from a new prison where many gang members were incarcerated. It also put a further strain on the PNH and their resources as they had to recapture prisoners. One and a half years after the earthquake only 629 prisoners had been recaptured out of the nearly 6,000 who escaped during the earthquake.[106] These escapes and uncontrolled releases also became an unintended method of 'rectifying' over-crowding. This added to impunity and undermined the rule of law.[107]

As a consequence of the lack of government support for prison reform, prison officers were continually severely under-resourced. This reduced the sustainability of some of the international support, for example, the prisons only used handwritten files, making the support for establishing a database ineffective.[108] Furthermore, prison officers often lacked capacity for 'self-defence and basic riot control, creating a system either that severely deprived the inmates or that encouraged the officers to use brutality'.[109] Abuse or CID was regularly used as punishment. Although this is prohibited under Haitian law it was still practised with impunity by government agents including prison officers.[110] This was combined with the exceptionally ineffective oversight of prison officers. The Inspector General's Office[111] had the task of ensuring the oversight of prison officers as well as the PNH, which it was not adequately able to do.

The combination of a skewed prioritisation of police support by international donors and MINUSTAH combined with a disregard for it by all Haitian governments meant much remained the same in the Haitian prison system.

Governance, democratisation and the criminal justice system

Improvement, or the lack thereof, in the criminal justice system can be linked to the ebbs and flows of the democratisation process. The democratisation process and the judicial system adversely affected each other. The absence of democratic strengthening delayed progress in justice reform. Programming to support judicial reform was focused on the extensive problems within the justice system but was not sufficiently viewed in the political context of an authoritarian regime transitioning towards democracy. Haiti was a state within which political individual power had been paramount without a history of political parties and organisations. To ensure political power control over the judicial system or the ability to manipulate it was viewed as critical. This did not change after 2004. The number of political parties increased considerably, yet this was not a reflection of broader democratic consolidation, but of individual candidates with narrow policies and political base. Moreover, not one Haitian government so far has implemented changes which have increased judicial independence thus serving as an effective constraint upon the executive. There was an absence of democratic consolidation which had an overwhelming effect upon the criminal justice system. Although lack of independence was acknowledged as the core problem in the judicial system, the democratic deficits underpinning this were not part of a holistic approach and programmatic efforts in both support to democratisation and judicial reform.

An issue that had a direct impact upon judicial reform was local elections. Article 175 of the Haitian Constitution stipulates that

> Supreme Court justices are appointed by the President of the Republic from a list submitted by the Senate of three (3) persons per court seat. Judges of the courts of appeal and courts of first instance are appointed from a list submitted by the Departmental Assembly concerned; justices of the peace are appointed from a list drawn up by the Communal Assemblies.

The transitional government did not comply with the constitution and directly selected Supreme Court justices, as well as judges to the lower courts, without nominations from the assemblies. This de-legitimised the judicial process.[112] But these were viewed as challenges to democracy rather than to the judicial system.

Holding these elections was critical to ensure these departmental and communal assemblies could nominate judges. Greater priority should have placed on conducting these elections by the government, thereby also contributing to the judicial reform process. But local elections were never prioritised by subsequent governments, either out of unwillingness or inability. In 2011 an unfortunate mirroring of events occurred when, unable to hold municipal elections, the government replaced locally elected authorities with political appointees, in those communes (129 out of 140) whose term had expired.[113] Article 175 continued to be breached. This also meant that managing the courts, judges, justices of the peace and their resources was left to the MOJPS,[114] consequently increasing the propensity for political manipulation and interference, and decreasing judicial independence. Not having the departmental and local assemblies contributed to the failure of judicial reform at the most basic level, that of independence. Even more concerning, it could be viewed as a vehicle for control over the judicial system by the political leadership.

Having non-political appointees is also important since justices of the peace are the primary point of contact for people facing the judicial system, especially in the rural areas. Having a weak local judicial system meant that local politicians and groups were able to use violent intimidation without repercussion.[115] The consolidation of democracy in the rural areas could have led to a strengthening of the criminal justice system and a strengthening of a decentralised democratic system, having an impact not only on the judicial system but also on prisons and police. But Haiti has historically been and continued to be highly centralised, where power was sought through control of the state apparatus, including all aspects of the rule of law sectors.

As discussed in Chapter 8, Haiti has had lengthy periods of time when there has been no prime minister, no government, no quorum in parliament for decision-making, and rule by presidential decree. There were seventeen ministers of justice in 1994–2011.[116] This has led to an inability to make decisions and decisions being postponed for long periods of time. Political leaders and various governments have all benefitted from keeping the criminal justice system dependent and weak to the detriment of the people of Haiti.

Conclusion

There was a profound need for reform of the judicial and penal systems in Haiti. Although it was not part of the initial mandates, it is important to underscore that judicial and penal reform was directly linked to instability and insecurity. A stable and secure environment was undermined through politicisation of the judicial system and mass escapes.

MINUSTAH's ability to progress in terms of judicial reform was hampered drastically by the transitional government's unwillingness to deal with the issue, the transitional government's abuse of the justice system for its own ends, the unwillingness by the judiciary to conduct a reform process, and the sensitivities surrounding external involvement in judicial reform. The high sensitivities surrounding 'reform' coupled with deep unwillingness both in government and the justice system, was exacerbated by MINUSTAH's lack of human and financial resources. Nevertheless, there have been numerous judicial reform projects in the past twenty odd years in Haiti, none of which has as yet achieved the objective of an independent functioning judiciary. In part this was because the support was not placed within the wider political and historical context; the governments and elites use of the judicial system to their own ends; and in the transition from authoritarianism to democracy the judicial system continued to be viewed as central to political power and control.

The critical lesson that should have been learnt from the interventions in the 1990s is that unless judicial reform is addressed and a coordinated coherent approach is applied then it will have an extremely negative effect upon the police and therefore reform of the PNH may largely turn out to be wasted. An effective functioning judicial system is critical to the PNH. Devoting more resources to judicial reform so as to ensure balanced progress in both police and judicial reform is core to progress. Moreover, the main problem that faced prison reform – overcrowding – stemmed from inadequacies in the judicial system. But it needed to be placed in the absence of the Haitian elites' will to ensure such reform. The basis for reform is that all must see the benefits of such reform; in Haiti political actors seemingly thought the advantages of controlling the justice system still continued to outweigh the disadvantages.

Notes

1 Report of the Secretary-General, The rule of law and transitional justice in conflict and post-conflict societies: S/2004/616, 23 August 2004.
2 T. Carothers, 'The Rule of Law Revival', *Foreign Affairs* vol.77, no.2, 1998.
3 The terms prison and prison reform are used throughout, rather than corrections and correctional reform because during the time in question there were no correctional facilities in Haiti – they were prisons. Penal and prison reform are used interchangeably.
4 Carothers sets out these three types of rule of law reform. Thomas Carothers, *The Rule of Law Revival, Promoting Rule of Law Abroad: In Search of Knowledge*, Washington DC: Carnegie Endowment for International Peace, 2006, p.7.
5 There has been much discourse surrounding justice reform, often discussed in conjunction with broader SSR efforts or as case studies, see e.g. B. Baker & E. Scheye, 'Multi-layered justice and security delivery in post-conflict and fragile states', *Conflict, Security & Development* Volume 7, Issue 4, 2007; V. O'Connor, 'Traversing the Rocky Road of Law Reform in Conflict and Post Conflict States: Model Codes for Post Conflict Criminal Justice as a Tool of Assistance', *Criminal Law Forum*, Volume 16, Issue 3, October 2005; A. Wardak 'Building a post-war justice system in Afghanistan', *Crime, Law and Social Change*, Volume 41, Issue 4, May 2004; D. Desai, D. Isser, M. Woolcock, 'Rethinking Justice Reform in Fragile and Conflict-Affected States: Lessons for Enhancing the Capacity of Development Agencies', *Hague Journal on the Rule of Law*, Volume 4, Special Issue 1, March 2012. The UN also developed a guide for it, see e.g. UNODC with USIP, 'Criminal justice reform in post-conflict states: A guide for practitioners', 2011.
6 Interview with former minister, Port-au-Prince, 1997.
7 Interview with justice sector official, Port-au-Prince, 1997.
8 Interviews with senior justice sector officials and public sector officials, Port-au-Prince, 1997.
9 The Haitian Constitution was amended in 2012, but these two articles remained the same.
10 Paras.9 (a), 9(b) and 10 respectively.
11 USD 70 million went to the police force (a total of USD 97 million). This does not include the USD 1.1 billion spent by the US military in 1994/95 as part of the multinational intervention force.
12 US General Accounting Office, Report to Congressional Requesters, Foreign Assistance, 'Any further aid to Haiti's justice system should be limited to performance related conditions', 17 October 2000, pp.1–4. For results see *USAID/ Haiti Status Report*, 27 June 1997, p.7
13 GAO (the US General Accounting Office), report, 2000 pp. 31–33.
14 L. Aucoin, J. Exumé, I. Lowenthal, H. Rishikof, *Assessment of the Justice Sector in Haiti*, prepared for USAID/HAITI, 6 November 1997, p.iii. See also, Amnesty International, *Haiti: Still Crying Out for Justice*, July 1998, p.12.
15 Interviews with MICIVIH representative, Port-au-Prince, 1998.
16 Interview with USAID representative, Port-au-Prince, 1998.
17 C. Jean-Baptiste, 'February 1986 – February 1996. A Decade of Struggle for Democracy and Justice', *The Peasant*, vol.3, no.1 (1996), p.2.
18 A. Fuller with P. Texier, M. Brosseau, D. Lemaire, and P. Pierre-Louis, 'Prolonged pre-trial detention in Haiti', Vera Institute of Justice, July 2002, pp. 7–8.
19 Ibid. p.ii.
20 SG report, S/1996/813, 1 October 1996, para.36.
21 Fuller, 'Prolonged', 2002, p i.
22 Also see the section 'Criminal prosecutions in Haiti' in Chapter 7.

132 Judicial and prison reform

23 Interviews with officials in Washington DC and Port-au-Prince, 1997.
24 See also Chapter 7.
25 See also J. Senat Fleury, *Challenges of Judicial Reform in Haiti*, 2008, p.61.
26 UN Security Council Resolution, S/RES/1542, 30 April 2004, 8(d).
27 UN Security Council Resolution, S/RES/1608, 22 June 2005, 2(d).
28 UN Security Council Resolution, S/RES/1702, 15 August 2006, 14.
29 Crisis Group, 'Keeping Haiti safe: justice reform', Briefing no.27, 27 October 201, p.15.
30 L.-A. Berg, 'All judicial politics are local: the political trajectory of judicial reform in Haiti', *Inter-American Law Review*, vol.44, no.1, 22 October 2013, p.7.
31 SG report, S/2010/446, 1 September 2010, para 33.
32 Interviews with Ministers, politicians and civil society, 2006.
33 Plan d'action du Ministere de la Justice de la Securité Publique dans le Cadre de la Réforme Judiciaire.
34 Interview with UNDP staff member, Port-au-Prince, November/December 2006.
35 SG report, S/2014/617, para.34.
36 SG report, S/2007/503, 22 August 2007, para.2
37 Crisis Group, 'Keeping Haiti safe: justice reform', Briefing no.27, 27 October 2011, p.8.
38 SG report, S/2012/128, 29 February 2012, para. 36.
39 Interviews with civil society, Port-au-Prince, 2008–10.
40 SG report, S/2008/202, 26 March 2008, para.34.
41 This was initially established in 1996, but was closed for many years after donor withdrawal and political turmoil.
42 Haiti Freedom House 2015 <https://freedomhouse.org/report/freedom-world/2015/Haiti> (accessed 7 March 2016).
43 Ibid.
44 See also Crisis Group, 'Keeping Haiti safe: justice reform', Briefing no.27, 27 October 2011, p.1.
45 See Chapter 7 for details on this trial.
46 For example, all judges, including justices of the peace, are required by law to hold a law degree, however, only an estimated 25 per cent of justices of the peace held such a degree in 2009. C. Stone, 'A new era for justice sector reform in Haiti', Working Paper, Harvard University, 10 July 2010, p. 9. This was very concerning in relation to human rights in particular as justices of the peace dealt with 80 per cent of all cases outside of Port-au-Prince. L. Cavise, 'Post-earthquake legal reform in Haiti: In on the ground', *Brook Journal of International Law*, vol.38:3, 2013, p.919.
47 Interview with member of government, Port-au-Prince, June 2006.
48 For example, USIP developed model codes for post-conflict criminal justice, which has been used as a law reform tool in several countries. H.J. Albrecht, L. Aucoin and V. O'Connor, 'Building the rule of law in Haiti: new laws for a new era', USIP Briefing, August 2009, pp. 6–7.
49 Code Penal, promulgated 11 August 1835. Code d'Instruction Criminelle, promulgated 31 July 1835.
50 Interview with senior justice section official, MINUSTAH, Port-au-Prince, November/December 2006.
51 For a more detailed overview of the drafting process see e.g. Leonard L. Cavise, 'Post-earthquake legal reform in Haiti: In on the ground', *Brook Journal of International Law*, vol.38:3, 2013.
52 Haiti Libre, Haiti – Justice: Draft revision of the Haitian Penal Code, 14 March 2015, http://www.haitilibre.com/en/news-13382-haiti-justice-draft-revision-of-the-haitian-penal-code.html. Accessed 1 July 2015
53 USAID, Office of the Inspector General, Audit of USAID/Haiti's justice program, Audit Report no. 1-521-07-008-P, 24 April, 2007, p.8.
54 Interviews with UNDP and MINUSTAH officials, Port-au-Prince, November/December 2006.

55 International Centre for Prison Studies, World brief, Haiti, accessed 30 June 2015. http://www.prisonstudies.org/country/haiti
56 Data collection on this is scarce and unreliable.
57 USAID, Office of the Inspector General, Audit of USAID/Haiti's justice program, Audit Report no. 1-521-07-008-P, 24 April, 2007, p.xxx
58 Ibid.
59 Ibid.
60 See e.g. SG report, S/2015/667, 31 August 2015, para.26.
61 It was also critical to limit vigilante justice. Two results of the dysfunctional justice system were that Haitians relied on other methods to handle disputes because of limited access to justice. This was, for a while, resulting in vigilante justice through an increase of lynching. In the first six months of 2007 there were 88 reported lynchings; and 28 non-fatal lynchings. SG report, S/2007/503, 22 August 2007, para.50. Reports of lynching were frequent in the following couple of years, but were considerably reduced thereafter.
62 A case tracking system was funded by the US and implemented through contractors, in 1997, in parts of the country, but these were never officially adopted by the government; and not used after the advisors left, the projects were closed in 2000. S. Beidas, C. Granderson, and R. Neild, 'Haiti' in C. T. Call (ed.) *Constructing justice and security after war*, Washington DC: USIP, 2007, p.111.
63 *von Neptune v. Haiti, Merits, Reparations, and Costs, Judgment*, Inter-Am. Ct. H.R. (ser. C) No. 180, 6 May 2008 <http://www.corteidh.or.cr/docs/casos/articulos/seriec_180_ing.pdf. Accessed 13 August 2015.
64 Human Rights Council, 'Draft Report of the Working Group on the Universal Period Review: Haiti,' 18 October 2011, para 88.63–88.73 <http://daccess-dds-ny.un.org/doc/UNDOC/GEN/G11/172/71/PDF/G1117271.pdf?OpenElement> (accessed
65 F. Dostoevsky, *The House of the Dead*, 1861, cited in F. R. Shapiro, The Yale Book of Quotations, 2006, p. 210.
66 This is only briefly mentioned as the UN did not have a mandate for prison reform.
67 Fuller, 'Prolonged detention', 2002, p.6.
68 ICRC resource centre, Update No. 96/1 on ICRC activities in Haiti, 18 June 1996 <https://www.icrc.org/eng/resources/documents/misc/57jn33.htm≥ (accessed 3 July 2015).
69 *The Miami Herald*, 'A look inside Haiti's jails', 25 March 2001, <http://latinamericanstudies.org/haiti/jails.htm> (accessed 2 July 2015).
70 Interviews with MICIVIH staff, Port-au-Prince, Gonaives, 1997–98.
71 *Inter-American Yearbook on Human Rights 1998* vol.2, Martinus Nijhoff, 2000, p.1930 para.35. In 1998, 108 new guards started working.
72 ICRC resource centre, Update No. 96/1 on ICRC activities in Haiti 18-06-1996 Operational Update <https://www.icrc.org/eng/resources/documents/misc/57jn33.htm≥ (accessed 3 July 2015).
73 *The Miami Herald*, 'A look inside Haiti's jails', 25 March 2001.
74 A. Fuller with Philippe Texier, Michel Brosseau, Dilia Lemaire, and Patrick Pierre-Louis, 'Prolonged pre-trial detention in Haiti', Vera Institute of Justice, July 2002, pp.16–17.
75 United States Bureau of Citizenship and Immigration Services, *Haiti: Information on conditions in Haitian prisons and treatment of criminal deportees (2nd Response)*, 12 February 2002, <http://www.refworld.org/docid/3dec98224.html> (accessed 22 October 2015).
76 UNHCR, RefWorld: 'Haiti: Information on conditions in Haitian prisons and treatment of criminal deportees (2nd Response)' <http://www.refworld.org/docid/3dec98224.html≥ (accessed 1 July 2015).
77 Fallon, 'Prolonged detention', 2002, p.17.

134 *Judicial and prison reform*

78 Cited in United States Bureau of Citizenship and Immigration Services, *Haiti: Information on conditions in Haitian prisons and treatment of criminal deportees (2nd Response)*, 12 February 2002, <http://www.refworld.org/docid/3dec98224.html> (accessed 22 October 2015).
79 UN Security Council Resolution, S/RES/1542, 30 April 2004, 7 I (d).
80 UN Security Council Resolution, S/RES/1702, 15 August 2006, 4.
81 Email interview, DPKO, June 2007.
82 UN Security Council Resolution, S/RES/2199, 10 October 2013, 10.
83 UN Security Council Resolution, S/RES/2180, 14 October 2014, 12.
84 An ECOSOC report recommended deepening their cooperation, Report of the ECOSOC Ad Hoc Advisory Group on Haiti 2–27 July 2012, p.1, para. 49
85 Crisis Group, 'Haiti: Prison reform and the rule of law', Briefing no.15, 4 May 2007, p 7.
86 Interviews with donors, June and December, Port-au-Prince, 2006.
87 Eight of the 16 mandated correctional officers in the first deployment were provided by Canada. 'Support for reform of Haiti's prison system', Embassy of Canada website, <http://www.canadainternational.gc.ca/haiti/eyes_abroad-coupdoeil/prisons.aspx?lang=eng> (accessed 2 July 2015).
88 Interviews with DAP officals, Port-au-Prince, June 2006.
89 Interview with DAP official, Port-au-Prince, November/December 2006.
90 Understanding needs was sometimes lacking in support in Haiti. For example, in the women's prison in Port-au-Prince a strong box to keep the keys to all the cells of the prison was installed, yet there was no running water in the prison. It cost as much to put up the strong box as it did the tap to ensure running water – the strong box had yet to be used months after it was installed.
91 von Neptune v. Haiti, Merits, Reparations, and Costs, Judgment, Inter-Am. Ct. H.R. (ser. C) No. 180, 6 May 2008 <http://www.corteidh.or.cr/docs/casos/articulos/seriec_180_ing.pdf> (accessed 13 August 2015).
Human Rights Council, 'Draft Report of the Working Group on the Universal Period Review: Haiti,' 18 October 2011, para 88.63–88.73 <http://daccess-dds-ny.un.org/doc/UNDOC/GEN/G11/172/71/PDF/G1117271.pdf?OpenElement> (accessed 13 August 2015).
92 Republic of Haiti Submission for the 112th Session of the United Nations Human Rights Committee, 8–9 October, 2014 Review of Haiti's Report under the International Covenant on Civil and Political Rights
Prison Conditions and Pre-Trial Detention in Haiti, Submitted by: Alternative Chance Boston College Law School Bureau des Avocats Internationaux Institute for Justice & Democracy in Haiti Université de la Fondation Dr. Aristide University of Miami School of Law Human Rights Clinic.
93 SG report, S/2008/586, 27 August 2008, para.41.
94 A survey found that prison officers regularly used torture or other abuses. Human Rights Watch, Haiti Country Summary, January 2010.
95 Human Rights Watch, 'World Report 2012, Haiti,' <http://www.hrw.org/world-report/2013/country-chapters/haiti?page=2> (accessed 14 July 2015).
96 C. Stone, 'A new era', p.10.
97 United States Department of State, Bureau of Democracy, Human Rights and Labor, Report on International Prison Conditions Global Conditions in Prisons and Other Detention Facilities, 2012 <http://www.state.gov/documents/organization/210160.pdf> (accessed 15 July 2015).
98 Submission for the 112th session of the UNHRC, 8–9 October 2014, 'Prison conditions and pre-trial dentition in Haiti', para.11.
99 'Tableau de bord de Gestion Administration Pénitentiaire', 31 October 2006.
100 'Prison Brief for Haiti', ICPS, School of Law, King's College, London, <http://www.kcl.ac.uk/depsta/law/research/icps/worldbrief/wpb_country.php?country=65> (accessed 17 October 2008).

101 Interview with senior prisons officer, MINUSTAH, Port-au-Prince, November/December 2006.
102 According to the International Center for Prison Studies as cited by C. Groden, *Time Magazine*, 5 August 2013 <http://newsfeed.time.com/2013/08/05/the-10-worst-countries-for-prison-overcrowding/> (accessed 2 February 2016).
103 Submission for the 112th session of the UNHRC, 8–9 October 2014, 'Prison conditions and pre-trial dentition in Haiti', para.18.
104 World Prison Brief, 'Haiti', <www.prisonstudies.org/country/haiti > (accessed 9 November 2015).
105 World Prions Brief, 'Haiti', <http://www.prisonstudies.org/country/haiti≥ (accessed 4 March 2016). Reports vary as to the extent of overcrowding from 200 to 400 per cent. Submission for the 112th session of the UNHRC, 8–9 October 2014, 'Prison conditions and pre-trial dentition in Haiti', para.17.
106 SG report, S/2010/446, 1 September 2010.
107 See also, Crisis Group, Prison reform, p.2.
108 Submission for the 112th session of the UNHRC, 8–9 October 2014, 'Prison conditions and pre-trial dentition in Haiti'.
109 Ibid. para.22.
110 Ibid. para.10.
111 See Chapter 5 for discussion of IGO (Inspector General's Office) and the problems of oversight.
112 A. Braden, B. Gardner, J. Gabello, 'The Independence of the Judiciary in Haiti under the Interim Government', School of Law Center for Internatonal Legal Education, University of Pittsburgh, 18 April 2006. The interim government further undermined the judicial system by removing five out of ten judges from the Supreme Court in December 2005. Associated Press, 'Haiti Supreme Court', 9 December 2005.
113 SG report, S/2013/139, 8 March 2013, para.29.
114 L.-A. Berg, 'All judicial', p. 12.
115 See also L.-A. Berg, 'All judicial', p. 24.
116 Ibid., p.28.

Bibliography

Albrecht, H.J., Aucoin, L., and O'Connor, V., 'Building the rule of law in Haiti: new laws for a new era', USIP Briefing, August 2009.

Amnesty International, 'Haiti: Still crying out for justice', July 1998. <https://www.amnesty.org/download/Documents/152000/amr360021998en.pdf> (accessed 30 Spetember 2016).

Aucoin, L., Exumé, J., Lowenthal, I. and Rishikof, H., *Assessment of the Justice Sector in Haiti*, USAID/HAITI, 6 November 1997.

Baker, B. and Scheye, E. 'Multi-layered justice and security delivery in post-conflict and fragile states', *Conflict, Security & Development* vol. 7, no. 4, 2007.

Berg, L.-A., 'All judicial politics are local: the political trajectory of judicial reform in Haiti', *Inter-American Law Review*, vol. 44, no. 1, 22 October 2013.

Braden, A., Gardner, B. and Gabello, J., 'The independence of the judiciary in Haiti under the interim government', School of Law Center for International Legal Education, University of Pittsburgh, 18 April 2006.

Call, Charles T., (ed.) *Constructing Justice and Security after War,* Washington DC: USIP, 2007.

Carothers, T., 'The rule of law revival', *Foreign Affairs* vol.77, no.2, 1998.

136 Judicial and prison reform

Carothers, T., *The Rule of Law Revival, Promoting Rule of Law Abroad: In Search of Knowledge*, Washington DC: Carnegie Endowment for International Peace, 2006.

Cavise, Leonard L., 'Post-earthquake legal reform in Haiti: In on the ground', *Brook Journal of International Law*, vol.38, no.3, 2013.

Code d'Instruction Criminelle, 31 July 1835.

Code Penal, 11 August 1835.

Crisis Group, 'Haiti: Prison reform and the rule of law', Briefing no.15, 4 May 2007.

Crisis Group, 'Keeping Haiti safe: justice reform', Briefing no.27, 27 October 2011.

Desai, D., Isser, D. and Woolcock, M. 'Rethinking justice reform in fragile and conflict-affected states: lessons for enhancing the capacity of development agencies', *Hague Journal on the Rule of Law*, vol. 4, no. 1, March 2012.

Dostoevsky, F., *The House of the Dead* (1861); cited in Shapiro, F.R, *The Yale Book of Quotations* New Haven, CT: Yale University Press, 2006.

Embassy of Canada, 'Support for reform of Haiti's prison system', <http://www.canadainternational.gc.ca/haiti/eyes_abroad-coupdoeil/prisons.aspx?lang=eng> (accessed 2 July 2015).

Fleury, J. Senat *Challenges of Judicial Reform in Haiti*, lulu.com, 2008.

Forum Citoyen pour la Réforme de la Justice, 'Pacte pour la réforme de la justice', June 2006.

Freedom House, 'Haiti 2015', <https://freedomhouse.org/report/freedom-world/2015/Haiti> (accessed 7 March 2016).

Fuller A., Texier, P., Brosseau, M., Lemaire, D. and Pierre-Louis, P. 'Prolonged pre-trial detention in Haiti', Vera Institute of Justice, July 2002.

Human Rights Council, 'Draft Report of the Working Group on the Universal Period Review: Haiti', 18 October 2011, <http://daccess-dds-ny.un.org/doc/UNDOC/GEN/G11/172/71/PDF/G1117271.pdf?OpenElement> (accessed 13 August 2015).

Human Rights Watch, 'Haiti country summary', January 2010.

Human Rights Watch, 'World Report 2012, Haiti,' http://www.hrw.org/world-report/2013/country-chapters/haiti?page=2 (accessed 14 July 2015).

International Centre for Prison Studies (ICPS), 'Prison brief for Haiti', School of Law, King's College, London, <http://www.kcl.ac.uk/depsta/law/research/icps/worldbrief/wpb_country.php?country=65>, (accessed at 17 October 2008).

ICRC resource centre, 'ICRC activities in Haiti', Update No. 96/1, 18 June 1996. <https://www.icrc.org/eng/resources/documents/misc/57jn33.htm≥ (accessed 3 July 2015).

Inter-American Court of Human Rights, 'Yvon Neptune v. Haiti, Merits, Reparations, and Costs, Judgment', (ser. C) No. 180, 6 May 2008 <http://www.corteidh.or.cr/docs/casos/articulos/seriec_180_ing.pdf> (accessed 4 July 2015).

Inter-American Commission of Human Rights, *Inter-American Yearbook on Human Rights 1998* vol.2, Leiden: Martinus Nijhoff, 2000.

International Centre for Prison Studies, 'World brief, Haiti', <http://www.prisonstudies.org/country/haiti> (accessed 30 June 2015).

Jean-Baptiste, C. 'A decade of struggle for democracy and justice', *The Peasant*, vol.3, no. 1, 1996.

Ministère de la Justice de la Securité Publique, *Plan d'action du Ministere de la Justice de la Securité Publique dans le cadre de la réforme judiciaire*, 2012–2016.

O'Connor, V. 'Traversing the rocky road of law reform in conflict and post conflict states: Model codes for post conflict criminal justice as a tool of assistance', *Criminal Law Forum*, vol. 16, no. 3, October 2005.

Stone, C. 'A new era for justice sector reform in Haiti', Working Paper, Harvard University, 10 July 2010.

'Tableau de bord de Gestion Administration Pénitentiaire', 31 October 2006.

United States Bureau of Citizenship and Immigration Services, 'Haiti: Information on conditions in Haitian prisons and treatment of criminal deportees (2nd Response)', 12 February 2002, HTI02001.ASM, <http://www.refworld.org/docid/3dec98224.html> (accessed 22 October 2015).

United States Department of State, Bureau of Democracy, Human Rights and Labor, 'Report on international prison conditions global conditions in prisons and other detention facilities' <http://www.state.gov/documents/organization/210160.pdf > (accessed 15 July 2015).

UNODC with USIP, 'Criminal justice reform in post-conflict states: A guide for practitioners', 2011.

USAID, *Haiti Status Report*, 27 June 1997.

USAID, Office of the Inspector General, 'Audit of USAID/Haiti's justice program', Audit Report no. 1-521-07-008-P, 24 April, 2007.

US General Accounting Office, Report to Congressional Requesters, Foreign Assistance, 'Any further aid to Haiti's justice system should be limited to performance related conditions', 17 October 2000.

Wardak, A. 'Building a post-war justice system in Afghanistan', *Crime, Law and Social Change*, vol. 41, no. 4, May 2004.

World Prisons Brief, 'Haiti', <http://www.prisonstudies.org/country/haiti≥ (accessed 4 March 2016).

UN documents

Report of the ECOSOC Ad Hoc Advisory Group on Haiti 2–27 July 2012.

SG report, 'The rule of law and transitional justice in conflict and post-conflict societies', S/2004/616, 23 August 2004.

SG report, S/1996/813, 1 October 1996.

SG report, S/2007/503, 22 August 2007.

SG report, S/2008/202, 26 March 2008.

SG report, S/2010/446, 1 September 2010.

SG report, S/2012/ 128, 29 February 2012.

SG report, S/2013/139, 8 March 2013.

SG report, S/2014/617, 29 August 2014.

SG report, S/2015/667, 31 August 2015.

SRSG report, S/2008/586, 27 August 2008.

Submission for the 112th Session of the United Nations Human Rights Committee, 'Review of Haiti's Report under the International Covenant on Civil and Political Rights Prison Conditions and Pre-Trial Detention in Haiti', Submitted by: Alternative Chance, Boston College Law School, Bureau des Avocats Internationaux, Institute for Justice & Democracy in Haiti, Université de la Fondation Dr Aristide, University of Miami School of Law, Human Rights Clinic, 8 & 9 October 2014.

UN Security Council Resolution, S/RES/1542, 30 April 2004.

UN Security Council Resolution, S/RES/1608, 22 June 2005.

UN Security Council Resolution, S/RES/1702, 15 August 2006.

UN Security Council Resolution, S/RES/2199, 10 October 2013.

UN Security Council Resolution, S/RES/2180, 14 October 2014.
UNHCR, RefWorld: 'Haiti: Information on conditions in Haitian prisons and treatment of criminal deportees (2nd Response)' <http://www.refworld.org/docid/3dec98224.html≥ (accessed 1 July 2015).

Media

Associated Press, 'Haiti Supreme Court', 9 December 2005.
Groden, C., 'The 10 worst prions for prison over-crowding,' *Time Magazine*, 5 August 2013 <http://newsfeed.time.com/2013/08/05/the-10-worst-countries-for-prison-overcrowding/> (accessed 2 February 2016).
Haiti Libre, 'Haiti – Justice: Draft revision of the Haitian Penal Code', 14 March 2015, <http://www.haitilibre.com/en/news-13382-haiti-justice-draft-revision-of-the-haitian-penal-code.html> (accessed 4 May 2015).
The Miami Herald, 'A look inside Haiti's jails', 25 March 2001, <http://latinamericanstudies.org/haiti/jails.htm> (accessed 2 July 2015).

7 Justice and reconciliation

Transitional justice – accountability for the past to ensure adherence to the rule of law in the future – is a core part of a peace building process. The UN has acknowledged and repeatedly emphasised the role it can play in ensuring sustainable peace and stability,[1] but the relationships between democratisation, security sector reform, disarmament, demobilisation and reintegration, and transitional justice have frequently been overlooked. The international community has often addressed transitional justice separately from other peacebuilding activities.[2]

Transitional justice was not formally identified as a part of the intervention mandate in Haiti. The subsequent analysis therefore aims to highlight the importance of including the issue of transitional justice in peace operations due to the connections with other issues that are normally, and were in Haiti, part of a UN peace operations mandate. Justice in this chapter refers to criminal justice for the perpetrators of the crimes committed in 1991–94. It is defined as action taken in a court of law or tribunal to assert the guilt or innocence of the accused for crimes perpetrated during the coup period.

This chapter argues that, particularly after 1994, transitional justice's absence was critically linked to the continued insecurity. The Haitian government attempted justice and reconciliation after 1994 through a truth and reconciliation commission. Other attempts at justice were minimal – there was also a distinct difference between the political will to pursue justice and the demand for it within Haitian society. This chapter establishes that reconciliation did not occur in the period between 1994 and 2000 and that the absence of some form of criminal justice was a contributing factor. In Haiti, a sense of justice was necessary for a process of reconciliation and without it the focus on reconciliation appeared hollow, furthering prevailing insecurity. Due to the change in the type of violence, transitional justice, in its more traditional definition, was not on the agenda after 2004. This chapter thus focuses on post-1994 efforts.[3] Because transitional justice was not tackled in any meaningful manner, it contributed to the gradual collapse of the democratic process. The issue of justice and reconciliation therefore needs to be discussed and is a lesson learnt not only for Haiti but also for other operations. This chapter discusses amnesties and reconciliation versus justice and that justice was paramount among the expectations of the Haitians. It sets out the flaws of the truth commission and the problems of domestic prosecution. It establishes that insecurity and fear prevailed in part because of the absence of any meaningful process of justice.

Transitional justice

There has been an increasing focus on transitional justice in peacebuilding since the early 1990s. It has been suggested that there are a number of imperatives to ensure some type of transitional justice in post-conflict societies.[4] This has led to a growing number of means and choices, both judicial and non-judicial, that governments in post-conflict societies and the international community can use to address past human rights violations in an effort to curb reoccurrence, enhance reconciliation and provide a measure of accountability. There has been a proliferation of judicial means including ad-hoc tribunals, hybrid and special courts. As the number of judicial means grew so did the discourse on non-judicial reconciliation mechanisms. Non-judicial means of accountability, such as truth commissions, were also increasingly promoted. Transitional justice has thus become part of the post-conflict peacebuilding process, where it is viewed as essential to reconciliation and the reconstruction of society after conflict.

The primary objectives of transitional justice are twofold: first, to begin processes of reconciliation among the parties to the conflict and the affected populations by establishing a process of accountability and acknowledgement; and second to deter reoccurrence, ensuring sustainable peace. Both judicial and non-judicial accountability can encourage reconciliation of post-conflict societies. However, reconciliation is a complex concept and not easily defined; it has been described in numerous ways from acknowledgement and repentance from the perpetrators and forgiveness from the victims,[5] non-lethal co-existence,[6] as democratic decision-making and reintegration,[7] and as four concepts namely truth, mercy, peace and justice.[8] Crucially, reconciliation is a process, which end-state can be reached by different means and lengths of time. This chapter distinguishes between national reconciliation and individual reconciliation. National reconciliation is achieved when societal and political processes function and develop without reverting to previous patterns or the framework of the conflict. Individual reconciliation is the ability of each human being to conduct his or her life in a *similar* manner as prior to the conflict, without fear or hate. This is an important distinction because each can come about independently of the other, or national reconciliation can come at the expense of individual reconciliation.[9] Moreover, it is important because frequently there is a gap between what political leaders seek and what civil society expects after conflict.

To what extent any transitional justice mechanism on its own is able to achieve non-reoccurrence of human rights violations can be questioned, but it is here the relationships to peacebuilding, state building, and other processes such as DDR and reform processes become particularly important. For example, to minimise the chances of institutional human rights violations, the government institutions responsible for the violations must be transformed. This is a vital step in ensuring non-reoccurrence. Transitional justice mechanisms such as truth commissions can provide recommendations for what changes and reform need to take place within government institutions that perpetrated violations against its citizens. Domestic and hybrid courts can potentially enhance and reform the judicial system whilst ensuring accountability. Vetting can ensure that former perpetrators are not allowed positions in government institutions, whether they are military, police or intelligence services, oversight mechanisms or any other form of government positions.

Reconciliation versus justice

At the time of the 1994 intervention, and in the first months thereafter, justice *and* reconciliation figured prominently in the discourse in Haiti, but reconciliation soon became the central tenet of the government. In President Aristide's first speech upon his return to Haiti, he told his supporters: 'no to violence, no to vengeance, yes to reconciliation'.[10] Civil society, though, never ceased to emphasise justice: 'the word was justice, not reconciliation, but nothing happened'.[11] In the end neither occurred.

There was a demand for justice for the coup era[12] as it was perceived that there could not be reconciliation without some form of criminal justice.[13] These demands for justice persisted and for example, the organisation Justice and Peace continued to denounce the Haitian authorities for not prosecuting human rights violators, and condemned that no serious initiative had been taken to obtain justice for the victims of the coup. At the end of May 1998, a picket line had been ongoing for thirty weeks, demanding justice and reparations for the victims of the coup. They emphasised the importance of arresting people for their roles in the coup, because they argued that if they were not it could be a harbinger of a new coup.[14] Reconciliation without some form of justice appeared difficult in a post-intervention Haiti. At least a symbolic form of justice for the mass population that had felt the brunt of the military repression was necessary for reconciliation to occur. Mainly people from the old regime, politicians and the international community supported the notion of reconciliation.[15] Reconciliation appeared in practice to be accepting impunity. There was a demand for justice among the Haitian people and the popular organisations. It was a demand that went unheard.

The major problem with focusing exclusively on reconciliation, rather than on justice and reconciliation, was the resurfacing of partisans of the old regime. They saw that no consequences came of their actions, and that they could continue their roles in Haitian society and political life much as before. The groups, which emphasised the importance of justice in Haitian society, all came from civil society, people who worked with civil society or in the justice sector. There was barely any mention of justice among politicians or the elite, who seemed to be, as one person put it: 'carrying on as nothing has happened'.[16] This can be explained by the fact that it was the impoverished Haitians who had endured most of the repression during the junta regime and, therefore, felt a need for justice. This need did not exist among the majority of the elite. Among the masses, however, justice for the coup period was a necessity, for there had been none.[17]

Amnesties versus expectations

There were high expectations in Haitian society of what change the UN peace operation would bring. The junta was to be thrown out, democracy restored and justice delivered. There was a hope of deliverance in the Haitian population. The Port-au-Prince agreement, largely, hindered the possibility of bringing to justice the main officers behind the coup: Raoul Cédras, Philippe Biamby and Michel François.[18] It facilitated, in particular, Cédras' exit from Haiti. The agreement stated that 'certain military officers of the Haitian Armed Forces are willing to consent to an early and honourable retirement'.[19] This provided amnesties to the main perpetrators of the coup.[20] This agreement provoked a strong reaction in the Haitian community both inside and outside Haiti. It was called a 'travesty of justice'.[21] Amnesties can explicitly be granted by political or military leaders, by the new or out-going regime, but can also be granted *de facto* by avoiding to apply any transitional justice mechanism whether judicial or non-judicial. In Haiti, a combination of these led to amnesties for the key perpetrators in the coup.

On 6 October 1994, in line with the Port-au-Prince agreement, the Haitian parliament approved the amnesty law for the military and specified that it affected 'all the crimes and related actions' of the military personnel who ousted Aristide.[22] This agreement potentially did save lives, in the sense that a forceful international intervention may have led to casualties.[23] Nevertheless, the fact that there were no criminal proceedings against any of the principal culprits of the coup would not only cost lives in the end, but also weaken the fundaments on which to build a new democratic society. There were many human rights violators who were not specifically mentioned in these agreements, and who therefore could have been prosecuted but were not. These, in particular, were the *Front National pour le Changement et la Democratie* (FRAPH) and the *attachés*.

The Haitian legislature also adopted a law on judicial reform in April 1998. It included provisions which stated that 'all crimes and misdemeanours committed between 30 September 1991 and 15 October 1994 are imprescriptible, regardless of their magnitude'.[24] This reflected the unwillingness of the Haitian government to handle the issues of justice and culpability. It meant that impunity would continue to reign in Haiti.

The National Truth and Justice Commission

The use of truth commissions (TCs) as a transitional justice mechanism has steadily grown since the early 1990s. Both the international community and post-conflict governments have frequently supported this form of truth-seeking. Truth commissions are often promoted as the primary vehicle to ensure reconciliation after conflict.[25] Truth commissions investigate past human rights abuses committed during conflict and civil unrest. Generally, they examine violations perpetrated by the military, government or other state institutions. They are non-judicial bodies, which can give recommendations, but they do not have the authority to punish. These recommendations can contain suggestions for broad reforms of state institutions and reparations for the victims. A truth commissions is a truth-seeking mechanism allowing the victims, and in some instances the perpetrators, to expose human rights violations. They are established and given authority by local governments or international organisations, sometimes by both. They are only operational for a limited time-period – commonly no longer than two years – and can be organised and structured in many different ways.

Truth commissions are often viewed as able to lay the ground for deep-seated institutional change within a post-conflict society. The reports of truth commissions commonly include recommendations for reform of the security sector, and if implemented truth commissions can promote significant change. Choosing this truth-seeking mechanism may ensure the beginning of transparency and oversight of the security sector. Moreover, by creating a historical record it can encourage a mind-set shift towards greater transparency and accountability. However, governments can use truth commissions as a vehicle for non-action, as a way of not making political contentious decisions, such as initiating criminal proceedings. They can become a political tool to avoid other forms of justice for the sake of stability. Furthermore, a government can ignore its recommendations and therefore no change may be instigated. The latter took place in Haiti.

Reconciliation is a primary objective of truth commissions; several truth commissions refer to it in their mandate or include it in their name. However, here the distinction between national and individual reconciliation becomes important. A truth commission aims to establish a general pattern of human rights violations and investigates the social and political factors leading to these violations, hence promoting national reconciliation. In pursuing this aim, truth commissions hear individual testimonies and may therefore be expected to obtain individual reconciliation for victims of abuse. Victims, realising that the focus is on national reconciliation, may be disappointed. Nevertheless, placing an individual case of abuse within a pattern of abuse can in some cases lead to individual reconciliation. It can create an understanding of why the individual had to suffer, as it is related to the fact that this was part of violations by state institutions perpetrated on, in many cases, a vast scale. Reconciliation is an extremely individual process and whether or not it will result from of placing the abuses in a larger framework will vary according to the personal experience of violations.[26]

The National Truth and Justice Commission was established by President Aristide in 1994. Its report was finalised at the beginning of 1996 and was entitled *Si M Pa Rele* (If I Don't Cry Out). The Commission was criticised for having taken so long in concluding their report. It was also blamed for not involving more human rights groups and popular organisations.[27] A principal flaw was the Commission's lack of power. It was completely different in this respect from, for example, the Truth and Reconciliation Commission in South Africa, which had the powers to hear offenders' testimonies and grant amnesties.[28] The Haitian Commission was appointed to write a report but apart from that they could take no other form of action. They only listened to the victims' testimonies. The Commission could have done a much more effective job with more extensive and broader powers.

Neither the report nor the Commission itself was the greatest problem; it was the total absence of follow-up. In the UN Secretary-General's report on Haiti in 1997, he pointed out that neither the Follow-Up Committee nor the Compensation Committee to help victims of the coup, which the report had recommended be set up, had been established.[29] The Follow-Up Committee only began its work in 1998. A factor was also the initial extremely limited distribution of the report. Only 75 copies were published, and until the end of 1998 it was only printed in French and not in Haitian Creole. It was only later with the assistance of the International Civilian Mission in Haiti (MICIVIH) that a second edition of 1,500 copies was published.[30] Victims told their story, but amidst minimal publicity, and without true recognition. The result was no dialogue in Haitian society. The fault lay with the Haitian government and their lack of will to pursue the recommendations provided by the Commission. A confidential appendix with the names of perpetrators of human rights abuses was attached, so that they could be prosecuted in a court of law, depending on the evidence produced.[31]

The Haitian government arguably chose a truth commission as a transitional justice mechanism because it did not have the political will to institute any other form of justice. They thought criminal prosecutions in particular might be destabilising. What they disregarded was that by not putting any processes of justice in place and rather embracing a political compromise, they encouraged impunity.

When a truth commission is chosen because it is less politically challenging, it can become a way to avoid addressing the issues of justice. Truth commissions can be an important measure of transitional justice, but should not be used to avoid accountability.[32] Yet, it becomes difficult to accuse the government of not addressing justice, because a truth commission has been put in place.[33] In such circumstances, if a truth commission is the only type of transitional justice mechanism chosen it not only reduces the impact it may have upon reconciliation in society, but it also raises the risk of continued distrust towards state institutions. A truth commission then does not have an effect upon reform because recommendations are avoided and the truth commission is used as a tool to placate the civilian population. Rather than ensuring stability it could increase vigilante justice perpetrated by victims feeling unfairly treated, and to continue behaviour of impunity by members of the security sector, which has seen no change towards accountability. A major benefit of truth commissions is that they have the potential of starting a process of security sector reform, and begin to create a mind-set shift towards accountability, but non-implementation due to absence of political will can undermine accountability, the belief in change and the transition to democracy.

Because the Haitian government did not have the political will necessary to implement the recommendations of the NTJC, they used it to show that a process of justice had occurred. However, this led to distrust and disillusionment towards both towards the commission and the government.[34] It also had a negative effect on police and judicial reform in Haiti, as there was no accountability for past crimes, which did nothing to engender change in the criminal justice system.

Domestic prosecution

The Rome Statute, even though it establishes the International Criminal Court, emphasises the primacy of nation states in ensuring justice and underscores state responsibility for crimes committed on national territory.[35] The Preamble to the Rome Statute states that 'it is the duty of every state to exercise its criminal jurisdiction over those responsible for international crimes'. This was of course not yet established when Haiti chose to address its human rights abuse through a truth commission, but customary international law also affirms that domestic courts should deal with certain crimes, including genocide and gross violations of human rights. In addition, international law establishes victims' right to seek redress for human rights violations and to have their case heard.[36]

International law had thus evolved, even in 1994, to support the premise that there is a responsibility of the individual state to prosecute gross violations of human rights conducted on its territory. Simultaneously strong criticisms have been voiced against the use of prosecutions.[37] Yet, what has been seen in post-conflict societies is an increasing demand for criminal prosecutions by civil society – whether in international tribunals, domestic courts or hybrid/mixed courts – following gross violations of human rights,[38] as well as an increase in domestic prosecutions for past human rights violations in post-conflict societies.[39]

Alongside the developments of the rights of victims and the state's obligations to protect its citizens, the rights of the accused have also evolved considerably to ensure their protection during criminal prosecution – this includes the right to a fair and public hearing.[40] The Office for the High Commissioner of Human Rights has called upon states to ascertain a fair and public hearing when trials are conducted to deal with past gross violations of human rights in a post-conflict context.[41] Breaches of the rights of the accused, when using criminal prosecution as a measure of transitional justice, undermine the justice process and it is imperative that the rights of both the victims and the accused are protected.

There are vast problems in using a domestic criminal justice system in dire need of reform to address justice for past crimes. Domestic trials against alleged perpetrators of war crimes and gross violations of human rights take place within the formal judicial system applying domestic laws, using national judges and prosecutors, and they have regularly been criticised as negatively affecting reconciliation and post-conflict reconstruction.[42] It is the potential for bias and unfairness of trials and the possibility of such trials leading to further destabilisation and continued conflict, which are voiced as objections to their use in a transitional justice context. In essence, the discourse on the suitability of domestic trials to deal with past crimes is on two levels: a) whether or not a punitive mechanism should at all be used in a post-conflict setting, and b) whether or not a domestic judicial system has the capacity, after prolonged conflict, to conduct fair and unbiased trials. The latter relates to the issue of security sector reform.

The level of corruption, functionality and trust in the system will influence a) whether domestic prosecution can and will be chosen as a mechanism of transitional justice, and b) whether it is viewed as politically expedient to apply such a mechanism. Judicial reform is a long-term process – how long-term is dependent upon the state of the judicial system – which can be contrary to the immediate demands for justice arising within a post-conflict setting. It is not necessary to fully reform or restore a judicial system prior to conducting domestic prosecution for past abuses; on the contrary domestic trials can also contribute to the development of rule of law.[43] These trials can positively influence the development of the judicial system and strengthen it by establishing accountability for past crimes, serving as a role model for the judiciary dealing with ordinary crimes, and ensuring an end to impunity. But the minimum requirements of a fair trial need to be guaranteed or these trials can undermine the rule of law.

In Haiti, with the army gone, the level of institutional political violence diminished, but without any justice or disarmament, the culprits of the three-year terror regime were still living among the population it had terrorised with the weapons they possessed. The absence of transitional justice became, therefore, a factor in the absence of public security. However, the government deemed prosecutions to further the risks to security.

Criminal prosecutions in Haiti

There was a fear by the government that criminal prosecutions would turn into retribution and lead to instability, leading to the emphasis on reconciliation. Yet it is in the vacuum of justice that retribution occurs. Without it, vigilante justice, that is retribution, can come to play a significant part. There were examples of this in Haiti, where known paramilitaries were taken and killed, Père Lebrun style, but President Aristide appealed to the population not to take justice into their own hands.[44] Aristide asked the people to refrain from this type of justice and to point out the *attachés* to the Multinational Force (MNF) instead of using street justice. When people complied and pointed them out, the US troops delivered them to the FAd'H, who let them go.[45] This further increased impunity, which in turn encouraged instability and insecurity.

Even if the Haitian government had more extensively sought a process of justice through the domestic courts, there was one important factor hindering this. In the first phase of the intervention, the MNF raided the headquarters of the FRAPH. They confiscated numerous documents (160,000), video films, tapes and photos, which contained the names of people involved in the coup, documented atrocities and filmed/taped evidence of torture sessions,[46] proving individuals' involvement in the illegalities and atrocities of the coup regime. The MNF sent this material and similar material seized from the FAd'H to the US and it was not returned to Haiti. It could have been used in a court of law to prosecute these individuals for crimes committed against the Haitian people. The removal of this material led to the inability of the Haitian government to report on the fate of the 'disappeared'.[47]

The confiscation of these documents led to a deterioration in the Haiti–US relationship.[48] The US government refused to return them on the grounds that they contained American names. After much pressure, the US government relented and agreed to return the documents, but erased any reference to American names.[49] The Haitian government refused to accept the documents in such condition and did not initiate any criminal proceedings based on them.[50] Haitians viewed the FRAPH documents as a crucial element in obtaining justice in Haitian society.[51]

Even though there was limited political will in the Haitian government to prosecute anyone who had taken part in the violations during the junta years, the government did attempt to bring some of the perpetrators to justice. For example, they requested the extradition of the former chief of police, J.M. François, from Honduras, on human rights charges; the extradition request also included the generals who participated in the coup. The Honduran court denied the request, because it did not meet the requirements outlined in extradition conventions signed by Honduras.[52]

The government also attempted to have Emanuel 'Toto' Constant, the leader of FRAPH, extradited from the US. The Haitian government demanded his extradition several times, but their request was denied on the grounds that Constant would not receive a free and fair trial in Haiti.[53] Because of the state of the judicial system, Constant might not have received a fair trial in Haiti for two reasons: out of a desire for retribution, or due to the extent of partisans of the old regime within the judicial system. Subsequently, in an interview in July 1998, Constant claimed that FRAPH was still operational and that he continued to be the head of it.[54] Whether correct or not, this sent a signal to all *macoutes*, *attachés*, *zenglendos* and paramilitaries that Constant was in effect 'untouchable'.[55] It demonstrated that impunity reigned. The lack of prosecutions led to a lack of accountability, encouraged the continued use of armed groups for political purposes, and encouraged FRAPH and *attachés* to destabilise the new government and undermine the democratisation process.

The Haitian courts, (as discussed in Chapter 6) at the time of intervention were not able to conduct trials such as Constant's, as the problems in the judicial sector were too expansive. For example, this was underscored by the case against the alleged killers of the Justice Minster Guy Malary, who was killed in 1993 and the case tried in 1996.[56] His alleged killers were acquitted, which illustrated the problems of the Haitian justice system and the ability of achieving justice within it for the crimes of the coup era.[57]

A successful court case was held over the Raboteau massacre. The Raboteau massacre took place on 22 April 1992 in Raboteau Gonaïves. In 2000, a Haitian court tried 59 people for their alleged roles in the massacre, 37 of them, including former coup leader Raoul Cédras, were tried *in absentia*. When preparations for the case started in 1998, the case was viewed as a test-case for Haitian justice.[58] Sixteen of those tried in person were convicted and sentenced to terms ranging from four years to life imprisonment. National and international monitors, including officials from the United Nations International Civilian Support Mission in Haiti (MICAH), observed the trial. The UN Special Rapporteur and Independent Expert on Haiti stated that the trial was a 'landmark for justice in Haiti' and was fair and transparent.[59] Unfortunately, in May 2005, the Supreme Court overturned all the sentences. There is reason to believe that the overturning of the sentences was politically motivated; moreover, it constituted a major setback in the fight against impunity in Haiti.[60] Thus what had been a landmark for justice was let down because of the flaws in the judicial system, which was open to corruption and political pressure. Even if the court had not overturned the judgement, because of the extensive problems in the prison sector actually none of the fifteen men were in prison when their sentences were overturned, all had escaped (apart from one who had died in prison).

Fear and insecurity

Due to the lack of criminal proceedings, fear among a part of the population continued to exist in Haitian society, even if the junta was removed. Fear and apprehension existed because there had been no punishment for human rights abusers.[61] When there is no punishment, as one put it 'anyone can do what they want'.[62] Fear, therefore, became prevalent. The oppressors were still at large to threaten and abuse. As a newspaper pointed out, it must inevitably ruin the spirit of the people to see the former members of the army, who had killed, tortured and raped during the coup years, walking around and demonstrating in the streets.[63] Reports were received by Amnesty International that the people who testified to the National Truth and Justice Commission received threats from their former abusers, some of whom were still living in the same neighbourhoods as the victims.[64]

Combined with the fact that few of these perpetrators were disarmed or demobilised and there was no effective reintegration back into Haitian society (Chapter 4), they became a constant part of the insecurity problem. Individuals who took part in the violence during the junta years, persistently continued to play a role in insecurity in the years that followed.[65] They were emboldened by the lack of justice and DDR, and thus little changed. The fear of the Haitian government that justice would increase instability was flawed; impunity in Haiti was a solid foundation for insecurity.

Conclusion

Insecurity in Haiti was closely intertwined with a lack of justice, and contributed to a society where public security was scarce and fear among the population prevalent because there was no justice administered to the perpetrators of the coup. As discussed in previous chapters, this insecurity was linked to disarmament and restructuring of the security forces. However, the absence of justice was one of the more important variables in the continued absence of public security in Haitian society post-1994 intervention.

The National Truth and Justice Commission could have been an important part of the process of justice. However, due to lack of political will to enforce the recommendations of the Commission and reluctance in granting it broader powers, it was flawed. There was a need for two parallel processes of justice: the work of the Commission and criminal proceedings against a few of the perpetrators of human rights abuses during the coup era. These two processes could have led to reconciliation within Haitian society, but the inherent systemic problems within the judicial structure limited this option. Not even today would the Haitian courts be able to deal with cases of this magnitude.

Justice is also essential for the further development of the democratisation process. Justice is at the core of the building of democracy; as pointed out above, with untouchables there cannot be democracy.[66] With the amnesties granted and more importantly supporters of the coup regime living in impunity, there were clearly untouchables in Haitian society. Therefore, to consolidate the democratic process, both the Haitian government and the international community should have prioritised some form of justice for the coup era. Throughout Haitian history, impunity has always been the prerogative of the dictatorial regimes.[67] In a democracy it should not be. On the contrary, justice, not impunity, is the central pillar in state of law. It can function as the base for equality in front of the law.[68] Impunity cannot be accepted in a democracy. Reconciliation of Haitian society was also a prerequisite for the process of democratisation to continue. Therefore, since the above argues that reconciliation could not be obtained without some form of justice, it follows that justice would have been necessary for the continued process of democracy. Justice was far from the only or the strongest element that contributed to the derailment of democracy in Haiti in the late 1990s, but it was an important one.

Another consequence was that by letting impunity reign, the population would stop believing in real change.[69] There was first talk of justice, but there was none. Then there was talk of reconciliation, but no serious efforts were made. It sent a signal to both the oppressors and the population that no real change was about to take place this time either. The focus on reconciliation emboldened the *macoutes*.[70] People needed to feel secure and in order to feel secure in Haiti some form of justice was required.

Notes

1 See e.g. Report of the Secretary-General, 'The Rule of Law and Transitional Justice in Conflict and Post-Conflict Societies', S/2004/616, 23 August 2004. Report of the Secretary-General to the Security Council, 'The rule of law and transitional justice in conflict and post-conflict societies', S/2011/634, 12 October 2011. UNA-USA, DPKO, *Program on Peace Building and Rule of Law*, Partnership Program on Peace Building and Rule of Law, 2003.
2 Perhaps with the exception of vetting of police and military personnel, which is where security sector reform and transitional justice overlap most clearly.
3 This chapter does not address the attempt to bring Jean-Claude Duvalier to justice, since it deals with crimes committed outside the period addressed in this book, as he ruled from 1971 to 1986. A case was brought against him by the Haitian authorities when he returned to Haiti in 2011. Haitian courts were unable to bring the case to trial prior to his death in 2014.
4 For this debate, see e.g. L. Vinjamuri and J. Snyder, 'Trials and Errors: Principle and Pragmatism in Strategies of International Justice', *International Security* 28/3, Winter 2003/4. P. Hayner, *Unspeakable Truths: Confronting State Terror and Atrocity*, New York: Routledge, 2001. C. Hesse and R. Post (eds), *Human Rights in Political Transitions: Gettysburg to Bosnia*, Boston: MIT Press, 2000. N. J. Kritz, *Transitional Justice: How Emerging Democracies Reckon with Former Regimes*, Washington,

150 *Justice and reconciliation*

DC: United States Institute of Peace, 1995. R. Mani, *Beyond Retribution: Seeking Justice in the Shadows of War*, Cambridge: Polity, 2001. J. Mendez, 'Accountability for Past Abuses', *Human Rights Quarterly* 19/2 1997. M. Minow, *Between Vengeance and Forgiveness: Facing History after Genocide and Mass Violence*, Boston: Beacon Press, 1998. D. Orentlicher, 'Settling Accounts: The Duty to Prosecute Human Rights Violations of a Prior Regime', *Yale Law Journal* 100 (1991): 2537–2615. C. Lekha Sriram, *Justice vs Peace in Times of Transition*, London: Frank Cass, 2004. R.G. Teitel, *Transitional Justice*, Oxford: OUP, 2002.

5 Monteville in K. Avruch & B. Vejarano, 'Truth and Reconciliation Commissions: A Review Essay and Annotated Bibliography', *The Online Journal of Peace and Conflict Resolution*, Issue 4.2, Spring 2002, p.4.
6 D. Crocker in J.D. Tepperman, 'Truth and Consequences', *Foreign Affairs*, March/April 2002, p.7.
7 Denis Thompson in ibid, p.7.
8 J. Lederach in A. Odendaal, 'For All Its Flaws. The TRC as a Peacebuilding Tool', *CCR*, vol. 6, no. 3/4, December 1997, p.1
9 This definition is set out in R. Kerr and E. Mobekk, *Peace and Justice: Seeking Accountability after War*, Cambridge Polity Press, 2007, p. 6.
10 'President Aristide Calls for Reconciliation and Justice on Returning to Haiti', Television National d'Haiti, Port-au-Prince, 15 October (1994), as translated in *SWB part 5*, 17 October (1994).
11 Interview with head of popular organisation, Port-au-Prince, 1997.
12 For example, peasants were demanding justice in the spring of 1995, with the MPP members presenting complaints to the local authorities. 'More News from MPP', *The Peasant*, vol.2, no.1, 1995, p.2. In commemoration of the killing of A. Izmery, a demonstration demanding justice was held on 11 September 1995. *Haiti Info*, vol.3, no.24, 16 September 1995, p.1. Several demonstrations were held denouncing the reconciliation policies of the government in September 1995. 'Le Coup d'État Continue', *Haiti Progrès*, 4–10 October 1995, p.1. The number of participants in these demonstrations cannot be confirmed.
13 Interviews with Haitian civil society, opposition politicians, officials, Port-au-Prince, Cap Haitien, Gonaives, 1997–98.
14 Ibid.
15 Interviews, Port-au-Prince, 1997–98.
16 Interview with leader of human rights organisation, Port-au-Prince, 1997.
17 Interview with women's group, who all had been active in the resistance against the coup, Port-au-Prince, 1998.
18 For discussion regarding the Port-au-Prince agreement see Chapter 2.
19 Port-au-Prince agreement para.3, September 1994.
20 Amnesty is defined as an act granting an individual or group immunity from criminal prosecution for crimes committed in the past. There are two types of amnesties: general amnesty, which covers all crimes committed in the given time period; and conditional amnesty, the perpetrator must here meet a number of conditions set out by the people granting the amnesty, individual responsibility is in this case assessed, which it is not in a general amnesty, but the perpetrator nevertheless escapes punishment. J. Alexander, *A Scoping Study of Transitional Justice and Poverty Reduction*, for Dfid, January 2003, p. 43.
21 'Area Haitians Echo Mistrust of Carter Pact', *The Washington Post*, 20 September 1994. Amnesty condemned the lack of justice in Haiti. Amnesty International, *Haiti: Still Crying out for Justice*, July 1998.
22 'Parliament Approves Amnesty Law', EFE News Agency, Madrid, 7 October 1994, as translated in *SWB part 5*, 8 October 1994.
23 The strength of the US forces compared with that of the Haitian Armed Forces combined with the fact that Cédras, according to a source close to him, wanted an

Justice and reconciliation 151

24 intervention (interview Port-au-Prince, 1997) begs the question whether there would have been real opposition.
24 Report of the Secretary-General, S/1998/434, 28 May 1998, 20.
25 For discussion on truth commissions, see e.g. Hayner, *Unspeakable*, R. Rotberg, D. Thompson, (Eds.), *Truth v. Justice: The Morality of Truth Commissions*, Princeton: Princeton University Press, 2010. Eric Wiebelhaus-Brahm, *Truth Commissions and Transitional Societies: The Impact on Human Rights and Democracy*, Routledge, 2010. Pricilla Hayner, 'Fifteen Truth Commissions – 1974 to 1994: A Comparative Study', *Human Rights Quarterly*. Vol. 16, 1994. Neil Kritz, *Transitional Justice: How Emerging Democracies Reckon with Former Regimes. Volumes 1–3*. Washington, DC: United States Institute of Peace Press, 1995. P. Ball & A.R. Chapman, *The Truth of Truth Commissions: Comparative Lessons from Haiti, South Africa, and Guatemala*. The Urban Morgan Institute, Baltimore: John Hopkins University Press, 2001. J.L. Gibson, 'Truth, Justice, and Reconciliation: Judging the Fairness of Amnesty in South Africa.' *American Journal of Political Science*, Vol. 46, Issue 3, 2002.
26 See also Freeman & Hayner, in D. Bloomfield, T. Barnes, L. Huyse (eds.), *Reconciliation after violent conflict: A handbook*, 2003, p.122.
27 Arthur, *After*, p.21.
28 H. Zehr, 'South Africa's Truth and Reconciliation Commission is an Unprecedented Experiment of Breathtaking Stakes', *Mennonite Central Committee, News Service*, 7 March 1997.
29 Report of Secretary-General, A/51/935, 26 June 1997. 'Le Ministère de la Justice Déclare Soutenir une Résolution des Victimes du Coup d'Etat', *Le Matin*, 15 May (1998), p.1.
30 Interview with senior MICIVIH representative, 1999.
31 Amnesty International, *Haiti*, p.8.
32 P. Hayner, 'Justice in Transition: Challenges and Opportunities', Presentation to 55th Annual DPI/NGO Conference, Rebuilding Societies Emerging form Conflict: A Shared Responsibility, United Nations, 9 September 2002, p.6.
33 See also Hayner, 'Truth Commissions: Exhuming the Past', *North American Congress on Latin America*, Sep/Oct 1998, p.2.
34 Interviews with representatives from civil society, 1998.
35 Rome Statute to the International Criminal Court, article 19. Rome Statute circulated as document A/CONF.183/9 of 17 July 1998 and corrected by process-verbaux of 10 November 1998, 12 July 1999, 30 November 1999, 8 May 2000, 17 January 2001 and 16 January 2002. The Statute entered into force on 1 July 2002. See also D. Orentlicher, *Independent Study on Best Practices, Including Recommendations, to Assist States in Strengthening their Domestic Capacity to Combat all Aspects of Impunity*, E/CN.4/2004/88, 27 February 2004, p.11.
36 See e.g. Universal Declaration of Human Rights, 1948, Article 8, ICCPR, article 9.
37 See e.g. M. Minow, *Between Vengeance and Forgiveness. Facing History after Genocide and Mass Violence*, Boston: Beacon Press, 1998.
38 For example, in South Africa, Timor-Leste, Haiti, Rwanda, Sierra Leone.
39 K. Sikkink and C. Booth Walling, 'Errors about Trials: The Political Reality of the Justice Cascade and Its Impact', Paper presented at the annual meeting of the APSA, 2005, p.10.
40 Universal Declaration, article 10.
41 Office for the High Commissioner of Human Rights, Resolution 2004/72, article 13.
42 See e.g. J. Snyder and L. Vinjamuri, 'Trials and Errors: Principle and Pragmatism in Strategies of International Justice', *International Security*, vo.28, no.3, Winter 2003/04, p.5 and p.25.
43 See also Smulovitz quoted in UNDP, *Access to Justice*, Practice Note, 9 March 2003, p.29.

152 Justice and reconciliation

44 L. Rohter, 'Haitians alarmed at unwillingness of US troops to disarm gunmen', *The New York Times*, 19 October 1994. Père Lebrun is a tyre filled with petrol put around a person's neck and set on fire. It was named after a tyre manufacturer. This was another reason why the interim police force was so frightened of policing the streets.
45 Ibid. This was due to the Port-au-Prince agreement, which stated that the MNF was to cooperate with the FAd'H. See Chapter 2.
46 'US Soldiers "Invade" FRAPH Headquarters; Front Leader Emmanuel Constant Reacts', Tropic FM Radio, Port-au-Prince, 3 October (1994), as translated in *SWB part 5*, 5 October (1994). Adama Dieng, the UN Human Rights Commission's independent expert on Haiti, in *The Haiti Support Group Briefing*, no.33, May 1999, p.4.
47 Amnesty International, *Haiti*, 1998, p.21. The Follow-up Committee of the NTJC demanded the return of the FRAPH documents, and suggested the creation of a special tribunal to facilitate the judgement of the accused of crimes during the coup era.
48 D. Farah, 'US–Haitian Relations Deteriorate: Disarmament Dispute, Contact with Ex-Ruler Infuriate Aristide', *The Washington Post*, 29 November (1995).
49 'US Makes a Mockery of Justice', *The Haiti Support Group Briefing*, no.29, August (1998), p.1.
50 Amnesty International, *Haiti*, p.20.
51 Interviews with leaders of grassroots movements and civil society organisations, Port-au-Prince, Gonaives, Cap Haitien, 1997–98.
52 'Haiti Requests Honduras to Extradite Former Police Boss on Human Rights Charges', La Prensa, Honduran Newspaper, 9 May (1998), as translated in *SWB part 5*, 12 May (1998). 'Honduran Court Rejects Haiti's Extradition Request for Former Chief of Police', *La Tribuna*, Honduran Newspaper, 21 May 1998, as translated in *SWB part 5*, 23 May (1998)
53 Interview with US State Department representative, Washington DC, 1998.
54 C. Orenstein in Emerge, cited in 'US Makes a Mockery of Justice', *The Haiti Support Group Briefing*, no.29, August 1998, p.1.
55 Interview with senior Haitian official, Port-au-Prince, 1998.
56 See R. Brody, 'Impunity Continues in Haiti', *NACLA Report on the Americas*, vol. xxx, no.2, September/October (1996), p.1.
57 I. Stotzky, *Silencing the Guns in Haiti, the Promise of Deliberative Democracy*, Chicago: The University of Chicago Press, 1997, p.135.
58 'Réflexions Autour du Procès du Massacre de Raboteau', *Le Matin*, 29 July 1998, p.5.
59 Amnesty International, 'Haiti: Obliterating justice, Supreme Court overturning sentences for Raboteau massacre is huge step backwards', 26 May 2005.
60 Ibid.
61 C. Kumar & E. Cousens, *Peacebuilding in Haiti*, International Peace Academy, 1996, p.7.
62 Interview with government official, Port-au-Prince, 1998.
63 'Quand le Fascisme Militaro-Macoute Relève la Tête', *Haiti en Marche*, 26 June – 2 July 1996, p.4.
64 Amnesty International, *Haiti*, p.9.
65 For examples see e.g. M. Deibert, *Notes from the last testament, the struggle for Haiti*, New York, Seven Stories Press, 2005.
66 Interview with government official, Port-au-Prince, 1998.
67 R. Courtois, *Le Matin*, 21 July 1998, p.1.
68 See also L. Hurbon, 'Le Crime, l'Oubli et le Pardon', *Chemins Critiques, Revue Haitiano-Caraibéenne*, vol.3, no.3, January 1997, p.17.
69 S. Castor, *La Formation de la Police. Un enjeu de la Transition*, Port-au-Prince: CRESFED, 1994, p.16.
70 'Duvalierists Unpunished and Unbowed in Borgne', *Haiti Progrès*, 3–9 July (1996), p.9.

Bibliography

Alexander, J. *A Scoping Study of Transitional Justice and Poverty Reduction*, London: DFID, January 2003.

Amnesty International, 'Haiti: Still crying out for justice', July 1998. <https://www.amnesty.org/download/Documents/152000/amr360021998en.pdf> (accessed 30 Spetember 2016).

Amnesty International, 'Haiti: Obliterating justice, Supreme Court overturning sentences for Raboteau massacre is huge step backwards', 26 May 2005 <https://www.amnesty.org/download/Documents/80000/amr360062005en.pdf> (accessed 30 Spetember 2016).

Avruch, K., and Vejarano, B. 'Truth and reconciliation commissions: A review essay and annotated bibliography', *The Online Journal of Peace and Conflict Resolution*, vol. 4 no. 2, Spring 2002.

Ball, P. and Chapman, A.R. *The Truth of Truth Commissions: Comparative Lessons from Haiti, South Africa, and Guatemala*. The Urban Morgan Institute, Baltimore, MD: John Hopkins University Press, 2001.

Bloomfield, D., Barnes, T. and Huyse L. (eds), *Reconciliation after Violent Conflict: A Handbook*, Stockholm: IDEA, 2003.

Brody, R. 'Impunity Continues in Haiti', *NACLA Report on the Americas*, vol. xxx, no.2, September/October 1996.

Castor, S. *La Formation de la Police. Un enjeu de la Transition*, Port-au-Prince: CRESFED, 1994.

Deibert, M., *Notes from the Last Testament: The Struggle for Haiti*, New York, Seven Stories Press, 2005.

Gibson, J.L. 'Truth, justice, and reconciliation: judging the fairness of amnesty in South Africa', *American Journal of Political Science*, vol. 46, no. 3, 2002.

Hayner, P., 'Fifteen truth commissions – 1974 to 1994: A comparative study', *Human Rights Quarterly*. vol. 16, 1994.

Hayner, P. 'Truth commissions: Exhuming the past', *North American Congress on Latin America*, Sep/Oct 1998.

Hayner, P. *Unspeakable Truths: Confronting State Terror and Atrocity*, New York: Routledge, 2001.

Hayner, P. 'Justice in transition: Challenges and opportunities', Presentation to 55th Annual DPI/NGO Conference, Rebuilding Societies Emerging form Conflict: A Shared Responsibility, United Nations, 9 September 2002.

Hayner, P., *Unspeakable Truths, Transitional Justice and the Challenge of Truth Commissions,* London: Routledge, 2010.

Hesse, C. and Post, R. (eds), *Human Rights in Political Transitions: Gettysburg to Bosnia*, Boston, MA: MIT Press, 2000.

Hurbon, L. 'Le crime, l'oubli et le pardon', *Chemins Critiques, Revue Haitiano-Caraibéenne*, vol. 3, no. 3, January 1997.

International Covenant on Civil and Political Rights, 1976.

Kerr, R., and Mobekk, E., *Peace and Justice: Seeking Accountability after War*, Cambridge: Polity Press, 2007.

Kritz, N., *Transitional Justice: How Emerging Democracies Reckon with Former Regimes.* Volumes 1–3, Washington DC: United States Institute of Peace Press, 1995.

Kumar, C. and Cousens, E. *Peacebuilding in Haiti*, New York: International Peace Academy, 1996.

Lekha Sriram, C. *Justice vs Peace in Times of Transition*, London: Frank Cass, 2004.
Mani, R. *Beyond Retribution: Seeking Justice in the Shadows of War*, Cambridge: Polity, 2001.
Mendez, J. 'Accountability for past abuses', *Human Rights Quarterly* vol. 19, no. 2, 1997.
Minow, M., *Between Vengeance and Forgiveness. Facing History after Genocide and Mass Violence*, Boston. MA: Beacon Press, 1998.
Odendaal, A. 'For all its flaws. The TRC as a peacebuilding tool', *Centre for Conflict Resolution*, vol. 6, no. 3/4, December 1997.
Orentlicher, D. 'Settling accounts: The duty to prosecute human rights violations of a prior regime', *Yale Law Journal* vol. 100, 1991.
Orentlicher, D., *Independent Study on Best Practices, Including Recommendations, to Assist States in Strengthening their Domestic Capacity to Combat all Aspects of Impunity*, E/CN.4/2004/88, New York: United Nations, 27 February 2004.
Port-au-Prince agreement, September 1994.
Rome Statute to the International Criminal Court.
Rotberg, R. and Thompson, D. (eds), *Truth v. Justice: The Morality of Truth Commissions*, Princeton, NJ: Princeton University Press, 2010.
Sikkink, K. and Booth Walling, C. 'Errors about trials: The political reality of the justice cascade and its impact', Paper presented at the annual meeting of the American Political Science Association, 2005.
Snyder, J. and Vinjamuri, L. 'Trials and errors: Principle and pragmatism in strategies of international justice', *International Security*, vol. 28, no.3, Winter 2003–04.
Stotzky, I., *Silencing the Guns in Haiti, the Promise of Deliberative Democracy*, Chicago, IL: The University of Chicago Press, 1997.
Teitel, R.G. *Transitional Justice*, Oxford: Oxford University Press, 2002.
Tepperman, J.D. 'Truth and Consequences', *Foreign Affairs*, March/April 2002.
Universal Declaration of Human Rights, 1948.
Wiebelhaus-Brahm, E., *Truth Commissions and Transitional Societies: The Impact on Human Rights and Democracy*, London: Routledge, 2010.
Zehr, H. 'South Africa's Truth and Reconciliation Commission is an unprecedented experiment of breathtaking stakes', *Mennonite Central Committee News Service*, 7 March 1997.

UN documents

Office for the High Commissioner of Human Rights, Resolution 2004/72.
SG report, S/1998/434, 28 May 1998.
SG report, A/51/935, 26 June 1997.
SG report, 'The Rule of Law and Transitional Justice in Conflict and Post-Conflict Societies', S/2004/616, 23 August 2004.
SG report, 'The rule of law and transitional justice in conflict and post-conflict societies', S/2011/634, 12 October 2011.
UNA-USA, DPKO, *Program on Peace Building and Rule of Law*, Partnership Program on Peace Building and Rule of Law, 2003.
UNDP, *Access to Justice*, Practice Note, 9 March 2003.

Media

Courtois, R. 'L'impunité est incompatible avec les principes démocratiques', *Le Matin*, 21 July 1998.
EFE News Agency, 'Parliament approves amnesty law', Madrid, 7 October 1994, as translated in *SWB part 5*, 8 October 1994.
Farah, D. 'US–Haitian relations deteriorate: Disarmament dispute, contact with ex-ruler infuriate Aristide', *The Washington Post*, 29 November 1995.
Haiti en Marche, 'Quand le fascisme Militaro-Macoute relève la tête', 26 June – 2 July 1996.
Haiti Info, vol. 3, no. 24, 16 September 1995.
Haiti Progrès, 'Le coup d'état continue', 4–10 October 1995.
Haiti Progrès, 'Duvalierists unpunished and unbowed in Borgne', 3–9 July 1996.
Haiti Support Group Briefing, 'US makes a mockery of justice', no.29, August 1998.
Haiti Support Group Briefing, no.33, May 1999.
La Prensa, Honduran Newspaper, 'Haiti requests honduras to extradite former police boss on human rights charges', 9 May 1998, as translated in *SWB part 5*, 12 May 1998.
La Tribuna, Honduran Newspaper, 'Honduran court rejects Haiti's extradition request for former chief of police', 21 May 1998, as translated in *SWB part 5*, 23 May 1998.
Le Matin, 'Le Ministère de la Justice déclare soutenir une résolution des victimes du coup d'etat', 15 May 1998.
Le Matin, 'Réflexions autour du procès du massacre de Raboteau', 29 July 1998.
Rohter L., 'Haitians alarmed at unwillingness of US troops to disarm gunmen', *The New York Times*, 19 October 1994.
Television National d'Haiti, 'President Aristide calls for reconciliation and justice on returning to Haiti', Port-au-Prince, 15 October 1994, as translated in *SWB part 5*, 17 October 1994.
The Peasant, 'More news from MPP', vol.2, no.1, 1995.
The Washington Post, 'Area Haitians echo mistrust of Carter pact', 20 September 1994.
Tropic FM Radio, 'US soldiers "invade" FRAPH headquarters; front leader Emmanuel Constant reacts', Port-au-Prince, 3 October 1994, as translated in *SWB part 5*, 5 October 1994.

8 Democratisation: strengthening good governance

Since the early 1990s promoting democracy and supporting democratisation efforts has been a central feature of peace operations and viewed as crucial to sustainable peace. In 1994 Haiti was the first UN intervention which had ever been explicitly mandated to restore democracy. It was the primary objective in the mandate, together with ensuring security and safety. Yet it unravelled. The democratisation process soon began to deteriorate and from the late 1990s was in severe decline – this was a result of both external and internal factors. The governments and political leaders increasingly politicised the security forces even if progress was made within these sectors. This ultimately contributed to the conflict in 2004 which precipitated the need for a new international intervention to support democracy. The second intervention in February 2004 came as a response to a breakdown in democratic governance and renewed crisis. The 2004 peace operation had several objectives; support for democracy was central as was security sector reform (SSR) and disarmament, demobilisation and reintegration (DDR). Democracy fundamentally rests on the government's ability to provide security, stability, the rule of law, justice, oversight and accountability. The renewed democratisation process from 2004 was very fragile.

Stability and security, building state capacities, security sector reform, and targeted development aid are key areas of support for the democratisation process. This chapter provides an overview of the first restoration of democracy in 1994, discusses the expectations of Haitians versus democracy restored, analyses the gradual unravelling of the democratic process and identifies democratic deficiencies. Subsequently the chapter analyses the political legitimacy of the post-2004 governments, tracing a gradual restriction on the democratic process. After decades of democratic transition it had yet to lead to stable governance.

Democracy and democratisation

Democracy and democratisation are 'essentially contested concepts' and there is no agreement how to measure democracy. The efforts of UN peacebuilding operations in this field must be viewed within this context of definitional ambiguity. This is exacerbated by the number of nationalities within any UN mission, each interpreting democracy and democratisation differently and many coming from countries with authoritarian regimes.

The contemporary model of democracy is representative democracy, where representatives are elected to govern and represent the majority. Schumpeter's much-quoted definition is 'the democratic method is that institutional arrangement for arriving at political decisions in which individuals acquire the power to decide by means of a competitive struggle'.[1] Another classical definition is Dahl's institutional definition of poliarchy, a political system which includes elected officials, free and fair elections, inclusive suffrage, right to run for office, freedom of expression, alternative information, and associational autonomy.[2]

These definitions focus on democracy as an institutional arrangement, but democracy is also 'a political system in which people have certain rights and obligations', where 'the responsibility of the rulers to the subjects' is the essence.[3] This emphasises the contract between the state and the individual. This is important, for without it democracy becomes solely a way of organising the state without emphasising the rights and obligations of the population. Democracy should be more than techniques for changing governments, it should be a system where people can determine their own destiny, where democracy has a social substance.[4] At the root of democracy lies the thought of popular power, an authority resting with the people.[5] Democracy is political empowerment. This is particularly important in post-conflict/post-authoritarian states, where democracy should include the participation of people at different levels, not only at the election booth, because the population have in these cases been held outside the processes of decision-making for long periods of time. Therefore, participation will define real change.

The most common understanding of contemporary democracy is *liberal democracy*. This includes a political system that is organised by way of free and fair elections, where representatives govern for a majority of the people and where the representatives have a responsibility towards the citizens to uphold their rights, where they are accountable and where participation at different levels is possible. At a minimum therefore democracy includes government based on majority rule and the consent of the governed, the existence of free and fair elections, the protection of minorities and respect for basic human rights, equality before the law, due process and political pluralism.

Democratisation

It is important to distinguish between democracy and democratisation. Democratisation is the process of moving towards a democracy. There are several explanations why democratisation comes about and is sustained. This includes, for example, the importance of the level of socio-economic development or level of modernisation as main indicators for successful democratisation,[6] which concludes that the better off the nation, the greater are the chances of sustaining democracy.[7]

None of these theories alone can explain the process of democratisation, or indeed what makes some states successful democracies whereas others fail. But they all point to important aspects of the process – namely economic development; social divisions such as class divisions; state and political institutions, that is, their general power in relation to civil society, which balances the power of the state; political culture and ideas (although this can be a consequence of democratisation); transnational and international engagements.[8]

One very important factor of democratisation is the will of the people to have a system other than an authoritarian one. The strength of the will for change within the population can be all-important in determining whether or not there will be a democratisation process. Without this will for change, it is doubtful whether this change would come about. Moreover, the occurrence of democratisation often depends on the historical context of the individual country. It is difficult to generalise about the construction of democracy, hence explanatory factors are frequently referred to as 'necessary but not sufficient'. It would be impossible to state that any factor was in all cases sufficient for democratisation.

Once democratisation has occurred, the need for consolidation arises. Six factors are argued to impact upon this. These are: legitimacy, including political, geographical and constitutional; consensus about the rules of the game and loyalty to those rules; policy restraint by winning parties; poverty and economic development; ethnic, cultural or religious constraints;[9] and education. In a recent post-conflict post-authoritarian context justice may play a critical role, as it did in Haiti. Illiteracy and poverty 'militate to a large extent against the full development of the democratic process' as democracy is founded on 'full bellies and peaceful minds'.[10] But these factors are just 'necessary but not sufficient' factors in the complex process of democratisation.

There have been criticisms of the above-discussed conditions for democracy and democratisation.[11] There are problems with the terms 'necessary but not sufficient', and a lot will depend on the individual case and the historic past. As has been stated: 'there can be no universal laws, or explanations of democracy as a general phenomenon'.[12] This is a problematic area in which to create conditions. Although some factors may be more important than others in creating, enhancing and consolidating the democratisation process, it might still not be valid to say that without these democratisation will not appear.

Due to these differences of interpreting and defining democracy and democratisation, when a state is assisted in creating or enhancing its democracy a different outcome can ensue than what was expected by that state and its population. Even if all were in favour of democracy, they rarely refer to the identical definition when promoting it.

Box 8.1 Governance structures in Haiti

- **Executive branch**
  Haiti is a semi-presidential republic with a president and a prime minister. The president is elected every five years by direct popular vote with absolute majority; two rounds of elections can be held if needed. The president can only sit for two terms. The prime minister is appointed by the president, from the majority party in parliament, but must be confirmed by parliament. Since 1994 several nominated prime ministers have been rejected by parliament. The cabinet is chosen by the prime minister in consultation with the president.

- **Legislative branch**
  Haiti has a bicameral legislature – the National Assembly – consisting of the Senate and Chamber of Deputies. The Senate consists of 30 Senators – three from each of the ten administrative departments. They are elected by absolute majority vote; two rounds of elections can be held if needed. They serve a six-year term; one third of the Senate is renewed every two years – one from each administrative department. The Chamber of Deputies has 99 members who are elected by absolute majority vote with the option for two rounds of elections. They serve a four-year term. There are no term limits for the Senate or the Chamber of Deputies.

- **Territorial administration**[13]
  There are ten departments in Haiti, each department is administered by a council of three members elected for four years by the Departmental Assembly. There are 140 communes. The communes have administrative and financial autonomy. Each Commune of the Republic is administered by a council, known as the Municipal Council, of three members elected by universal suffrage. The mandate of the Municipal Council is four years and its members can be re-elected indefinitely. The communal section is the smallest administrative unit, of which there are 570. The administration of each communal section is assured by a council of three members elected by universal suffrage for a term of four years. They can be re-elected indefinitely.

There are a vast number of political parties. In the 2015 legislative elections there were 128 parties with registered candidates. In 2010, 16 parties were represented in the National Assembly.

Democracy promotion in Haiti

When Aristide was elected in 1990 he was the first democratically elected President in Haiti.[14] It is in this historical context of authoritarianism, dictatorships and extremely politicised armed forces that had controlled Haitian political life since its inception, that the UN's support to democratisation should be viewed.

Restoring democracy – promoting elections

The objective of the first peace operation, as established by UN Security Council Resolution 940, was 'the prompt return of the legitimately elected President and the restoration of the legitimate authorities of the Government of Haiti, and to establish and maintain a secure and stable environment that will permit implementation of the Governors Island Agreement',[15] in short, the restoration of democracy. This was primarily defined as the return of the legitimately elected government and the holding of elections. This definition of democracy and democratisation did not reflect the views of the majority of Haitians. This was soon to lead to a number of serious problems. The principal bilateral donor to support for democratic consolidation in Haiti during this time period was the US.

Dwindling participation

Despite considerable international support, participation in the democratic process decreased consistently through the years after 1994. This was a result of disillusionment with the process due to democracy defined as elections only, lack of civic education, lack of political legitimacy due to fraud and irregularities, lack of transitional justice, insufficient security and stability, and no economic development, in sum fewer overall changes than had been expected.

Participation in the first municipal and legislative elections was marred by difficulties including postponement, electoral fraud, missing electoral cards and calls for a boycott of the elections by a number of parties.[16] In the run-off elections, which Jean-Bertrand Aristide's party *Organizasyon Politik Lavalas* (OPL) won, and the other parties boycotted, participation was very low although the numbers were disputed.[17] The international community acknowledged irregularities, but felt it would be disadvantageous to annul them, and it was stressed that they had been the 'freest and least violent' in the country's history.[18] There were three main reasons for low participation: people were not accustomed to participating in a second round of elections, the accusations of irregularities led people to withdraw from the process, and inadequate knowledge regarding the different types of elections, as previously only presidential elections had been held.

In the presidential elections in December 1995 there was only 15 per cent participation – the reason being that the majority of Haitians wanted Aristide to continue as president for the years he had been in exile, but one of the conditions for his return was that his years in exile would count towards his presidency.[19]

René Préval was elected, but there was no other real alternative as he had the support of Aristide.

By 1997, in the parliamentary elections, participation was at a mere five per cent.[20] This was due to a general disillusionment arising from a low level of confidence in the government, the political parties did not represent the views of the electorate, and the elections were not considered free and fair. Prime Minister Rosny Smarth stated that the low participation was because of lack of information; others emphasised that there had been no campaign to motivate the electorate.[21] People simply began to question democracy as well as the electoral processes, best illustrated by a headline that read: 'Democracy on course without the people'.[22] The elections were plagued by irregularities and declared fraudulent by international observers.

The UN presence brought about the freedom to join and form political parties and organisations. The political discourse at the time was vibrant and political parties in opposition as well as citizens could critique government policies without fear of reprisals. However, there was a lack of capacity to fully participate and effectively communicate their displeasure about government policies. Speaking out against the government was not suppressed at the time, and the UN ensured this through its presence. The people's discontent with the democratisation process was shown through the non-participation in elections.

Democracy restored or pépé democracy?[23]

The low voter turnout in the different elections was not a reflection of Haitians lack of support for democracy, but because Haitians defined democracy differently from the UN and other donors – as participatory democracy. As was underlined, people 'made a clear distinction between elections, which are generally used by the elites to further their own agenda, and democracy, which is measured by the people's participation in the political, economic and social affairs of their country'.[24] A former prime minister in Haiti stated it was a big mistake to focus only on elections, because they make no difference in people's lives.[25] When they received elections only they became disillusioned.[26] Participation at all levels is a cornerstone of democracy and as has been pointed out, without it 'no regime can be a democracy'.[27] But participation is more than elections. Elections are critical to show that there is some change in a post-conflict/post-authoritarian state – and they have been promoted consistently by the UN and other actors in the international community in interventions in fragile states. Yet they are not sufficient for democracy to take hold. It was not what was expected from a return to democracy. Arguably, defining democracy narrowly through elections created further problems.

Haitians wanted to create their own type of democracy, for example, it was suggested that representative democracy could take the form of cooperation with NGOs and human rights organisations, bringing government into closer contact with the different sectors of society.[28] The reality after the first elections fell far short of this. There was a lack of influence over the shape of their new democracy. There were four main Haitian perspectives on the UN and international support to the democratisation process. First, parts of the grassroots and popular movement argued that the type of system that had been returned with the intervention was not a democracy, but controlled by the Haitian elite.[29] This argument was rooted in the absence of justice for crimes committed during the junta years.[30] They called the Haitian republic a *macoute* republic.[31]

Second, it was referred to as a 'flap-flap' republic, or a *pépé* democracy, that is, a second-hand democracy from abroad. It had the characteristics of a democracy, but it was not rooted in the Haitian reality or perspectives and definitions of what type of democracy and democratisation process was needed.[32] What was special about 1986–91 was that people from the grassroots became organised and involved, and there was pro-democracy activity at this level. The top-down electoral model seemed to put a stop to that, and hence inadvertently served the aims of the coup.[33] A former prime minister defined it as 'a functional anarchy'.[34]

Third, one section of society emphasised the increased freedoms that the UN presence had brought including free press, free movement and holding of elections, but underscored that building democracy is a lengthy process.[35] The freedom of speech, possibility of redress, an ability to rely on the law had been brought about by the UN, but there was a fear that this could be threatened by drug empires, fanatical groups and expositions of personal political power.

Fourth, parts of the elite, who had been against the intervention, stated that it was not a democracy, because it was completely controlled by the international community, primarily the US.[36] They argued that the intervention and restoration of democracy was a means for the US to reassert its influence in Haiti's domestic politics.

These different perceptions of democracy were in part a result of divergent definitions of democracy. This is inevitable. But there was agreement on one issue, across class and political affiliations: democracy had far from succeeded. The slow pace of meaningful change in the factors that underpin democratisation was the principal cause of this disappointment, robbing the process of legitimacy.

Political infighting

It was not only disappointment with the singular focus on elections and the government that led to increasing disillusionment with the democratisation process, but also the consistent in-fighting of the political organisations. There was a split within OPL, which led to the creation of *Famni Lavalas* (Lavalas Family).[37] This split played a major part in the ensuing and continuous political crisis in the country. With OPL in power, *Famni Lavalas* was created by Aristide in October 1996 and made a political party in time for the elections in 1997. Divisions also began to appear among the parties on the left, which had previously been supporters of Lavalas.[38] There were growing differences between the organisations even before the elections[39] and these widened soon after. The election was primarily a contest between *Lafamni* and OPL, given that the other major parties decided on a boycott.

The political crisis was exacerbated by the inability to agree on a prime minister. The government had been without a prime minister since 9 June 1997, when Rosny Smarth resigned after months of increasing pressure to do so. When he stepped down he acknowledged that the government had not fulfilled the expectations placed on it. He continued to deal with day-to-day matters while waiting for a replacement to be appointed, but stepped down when no one had been appointed by 20 October.[40] President Préval named three people for the position: Eric Pierre, Hervé Denis (twice) and Jacques Alexis, but all were rejected by parliament.

Haiti was de facto without a government from June 1997 to January 1999 when President Préval appointed a prime minister, dissolved parliament and began ruling by decrees. At that point he became one of only nine elected officials in the whole of Haiti.[41] This was unconstitutional. Article 165 of the Haitian constitution states that 'in case of resignation of the Prime Minister the government stays in place until the nomination of a successor to deal with day to day matters'. This was referred to as a coup by some sectors of Haitian society. By this stage both internal and external accountability had become limited. Answering to their voters and to other officials and state institutions regarding decisions taken was minimal to non-existent.

Political legitimacy and state capacity

Political legitimacy is a central factor in the process of democratisation. Political legitimacy is a complex concept, which is difficult to define and measure. Although it has been closely coupled with the socio-economic success,[42] new regimes need to develop a degree of autonomy of this,[43] and develop alternative credentials like guaranteeing there will be no abuse of power,[44] or creating a belief that no other system can do better.[45] Political legitimacy also refers to 'the extent to which the electorate regards the government in power as being entitled, procedurally, to be there'.[46] Even so, 'the more shallow, exclusive, abusive and ineffective the regime, the greater the probability of broad popular disillusionment with it over time'.[47] But how do you give legitimacy to any 'political authority after many years of rule that had no legitimacy'?[48] The answer arguably lies in a more participatory model as emphasised by the grassroots. In Haiti there was a lack of belief that the government at the end of the 1990s was entitled to be there; it was unable to provide services and it was exclusive, ineffective, and corrupt[49] and in part abusive – political legitimacy was steadily eroding.

The influence of the international community was another important factor in legitimacy, as international involvement has not always been positive for democratisation in Haiti. Haiti's democratic process has always been influenced by its democratic neighbours, chiefly the US. This close link with the US has historically had a negative rather than a positive influence on democracy and democratisation. The US has supported numerous dictatorships, including the Duvaliers and General Namphy, and was against the election of Aristide in 1990. Not surprisingly the US government's role in the democratisation process was viewed as ambiguous. The UN's role however, was not viewed with similar suspicion. Haitians clearly distinguished between the different international donors and organisations.

Closely intertwined with political legitimacy is the capacity of the state and the government to provide services. The state's capacity to provide services and public goods was very inadequate, infrastructure was exceptionally bad, improved security was a result of UN presence, and welfare, such as it was, was provided by external agents, including the UN. The lack of change in the state's capacity to deliver public services and goods was an important reason for the population's disillusionment with democracy. They had expected change and improvement in their circumstances, but, apart from increased security and freedoms brought about by the UN, had found little improvement in terms of jobs, economic development, justice, education, health and welfare in the nearly six years of democracy.[50] By 2000 the Haitian state had limited capacity and was still in dire need of further capacity-building. Although the UN missions had focused on capacity-building in certain areas, others had been marginalised. Critically, the state and bureaucratic apparatus lacked capacity to effectively implement their decisions and suffered from corruption.

Democratic deficits

The international community was not perceived to be the reason for the continuous political crisis in Haiti. The blame was placed on the Haitian government, the political infighting, the split in the Lavalas movement and the lack of change. The road to democracy however, was made more difficult by the inability of the international community to consolidate the intervention particularly through more effectively supporting security, justice and economic development. UN missions cannot establish democracy in any country, but can only support the processes that facilitate democratisation taking place. It is how this dividend is utilised by national actors which will determine whether democratisation will take root. Haiti lacked several of the fundamental factors on which to build a democratic society – principal among them were security, justice and economic development.[51]

Security is an essential element for democratisation. In post-intervention Haiti security was defective and the state did not have a monopoly of power. The security situation improved immensely after the intervention in 1994 due to the UN presence, which critically eliminated institutional violence conducted by the Armed Forces of Haiti. But there was a rapid increase in crime, as well as instability, political crime and armed groups forming, that the interim and later the new Haitian police force were not able to deal with. This situation was exacerbated after the new police also began to be involved in criminal activities. Security was emphasised as being the first duty of a government, in which the Préval government had failed.[52] This was exemplified through the pre- and post-election violence. The failure of the disarmament process was one cause that induced and exacerbated this climate of insecurity.[53] Security was a primary objective for the UN in the context of holding free and fair elections. But providing security for the elections themselves was less connected to the broader security sector reform (SSR) processes in, for example, ensuring that there was no or limited potential for politicisation of the security forces. The possibility of this was acknowledged, but because the elections were needed to be held fast these processes ran at different speeds. It was the potential for politicised insecurity that needed addressing and which needed a deeper rethink of what democratisation is and how to support it in a post-authoritarian and fragile state. It was about more than elections without violence. Violence, gangs and armed forces have always been used in Haitian politics – the awareness of this should have translated more effectively into support and programming in democratisation and SSR.

The absence of security in Haiti was closely intertwined with a lack of transitional justice.[54] Demanding justice was another way of demanding security in Haiti. The lack of transitional justice in Haiti contributed to insecurity, as the supporters of the coup regime lived in impunity. It also meant that former human right violators and coup participants took part in the democratisation process, by both standing in the elections and seeking to influence the democratic process.[55] This was one factor among many that contributed to the democratic unravelling.

Economic development is central to the consolidation of democratisation and in Haiti a more level playing field in the economy needed to be created. There was over 70 per cent unemployment; limited access to power, water, education and health facilities; poor infrastructure; and the vast majority were living below the poverty line. Some Haitians argued that without economic development there could be no democracy in Haiti.[56] As others have also argued 'people on the border of or below subsistence minimum cannot really exercise their democratic rights, even if they were allowed to'.[57] Economic marginalisation inevitably leads to political marginalisation.[58] As a USAID document stated: 'Haiti's fledgling democracy cannot be sustained in the absence of economic growth'.[59] The economic situation was closely tied up with democratisation because people had expected to see an improvement in their living conditions, which did not come about.[60] This increased disillusionment with the democratisation process. Democracy needs some measure of economic growth, but the post-intervention years failed to accomplish this.

Economic growth through privatisation and structural adjustment programmes was proposed by the International Monetary Fund (IMF) and the World Bank. These policies were part of the agreements with the return of Aristide. In August 1994 the government met with the IMF, the World Bank and bilateral donors including the US, Canada and France. A plan was signed, which committed the government to the implementation of privatisation when it was returned to power. These agreements were confirmed in January 1995. At first the government hesitated over implementing the economic reforms, until pressed to move forward when millions of dollars in aid were withheld. The reluctance of the government to fully comply with these plans was partly due to the negative attitudes of the population. Privatisation[61] of the economy was highly unpopular in Haiti. The main reason for the opposition was based on suspicions that these measures would benefit only the elite and foreign business interests. The World Bank stated that 'privatisation is a politically sensitive issue in Haiti'.[62] It was such a politically sensitive issue that the government was refraining from using the concept, but rather, chose the word 'modernisation' of public enterprises. It led to the resignation of Prime Minster Smarck Michel, who felt there was so much resistance to these measures and that he was the only one in the government working for them.[63] Aristide continued opposing these policies after his term had ended, contributing to the split between him and Préval, as Préval was attempting to implement these economic policies. The World Bank subsequently concluded that corruption and cronyism between the private and public sectors 'may be such that privatisation may well not enhance the prospects for sustained, equitable development and may even make them worse'.[64] Due to few state capacities to run these companies nationally, privatisation seemed a natural solution, but this disregarded the fact that only a few families ran Haiti's economy and therefore a more equitable distribution of resources could be placed in doubt if they were privatised. This was one of the principal reasons for opposition to the plans.

Poverty was closely tied to social divisions, which continued to be vast and difficult to overcome, especially with the lack of economic development. These divisions were a significant factor, which created a problem for the democratisation process. These were deep enough to have been characterised as social apartheid.[65] It was emphasised that to fulfil the social contract the governments must make the elite 'change their perspective and restrict their historic capacity for social repression', but also 'contain the anger of the urban poor'.[66] A member of the elite stated that '(we) cannot forgive what the people did to us in 1990 – they voted against us' and 'democracy is for political families.'[67] This was an attitude voiced repeatedly by the elite, namely that 'the Haitian population is not ready for democracy'.[68] There were no ethnic, cultural or religious divisions that served as constraints. Rather the constraint was embedded in class, which was expressed in all political and economic processes.[69] This was not addressed in the UN's support for democratisation, primarily because it was defined as elections. The UN mission worked closely with the elite which disenfranchised the majority of Haitians, moreover, the majority of the elite had supported the coup. Democratisation in Haiti was originally a grassroots movement. But given that the elite held senior positions and were leading in the economic sphere they became the UN's principal interlocutors. The impact of this relationship in this context was significant, but the implications was either not sufficiently understood or adequately addressed. The majority of the elite at the time had a different agenda than democratisation – yet it was they whom the mission worked the closest with. Quite what a large role social divisions played in Haiti's democratisation process was underestimated.

Democratisation unravelling – consolidating authoritarianism

New elections were originally scheduled in 1999, but were postponed twice. Local and municipal elections were scheduled for 19 March and 30 April 2000 respectively, but were yet again postponed until finally they were rescheduled for 21 May and 25 June. The elections were to fill the Senate and the Chamber of

Deputies, but there were numerous pre-election problems. The registration to vote began late. It was decided that voter identification cards with photographs should be issued, to deter fraud. But there was a lack of materials to make the voter registration cards.[70] Also there were not enough registration offices, particularly in the countryside and in poor urban areas. This fuelled anger and subsequently led to demonstrations; as one demonstrator put it: 'Why should we have to fight to be able to vote?'[71] It was also argued that the lack of registration offices was a deliberate tactic to hinder the urban poor and people in the countryside in casting their votes, and to undermine more progressive parties.[72]

Electoral officials declared 2.7 million voters registered, out of approximately 4.5 million eligible voters.[73] Later the Provisional Electoral Council (CEP) and the Organization of American States (OAS) claimed that 93.27 per cent of the potential electorate had registered.[74] Both the numbers of eligible voters and registered voters became disputed.[75] A group of independent observers argued that as many as 25 per cent of eligible voters may have been excluded from registration.[76]

Another problem was that this pre-election process was marred by political violence. There were more than 70 violent incidents relating to the elections and 15 politically motivated killings.[77] The first round of elections was held on 21 May amidst relative calm and few incidents of violence, although there were allegations of fraud and stuffed ballot boxes. Circumstances were chaotic around the beginning of the vote count the following day, such as ballots and ballot boxes being 'strewn all over the streets'.[78] There were reports that in some places gunmen stormed polling stations and removed the ballot boxes.

Famni Lavalas won a seemingly impressive victory, but the result was criticised by the international community and declared invalid by the opposition party leaders.[79] The head of CEP fled to the US after receiving death threats, explaining he would not release the election results with all their irregularities.[80] The OAS, UN and US continued to apply pressure to have the results recalculated, yet the CEP formally declared Lavalas the winner of the elections, giving the party control of the Senate. Other Haitian groups added their voice to the opposition and international community in condemning the results of the elections.[81] The runoff elections were postponed, then held on 9 July; they had a very low turnout and were boycotted by the opposition. The OAS refused to observe the second round, stating that the first round was not free and fair.

The result of this flawed election was that Famni Lavalas won control of both houses of Parliament and 77 per cent of the city halls and a majority of the urban and rural councils.[82] On 28 August the Haitian parliament was sworn in despite international and local protests. These elections served only to further political controversy and to invite the renewal of international economic sanctions. In September demonstrations took place against the government and the newly instated Parliament. The presidential elections held on 26 November 2000 returned Aristide with 91.6 per cent of the vote. All major parties boycotted the elections.

The string of postponements of the elections and related problems with the electoral process did not just indicate flaws in the democratisation process, but underlined the re-emergence of the old patterns of governance in Haiti. This re-emergence was evident in the police, private sector and among the political class. There was a non-compromising divide-and-rule mentality aimed at obtaining the most power for oneself. The familiar processes of power, attitudes set against compromise and cooperation re-emerged. The country was said to be blocked by blindness and egoism.[83] This was reflected in the political crisis. Personal agendas were carried forward, which for example explained the failure to agree on a prime minister. But this was taking place under the guise of democracy, which made it harder to rid the system of them. As was underscored, it becomes more difficult to know your enemies in a 'democracy'.[84]

When the fifth UN peacekeeping mission left Haiti in February 2001 democratisation was unravelling, authoritarianism was resurfacing and politicised violence was rife. By 2002 Haiti was deemed 'not free' on the democracy index.[85] The first intervention to restore democracy had unravelled. Democratisation this time had failed.

Democracy resurrected

The period after the re-election of Aristide in 2000 was characterised by violence and armed gangs. Famni Lavalas, Aristide's political party, as well as other political and non-political groups, began to rely on young armed men to control the community – this was to provide security but also to ensure that no other groups operated in those areas for both political and financial reasons. The situation in the country was especially chaotic in 2003, when armed groups, former members of the armed forces and armed Aristide supporters regularly clashed and were uncontrolled in much of the country.[86] The democratisation process had effectively stopped in the years without UN presence and violence for political purposes and intimidation was ever-present. This was the complex context in which the UN intervened with a new democratisation mandate.

Support for democracy

UN Security Council Resolution 1542 adopted on 30 April 2004 established UN Stabilisation Mission in Haiti (MINUSTAH) which replaced the Multinational Interim Force (MIF) on 1 June 2004. MINUSTAH's first mandate stipulated that the mission should 'support the constitutional and political process underway in Haiti, including through good offices, foster principles and democratic governance, and institutional development' and assist the transitional government in organising, monitoring and carrying out free and fair elections.[87] The Security Council also asked the UN, the OAS and the Caribbean Community (CARICOM) to work with Haitians in promoting the rebuilding of democratic institutions, as well as assisting in developing a strategy to combat poverty and socio-economic development.[88] MINUSTAH's mandate was renewed on 15 August 2006 and included assisting in holding free and fair elections, and supporting institution building.[89] All subsequent resolutions reinforced MINUSTAH's support to the political process and institutional capacity-building.

MINUSTAH provided technical assistance to institutions, including the parliamentary chamber's strengthening legislative capacity; supported the Ministry of Interior and local government on budget and financial management, renovation of mayoral offices; enhancing outreach from mayors to government; provided capacity-building to the Ministry of Interior; as well as technical advice to departmental and commune-level authorities. Throughout, MINUSTAH provided all elections with technical, logistical and security support.

The major bilateral donors were the US and Canada, but the EU, World Bank, OAS, BID, IMF, and UNDP also supported the democratisation process. The broad aims were to end the crisis, ensuring stability and security, creating a stable state and strengthening democracy. The goals were substantial considering the level of institution and capacity-building necessary and dependent upon Haitian political will and civil society support for international influence and the economic elite's and armed actors' will to support it. Good governance is dependent upon good leadership and this needed to be provided by the Haitians. A peace operation with short-term mandates can support good leadership, but the will for change rested with the Haitians.

Holding elections and ensuring political legitimacy

A core part of MINUSTAH's mandate was to ensure that free and fair elections were held. In principle, since 2004 there had been free competition between the different parties. The UN presence ensured that participation in the different democratic processes was possible and that there was no longer persecution because of political beliefs. Political discussion in Haiti increased immensely after 2006, and critiquing the government and its policies became frequent, underlining the freedom of expression and freedom of the press that existed, in addition to rights such as freedom to form and join organisations. This was a substantial change from prior to February 2004 when, for example, journalists were targeted for disagreeing with or critiquing the government. During Aristide's government from 2000 there were attacks and threats against journalists who reported on demonstrations, and targeted attacks resulting in journalists going into exile.[90] Moreover, it was also a great change from the transitional government, which targeted former-President Aristide's supporters.[91]

However, elections were plagued by difficulties, decreasing participation and increasing allegations of fraud. The first round of presidential and legislative elections was held on 7 February 2006 and participation was 60 per cent. This was an incredible increase compared with the elections held in 2000. Rene Préval was elected.[92] Préval obtained 48.8 per cent of the votes, but over 50 per cent was needed to avoid a second round of voting. The Electoral Council ignored the electoral law, and counted the blank votes and divided them up between different candidates. This increased Préval's support from 48.8 to 51.2 per cent. People took to the streets to support Préval and to refuse a second round of elections. The elected government was perceived as legitimate, as entitled to be there, and not abusing its power. Nevertheless it was perceived to be inefficient in addressing issues that concerned most Haitians: economic development, job creation and education, which undermined political legitimacy. Moreover, many run-off elections were postponed. The government saw little use in supporting local and municipal elections.[93] This undermined both local democratic change and judicial independence.[94]

Political instability increased as a result of the April 2008 riots, which resulted in the prime minister resigning. Parliament rejected President Préval's first nomination for a new prime minister, and only after several months of political wrangling was a new prime minister, Michèle Pierre-Louis, accepted by parliament and she took office on 5 September 2008. This ended a five-month impasse during which time Haiti was effectively without a government – mirroring events in the 1990s. Senate elections, which should have been held in 2007, were not held until 2009; in the meantime the seats were empty, further undermining parliamentary control of the government, political legitimacy and the democratisation process. In the Senate elections many candidates were not allowed to take part, ostensibly for procedural reasons, but they were predominantly Fanmi Lavalas candidates; this was strongly criticised by local and international organisations. It also meant voter anger was expressed through non-participation, not violence, and as a result the turn-out dropped significantly and was estimated to be as low as 8–10 per cent, and the UN stated that ballots were stolen as well as destroyed.[95]

As a result political legitimacy decreased prior to the elections in 2010. The subsequent general elections, parliamentary and presidential, were due to be held in early 2010, but due to the earthquake were postponed until November 2010. Although necessary, this triggered concern since the mandates of the Deputies and one third of the Senate expired in May – this was handled by confirming a State of Emergency law. The three main candidates in the Presidential elections were Michel Martelly, Mirlande Manigat and Jude Celestin – the latter from the sitting party Unity. Allegedly Manigat received the majority of the vote in the first round of elections, followed by Celestin and Martelly. The elections were deemed fraudulent by the UN and marred by intimidation both during and leading up to the elections.[96] Violence was perpetrated by supporters of all candidates. After this first round of elections there was violence in the streets in response to the results and allegations of fraud. The violence effectively closed down several towns. An OAS report recommended that Michel Martelly should be placed as second-ranking, the Provisional Electoral Council (CEP) accepted the findings and thus Martelly became part of the run-off. The second round was postponed by two months as a result of the violence. The second round of presidential elections were held in March 2011; Michel Martelly won by 67.5 per cent (*Repons Peyizan*), his opponent Mirlande Manigat (*Rassemblement des Démocrates Nationaux Progressistes*) receiving 31.74 per cent. The participation was extremely low for a presidential election, only 22.5 per cent – in addition a large number of votes were discounted as they were never received by the CEP or due to irregularities. One report stated that this was as much as 13.2 per cent of the vote.[97] The second round was declared by the OAS to be an improvement on the first round, better organised and peaceful.[98]

The first months of the presidency was marred by the failure to agree on a prime minister; and 100 days into the presidency the government was still without

Democratisation 171

a prime minister after parliament had rejected two of Martelly's candidates. Only in September was Martelly's third candidate for prime minister, Garry Conille, ratified by the Chamber of Deputies and the Senate. Yet only a few months later in February 2012 Conille resigned as prime minister. Haiti was yet again without a prime minister. It was only in May that a new prime minister, Laurent Lamothe, took office.

Tensions were profound in the legislative bodies throughout this period, as well as between the legislative, executive and judiciary bodies. The work of these bodies was severely hampered by the constant delayed elections as a quorum for decision-making frequently was never reached. Moreover, as with the previous government, local elections were postponed repeatedly, leading to an absence of locally elected mayors and community representatives. This situation was further compounded by parliament accusing President Martelly of holding dual citizenship (illegal under the Haitian constitution); this halted progress on a number of issues including adoption of the national budget and agreement on when the next local elections were to be held.[99] Friction was exacerbated by reports of advisors and associates of President Martelly allegedly being involved in criminal activities, and allegations of judicial interference by the government leading to court cases against these individuals stalling or falling away.[100] By mid-2015 no legislative or municipal elections had been held since 2011. This ultimately undermined not only local democratic change but also the political legitimacy of the national government. As a result of their inability to hold municipal elections the government replaced locally elected authorities with political appointees in those communes (129 out of 140) whose term had expired in 2011. This fostered further tensions[101] and a lapse in the democratisation process. Moreover, local authorities were employing armed elements for their own protection and as 'law enforcers',[102] further undermining political legitimacy at municipal level. All these issues drastically affected the government's political legitimacy, as they seemed at best unable or at worst unwilling to hold legislative and municipal elections. It also fuelled anti-government demonstrations throughout the country, particularly in autumn 2013. The exceptionally low voter turnout in almost all elections after 2004, except the first presidential elections, demonstrated the majority of Haitians' profound disillusionment with the democratisation process.

As a result of the political stalemates, Parliament was dissolved in January 2015 and the President began ruling by decrees, leaving only eleven elected officials in the whole country. The prime minister had resigned in 2014 – again an unfortunate reflection of events in the late 1990s. Even though legislative elections were finally held in August 2015, they were marred by irregularities, violence, vandalism and theft, and had to be cancelled in several areas.[103] Moreover, participation was at a mere 18 per cent. A second round of legislative elections and first round of presidential elections were held in October, but were also mired in allegations of fraud. The official results indicated that Jovenel Moise, the candidate of the governing party, was leading with 32.8 per cent, followed by Jude Celestin (25.3 per cent), Moise Jean Charles (14.3 per cent) and Maryse Narcisse (7 per cent). This was severely disputed and alleged to be fraudulent. A survey on voting patterns conducted after the elections found very different results, supporting the claims of vote rigging.[104] The dispute over who had won the first round of presidential elections led to violent demonstrations, where some opposition supporters chanted 'netwaye zam nou' (we are cleaning our guns).[105] It also meant further disappointment with the government and the democratic process, as seemingly elections did not determine who would run the country.[106] This was also exemplified by the low voter turnout which was an estimated 28 per cent.[107] After the results a survey found that people who had witnessed fraud or intimidation were less likely to feel that their voted counted or that voting was important because it determines who runs the country.[108] Unfortunately the international response was timid, underscoring that the elections were less violent than the August elections rather than focusing on the irregularities. There was an emphasis on highlighting that the elections were held as progress, rather than it in many ways indicated a derailing of the democratisation process. In what can only be described as very close interference in the national election process, the US dismissed the fraud allegations and called for a resumption of the electoral process.

The controversy surrounding these elections led to postponement of second round of elections. Martelly's term ended 7 February 2016 without a second round of presidential elections held. He made an agreement with parliament before leaving which left his prime minister in charge; and an interim president, Jocelerme Privert, was sworn in 14 February, with a mandate for 120 days, until new elections were to be held. These were scheduled for 24 April 2016, but did not take place due to the continued political infighting. A new commission was established to determine who should be in the presidential run-off. But on 25 April Privert suggested to hold the run-off 30 October, at the same time as the Senate elections. His interim presidency ended 14 June but weeks after in late July his mandate had not been extended nor another elected in his place. Haitian lawmakers effectively blocked any decision on this issue through failing to assemble a quorum. In late July Privert set the 9 October[109] as the date for the new elections; this was criticised by many in Haiti as he no longer was de jure interim president, drawing the legitimacy of this order into question. It seemed very little had changed from the nineties to 2016. After decades of Haitians fighting for democracy and seven UN missions promoting democratisation the political scene was eerily reminiscent of the late nineties.

Accountability of elected officials

Throughout the post-2004 period there was inadequate external accountability, and civil society was not sufficiently strong to exert the kind of pressure needed to function as accountability and oversight mechanisms. There were a vast number of civil society groups and organisations in Haiti, but many lacked the capacity to act as oversight mechanisms. MINUSTAH made considerable efforts in this regard, through for example, the Civil Affairs section which was present in all the departments of the country and worked with civil society and local authorities to ensure transparency by local authorities, greater access by civil society and improved communication between authorities and civil society. In many contexts accountability is easier to achieve at the local level because it is easier to facilitate access. In Haiti with a tradition of actors controlling rural areas, with the support of armed groups as 'law enforcers', this became more difficult. The multiple demonstrations at national level could in one way be interpreted as a form of accountability, as they targeted the government for their failure to deliver. However, although demonstrations and the freedom to hold them characterises a democracy, violence, destruction and riots to depose elected officials do not.

MINUSTAH provided capacity-building of parliamentarians and state officials, but internal accountability of the government was difficult since for long periods of time parts of the legislature were either not at full quorum or due to delayed elections not seated. Albeit there was a level of accountability by parliament, for example, a vote of no confidence against the prime minister was raised in 2008, but was defeated. Parliamentary accountability was further eroded through the dissolution of parliament, when the President ruled by decree, in effect ensuring no accountability of the sitting government. Given that for long periods parliament was not seated, it was simply impossible to function as an oversight mechanism of government. The level of capacity-building of parliamentarians matters little if they are not allowed to sit.

Democratic interdependencies and shortfalls

After 2004 Haiti continued to lack the foundations on which to build a democratic society. The complex interdependence between democracy, security, state capacities (state capacities in service delivery of the rule of law in particular), economic development and political will to develop a democratic society all strongly influenced the democratic process.

Security

There was violence throughout the UN presence in Haiti, but there was a level of security that, for example, permitted the holding of elections. A complete secure and stable society was not necessary for a continued democratisation process or state building in Haiti, but a level of security was necessary for the democratisation process to move forward. The continued violence and insecurity did not stop the democratisation process or state-building, but it served to slow it down. But the slow pace of democratisation cannot be blamed singularly on the issues of insecurity.

Conversely, democracy also strengthened security in the sense that when the non-elected transitional government was in power they used violence, pursued Aristide supporters and illegally arrested and detained political prisoners. This stopped after the democratic elections and with the new government in place. Furthermore, even though the transitional government strengthened the democratisation process by agreeing not to run for office in the elections, as a result there was little incentive for them to begin to build institutions and ensure

174 *Democratisation*

state capacity-building, for example, by committing and supporting security and justice reform. The transitional government's aversion to state capacity-building had an adverse effect upon the democratisation process and complicated the situation for the subsequently elected government.

State capacities

Lack of state capacity was one of the major problems in Haiti.[110] This was not only due to a lack of qualified personnel, but because of inadequate funds and the fact that so many issues needed to be addressed concurrently. The inability of the Haitian government to provide services to its people fundamentally weakened the shaky foundations of the democratisation process. State capacities in a narrow sense were in many ways given more attention than support for democracy – through training and mentoring. More specifically certain parts of building state capacities, such as policing, were given a lot of attention whereas other state capacities were more marginalised.

The civil service suffered from corruption and ineffectiveness. There were few qualified personnel, inadequate infrastructure, and insufficient resources. Consequently the state had very low capacity in its ability to provide services and public goods. To provide even the minimum of infrastructure and welfare the state continued to be heavily dependent upon foreign aid and assistance. After the earthquake, state capacities were even further eroded, an estimated one third of civil servants perished, many government buildings were destroyed or damaged, including all Ministries except one, leading to even heavier reliance upon external support. The weak state, the government's inability to be a service provider to its population in any area, lack of Haitian resources and Haitian capacity in turn weakened political legitimacy and affected democratisation.

As regular demonstrations and opposition showed, people grew tired of the lack of outputs. Haitians had, again, expected change with a resurrected democracy, but change was slow. But this unhappiness was also arguably intensified by imperfect understanding of problems faced by the state and government, in part due to lack of transparency. The state did not lack the will to deliver in all areas, but it lacked the capacities to do so. Expectations of rapid change were understandably higher than what was possible within the context, but in addition there was not always the will to provide services or ensure a more equitable distribution of resources.

Economic development

Economic development and further economic equality is central to democracy. The socio-economic situation when MINUSTAH deployed was one of extreme poverty, disparity, inequity and despair. Haiti was, as it always had been, the poorest country in the Western Hemisphere.

An aid embargo had been put in place between 2001 and 2004 as a result of the disputed presidential elections in 2000. This devastated Haiti's already frail economy.[111] It was a major factor behind economic stagnation,[112] and did little to aid the progress of democratisation. On the contrary the embargo led to a further economic decline and was a factor in the heightened internal conflict culminating in the violence in February 2004. As Jeffery Sachs stated 'US officials surely knew that the aid embargo would mean a balance-of-payment crisis, a rise in inflation and a collapse of living standards, all of which fed the rebellion against President Aristide'.[113] It is impossible to say whether or not continued aid during this time period would have increased democratisation, as it had been in severe decline since the late 1990s. It is doubtful that it would have had a strong positive impact upon democracy-building; most possibly it would only have ensured a strengthening of the government.

After 2004 the macro-economic indicators steadily improved, mainly after 2007, for example the Haitian gourde stabilised, and there was a reduction in inflation.[114] This gain was soon reversed and inflation doubled to 15.8 per cent in June 2008. Real growth in the gross domestic product (GDP) rose to 3.2 per cent, which was its 1991 level. But due to population growth, per capita GDP was in fact 23 per cent below its 1991 level and critically 38 per cent below its level in 1980.[115] Thus the majority of the population remained in abject poverty. There was a lack of employment opportunities and 76 per cent of Haitians continued to live on less than US$2 per day.[116] Improvements in basic services continued to be very limited. There was also a price increase on staples such as rice and flour, which culminated in food riots in April 2008. Consequently in 2007–08 Haiti ranked 146th out of 177 states on the human development index.

To help Haiti's dire financial crisis the country's US$1.2 billion multilateral debt was cancelled on 30 June 2009. This was followed up by a cancellation of its entire bilateral debt of over US$214.73 million. This was done to release government investment in the budget for the next six years. In addition, to boost economic development one effort was focused on textile manufacturing and, for example, the US Congress established duty-free access to the industry to create jobs. But the garment industry only constituted a small percentage of the GDP. It alone could not assure a way out of poverty. Although manufacturing can be important in increasing employment, manufacturers ultimately hire such a small percentage of the workforce that they could not 'absorb more than a fraction of the new entrants'.[117] A focus on assembly sector industries also meant that a low minimum wage was critical for competitiveness. In 2009 parliament suggested an increase in the minimum wage to G200 per day, but it was suggested this would be negative for foreign investment and undermine Haiti's competitiveness. The president conveyed these concerns in a letter to parliament; subsequently the Chamber of Deputies voted for an increase to only G125 per day.[118]

As a result of debt cancellations there had been some improvements in the Haitian economy, at least in the macro-economic situation, when the earthquake hit. This rapidly changed the situation. But even when the earthquake struck nearly 70 per cent of Haitians were unemployed. In response to the earthquake, donors pledged US$6.5 billion in aid for activities in 2010–12; by April 2012, 45 per cent of the pledges had been disbursed. Donors disbursed an additional US$760.5 million for recovery efforts and US$3.5 billion for humanitarian assistance.[119]

One UN strategy to support the economy after the earthquake was temporary job creation and more than 470,000 jobs were created.[120]

Three years after the earthquake the IMF assessed the macro-economic situation as stable, but economic growth was lower than projected; revenue collection was below budget targets, which, combined with declining international aid, exacerbated a difficult economic situation. Moreover, hurricanes and tropical storms continued to affect the economy in this period and there was a slow recovery of agricultural production. This also meant that Haiti continued to face food insecurity. The Poverty Reduction Strategy Paper set out a three-year development plan, which aimed to make Haiti an emerging country by 2030.[121]

There was macro-economic growth in 2014 and 2015 and inflation remained moderate in the early part of 2015, but nearly doubled from April to December 2015 (from 6.6 per cent to 12 per cent).[122] The macro-economic growth had insignificant impact upon the daily lives of Haitians, for example, a report found that in Cite Soleil only 26.4 per cent of men and 11.8 per cent of women were working, but only 14.1 per cent earned enough to feed their households.[123] Overall in 2015, 70–80 per cent of the population lived below the poverty line, surviving on less than US$2 per day, and Haiti fell to 163 on the Human Development Index in 2014. The HDI masks inequality in human development across the population; this has been adjusted for since 2010 and in the case of Haiti when the value is discounted for inequality it falls by 38.8 per cent.[124] Critically Haiti's GNI per capita decreased by 42 per cent between 1980 and 2014.[125] Thus, the majority of Haitians continued to live in abject poverty, and many continued to rely on remittances from abroad, which generated about 20 per cent of Haiti's GDP. There were improvements such as in education enrolment.[126] Education is crucial to increasing equality and reducing poverty, in the long term it may mitigate crime and conflict. But most education in Haiti was private, which restricted enrolment particularly in the absence of other socio-economic improvements. Prices for basic food products were 30–60 per cent higher compared with other countries in the region, because they are controlled and sold in concentrated markets.[127] Nevertheless extreme poverty declined from 31 to 24 per cent in 2012.[128] President Martelly set out his government's four E's plan to support development: education, employment, environment and the rule of law (*etat de droit*); a fifth, energy, was also introduced. Yet progress remained minimal. Rule of law had the most progress mainly due to international and MINUSTAH support.

Socio-economic divides

The vast socio-economic differences did not change post-2004. The richest 1 per cent owned the same wealth as 45 per cent of the poorest population.[129] The economic market continued to be controlled by a few families which reduced competition and solidified non-transparent business practices.[130] These families have in many cases been economically dominant for decades. Economic mobility has always been very rare. The political elite have traded favours for support by the economic elite and cronyism held back economic development. Economic development is vital to democratisation, but there can be no economic development if there is no political will to change. Vested political and economic interests have fuelled each other, increasing political instability in combination with regular natural disasters preventing any meaningful development. There have been few, if any, government led pro-poor and inclusive initiatives aimed at improving conditions for all, which are necessary to ensure economic growth.[131] Haiti's long history of authoritarianism has meant there is no previous history of governments providing services to its population, or indeed seeking sustainable growth. These inequalities, many would argue, rooted in historic social differences, have yet to be overcome.

Poverty in rural areas was more extensive than in urban areas. Therefore the extreme poverty in rural areas was a major factor in the rapid growth of the urban population. This urbanisation meant large numbers of unemployed disenfranchised youth, who were marginalised politically and economically as the urban areas could not absorb them. They were without social and family ties, which in many cases were substituted by armed gangs. It also meant that they were easier to mobilise by political forces, and engaged in and contributing to political instability and violence. The lack of economic development thus had an impact upon security and stability.

Haitian politics and governance were drivers for success or failure in economic development, as in all other efforts discussed in this book. The constant postponement of elections resulting in regularly few seated parliamentarians negatively affected economic development and the conflict between parliament and government hampered implementation of economic development projects. There were few to consistently lead or with decision-making power due to these problems of governance.

A democracy in decline?

There has been significant change in Haiti's democratisation process since 2004, but as the events in 2010 and 2015 underscored, much remained the same. Domestic democratic change on the key dimensions of rule of law, participation, competition and accountability improved for a while – but crucial areas were in need of substantial change at both national and local levels. Unfortunately the democratisation process seemed to further decline after 2012.

The result overall can only be described as a decline in democratisation. As of 2015, Haiti did not satisfy the criteria (rule of law, participation, competition, vertical and horizontal accountability) of a 'full' democracy. There are numerous tools to measure the level of democracy and democratisation. Most of these show that there was a considerable improvement in the democratisation process following the first elections after 2004. But these also established that it yet again decreased after the second presidential elections. For example, Freedom House ranked Haiti as not free (6.0 on both civil liberties and political rights) in 2004–06. This changed to partially free (5.0 on civil rights and 4.5 on political rights) in 2007–14, although notably in 2015 political rights had decreased to 5. Global Democracy Ranking showed a decrease in democratisation from 2008–09 to

178 *Democratisation*

2011–12 from a listing of 102 to 104. The Democracy Index in 2014 defined Haiti as an authoritarian regime based on an assessment of the electoral process and pluralism, functioning of government, political participation, political culture, and civil liberties.[132] According to the Democracy Index, Haiti's score has decreased every year since 2008.[133] The Transformation Index on Democracy Status shows it as increasing each year from 2006 to 2010, but it dips significantly in 2012 (from 5.1 to 3.7).[134] These tools all use somewhat different ways of measuring democracy and democratisation but nonetheless all reach the conclusion that democratisation has decreased in the latter years in Haiti. One reason was at first the impact of the earthquake. However, the fact that five years after the earthquake, and twelve years after renewed UN peace operations in Haiti, democracy was decreasing was worrying considering that MINUSTAH was drawing down its presence in Haiti.

The World Bank's governance indicators reflect a similarly bleak picture. For example, the aggregate indicator for voice and accountability establishes that it was lower in 2013 (26.1 per cent) compared with in 2009 (29.9 per cent) and even marginally lower than in 1996 (26.4 per cent). The political stability and absence of violence indicator only slightly improved from 2000 (24.5 per cent) to 2013 (25.1 per cent) – which is significant considering that in 2000 the democratisation process was unravelling. Government effectiveness marginally decreased from 2000 (3.9 per cent) to 2013 (3.8 per cent); this was a sizable decrease from 2008 (7.3 per cent), and even more so from 1996 (9.3 per cent). The rule of law indicator showed a slow but steady increase from 2006 (4.3 per cent) to 2013 (7.6 per cent), which was also an increase from 1998 (4.2 per cent). This underscores that persistent international and UN support in the rule of law, especially the police, has had some effect. Control of corruption had also increased from 2006 (4.9 per cent) to 2013 (11 per cent), although it was not a steady increase and dipped after the earthquake,[135] signifying how easily progress in this area could be reverted.

The social contract between the state and its people had simply yet to be established even after years of democratisation efforts. Economic growth, equity and political and economic equality are just parts of what needs to be established. This will take years. However, there has been limited progress in all parts of this in Haiti. Critically there has yet to emerge a political leader with the ability to unite the different sectors of Haitian society and thus begin to find solutions for the entire country.

In its support for Haitian democratisation MINUSTAH faced the constraints of resources, both financial and human, as well as time. Although the mission has continued to be renewed it is a peacekeeping mission which inherently means it does not have a twenty-year perspective. Moreover, even if the mission were to stay in Haiti for a very long time, each renewal is only for one year at a time, which limits long-term planning. It is further complicated by the fact that peace operations are on the invitation of the government. When that government is undermining the very mandate of the mission, it becomes critically difficult to keep a balance between diplomatic pressures and implementation of the mandate. Ultimately it is not the task of a peace operation to establish a democracy, but to ensure that aspects to facilitate this process are in place.

Conclusion

There is no doubt that the situation in Haiti improved after the UN deployment in 1994. The military dictatorship was removed and an elected government came into office. However the process of democratisation did not succeeded. Too many factors were absent, most importantly justice, security, and economic development. Disillusionment was created as a result of the singular focus of democracy defined as elections. Haitians had expected and wanted something more – participation. It resulted in the re-emergence of the old patterns of governance. Five years after the 1994 intervention to restore democracy in Haiti, the country had been without a prime minister since 1997, the president was ruling by decrees, the police force was unravelling and accountability was limited. As was underscored, 'all major donors worked on democratisation, yet Haitian democracy was nowhere to be found'.[136] The problems that Haitian society faced were not the fault of the UN and the international community, but much more should have been done than focus on elections to ensure a full transition to sustainable democracy. There was indeed only a functional anarchy.

Elections alone can be problematic. If they limit participation in the broader political processes then they become meaningless, and rather than contributing to security can undermine it when persistent allegations of fraud prevail. This leads to disillusionment with the process of elections and thus also with democratisation as this is the only part of a democratisation process that the population sees. In Haiti, there needed to be many more opportunities for direct participation in political affairs to ensure meaningful change in people's lives.

The UN however, cannot establish democracy in any country, but can only provide stability and support processes underpinning democratisation. There needs to be national political will by the government and political and economic elites to enhance and consolidate democracy. In Haiti this will was far from consolidated among all participants in the process. Transitioning from authoritarianism to a stable democratic society takes time. A culture of pluralism and equity needs to take root. Haitians have fought for and wanted an equal democratic society for a long time; but spoilers persisted, many of whom could be found within government.

Sadly in many ways post-2004 democratisation efforts mirrored events in the 1990s, with delayed elections and fraud, friction between parliament and president, minimal participation in elections, and limited economic development. After nearly thirty years of democratic aspirations, which began in earnest in 1986, in October 2016 there was no elected president and the date for presidential elections had been postponed since January – at best the process could be described as stalled, at worst as failing. In

the context of a planned MINUSTAH withdrawal the future of democratisation in Haiti in October 2016 could only be characterised as bleak.

Notes

1. J. Plamenatz, *Democracy and Illusion, An Examination of Certain Aspects of Modern Democratic Theory,* London: Clarke, Double and Brendon, 1973, p.116.
2. L. Laakso, 'Whose Democracy? Which Democratisation?', in J. Hippler (ed.), *The Democratisation of Disempowerment. The Problem of Democracy in the Third World,*

180 *Democratisation*

London: Pluto Press, 1995, p.211. Dahl emphasises that these are necessary, but not sufficient for attainment of democracy.
3 Plamenatz, *Democracy*, p.39.
4 J. Hippler, 'Democratisation of the Third World after the End of the Cold War', in Hippler (ed.) *Democratisation*, p.27.
5 A. Arblaster, *Democracy*, Milton Keynes: Open University Press, 1987, p.8.
6 D. Potter, 'Explaining Democratisation' in D. Potter, D. Goldblatt, M. Kiloh, P. Lewis (eds.), *Democratization*, London: Polity Press, 1997, pp.10–22.
7 Ibid.
8 Potter, 'Explaining', pp.24–30.
9 A. Leftwich, 'From Democratisation to Democratic Consolidation' in Potter, Goldblatt, Kiloh, Lewis (eds.), *Democratization*, pp.524–531.
10 A. Gitonga, 'The Meaning and Foundations of Democracy' in W. Oyugi, A. Odhiambo, M. Chege, A. Gitonga (eds.), *Democratic Theory and Practice in Africa*, London: James Curry, 1988, pp.16–19.
11 A. Edwards, 'Democratisation and Qualified Explanation' in ibid., pp.89–105.
12 P. Cammack, 'Democratisation and Citizenship in Latin America', in ibid., p.178.
13 The Haitian Constitution 2012, articles 61–84.
14 For details see Chapter 2.
15 Security Council Resolution, S/RES/940, 1994 para.4.
16 'Electoral Council Confirms Case of Electoral Fraud, but Denies pro-Lavalas Claim', Radio Metropole, Port-au-Prince, 5 April 1995, as translated in SWB part 5, 7 April 1995. 'MRN Leader Calls for Boycott of Elections and Dissolution of Electoral Council', Radio Metropole, Port-au-Prince, 21 June 1995, as translated in SWB part 5, 24 June 1995. See also, 'Vingt-deux Partis Réclament l'Annulation des Élections', *Le Matin,* 5 July 1995, p.1.
17 'Low Voter Turnout Reported in Second Round of Elections', Notimex News Agency, Mexico City, 17 September 1995 as translated in SWB part 5, 19 September 1995.
18 'Aristide Wants Talks to Ensure Better Organisation of Second Round of Elections', EFE News Agency, Madrid, 28 June (1995), as translated in SWB part 5, 29 June (1995). 'Aristide Set to Announce Solution to Electoral Crisis', AFP, Paris, 27 July (1995) as translated in FBIS-LAT, 27 July (1995).
19 Interviews with civil society, political leaders, Port-au-Prince, Gonaives, Cap Haiten, Jacmel, 1997.
20 The estimated amount of participation varies, e.g. the International Civilian Mission in Haiti (MICIVIH) stated it was 12 per cent.
21 'Prime Minister Says Low Voter Turnout Result of Lack of Information', Signal FM Radio, Port-au-Prince, 7 April 1997, as translated in SWB part 5, 9 April 1997.
22 'La Démocratie en Cours, Sans le Peuple', Le Nouvelliste, 7 April 1997, p.1.
23 There are numerous views on the nature of Haitian politics. The focus of this section is the Haitian perception at the time of their own situation based on extensive interviews. For other accounts see e.g. D. Nicholls *From Dessalines to Duvalier: Race, Colour and National Independence in Haiti*, London: Macmillan, 1996. Also Dupuy, Haiti, and Perusse, Haitian.
24 'Special MKNKP Congress and March. Peasants Demand Justice, Land Reform, Political Participation', *The Peasant*, vol.2, no.1, spring 1995, p.2.
25 Interview with former Prime Minister, Port-au-Prince, 1998.
26 Interviews with civil society groups and organisations, Haiti, 1997–98.
27 L. Diamond and L. Morlino, 'The Quality of Democracy', *Journal of Democracy*, vol.15 no. 4, 2004.
28 C. Werleigh, Catholic Institute for International Relations Conference, London, 19 November 1998.
29 Interviews Haiti, 1997–98.
30 See Chapter 6.

31 Interviews with popular movements, Haiti, 1997–98. Macoute refers to the Tonton Macoute, the militia created by Francois Duvalier, which conducted ruthless repression of the civilian population. When used in this connection it means that these elements were still present in the state and government system and part of the ruling class.
32 Interviews with civil society and political officials, 1997–98. Pépé refers to the second-hand clothes that can be bought in the streets, which often have been given from abroad.
33 Interviews with civil society and political officials, 1997–98.
34 Interview with former Prime Minister, Port-au-Prince, 1998.
35 Interviews, Port-au-Prince, 1997–98.
36 Interviews, Port-au-Prince, 1997–98.
37 OPL changed the name to Organisation de Peuple en Lutte, that is Organisation of the Struggling People.
38 'Alliés d'Hier, Adversaires d'Aujourd'hui', *Le Nouvelliste*, 12 November 1996, pp.1–2.
39 'Report on Growing Differences between pro-Aristide Organisations', Radio Metropole, Port-au-Prince, 21 January 1997, as translated in SWB part 5, 25 January 1997.
40 'Rosny Smarth Arrête de Traiter les Affaires Courantes et Quitte la Primature', Collectif Haiti de France, Une semaine en Haiti, no.385, 28 October 1997, p.1.
41 C. Orenstein, 'The Roads Built in Haiti Only Go So Far', *The Washington Post*, 30 January 2000, p. B05.
42 J. Linz & A. Stepan, 'Democratic Consolidation or Destruction' in R.A. Pastor (ed.), *Democracy in the Americas. Stopping the Pendulum*, London: Holmes & Meier, 1989, p.43.
43 J.C. Torres, 'The Politics of Economic Crisis in Latin America', *Journal of Democracy*, vol.4, no.1, January 1993, p.113.
44 Linz & Stepan, 'Democratic', p.43.
45 J. Linz, 'Legitimacy of Democracy and the Socio-Economic System' in M. Dogan (ed.), *Comparing Pluralist Democracies. Strains on Legitimacy*, London: Westview Press, 1988, p.65.
46 A. Lefwich, 'From Democratisation to Democratic Consolidation' in Potter, Democratisation, p.526.
47 L. Diamond, 'Democracy in Latin America. Degrees, Illusions, and Directions for Consolidation', in T. Farer (ed.), *Beyond Sovereignty. Collectively Defending Democracy in the Americas* London: The John Hopkins Press, 1996, p.75.
48 L. Hurbon, 'The Hope for Democracy', *The New York Review of Books*, 3 November 1994, p.39.
49 Corruption was a key issue in lack of legitimacy. People referred to the extensive corruption, calling the government and civil servants *gran manje* (big eaters). In the carnival of 1997 an anti-government theme emerged, which showed the population's perception of the government as being no different from their predecessors. For example, the leader of *Mouvman Péyizan Papaye* (MPP) withdrew from the Lavalas movement comparing it to the *macoute* regime of the Duvaliers. 'MPP Leader Explains Reasons for withdrawing from Lavalas Movement', Signal FM Radio, Port-au-Prince, 17 March 1998, as translated in SWB part 5, 19 March 1998.
50 Interviews with civil society in Haiti 1997–98.
51 These were repeatedly pointed out in interviews, Port-au-Prince, Cap Haitien, Gonaives, Jacmel, 1997–98.
52 'The Results of an Imposed Democracy', *Haiti Observateur*, 28 August – 3 September 1996, p.15.
53 See Chapter 4.
54 Justice in this context refers to criminal justice for the perpetrators of the crimes committed in 1991–94.

55 See also Chapter 6.
56 Interviews with civil society and politicians, 1998.
57 Hippler, 'Democratisation', p.28.
58 See also, ibid.
59 The USAID FY 1998 Congressional Presentation, *HAITI*, <http://www.info.usaid.gov/pubs/cp98/lac/countries/ht.htm> (accessed 23 July 1999).
60 Interviews Port-au-Prince, Jacmel, Cap Haitien, Gonaives 1997–98.
61 The government aimed to privatise nine state-owned companies: the telecommunications company, the electricity company, the ports, the airports, the cement factory, the flour mill, the National Bank of Credit, the Haitian Popular Bank and the ENAOL.
62 Diana Chung, *The Development Challenge in Haiti*, The World Bank Group, 1997 <http://www.worldbank.org/html/extdr/offrep/lac/haiti.htm> (accessed 3 May 1998).
63 Interview, Port-au-Prince, 1998.
64 Quoted in T. Buss (ed.), 'Why foreign aid to Haiti failed', National Academy of Public Administration, February 2006, p. 18.
65 Interview with Haitian scholar, Port-au-Prince, 1997, and M. Trouillot, 'Aristide's Challenge', *The New York Review of Books*, 3 November 1994, p.40.
66 Trouillot, 'Aristide's', p.40.
67 Interview, Port-au-Prince, 1997.
68 Interview, Port-au-Prince, 1997. This was reinforced by subsequent interviews 1997–98.
69 The concept of class to some extent includes the concepts of religion and culture in Haiti, but it is the class division which is essential. See Chapter 2.
70 'Protesters Block Haiti National Highway', Reuters, Port-au-Prince, 9 February 2000.
71 'Race Against time Until the Elections', Haiti-Correspondance, serie 2, no.52, 28 February 2000.
72 'The "Electoral Coup d'Etat" Takes Shape', Haiti Progrès, 23–29 February 2000.
73 'Just Weeks Away Haiti's Election Cloaked in Doubt', Reuters, Port-au-Prince, 25 February 2000.
74 'OAS Rubberstamps CEP Election Figures', Haiti Progrès, 10–16 May 2000.
75 Interviews with grassroots and human rights spokespersons in Haiti, telephone, 2000.
76 International Coalition of Independent Observers, 'Pre-election Statement', 19 May 2000.
77 M. Norton, 'Blast Damages Haiti Election HQ', Associated Press, 18 May 2000.
78 M. Faul, Associated Press, 22 May 2000.
79 Trenton Daniel, 'Haitian Opposition Leaders Attack Electoral Process', Reuters, 5 June 2000.
80 Trenton Daniel, 'Haiti Election Chief: Urged to Change Results', Reuters, 21 June 2000.
81 Michael Norton, 'Haitian Groups Condemn Election', Associated Press, 24 June 2000.
82 Michael Norton, 'Haitians Vote for Lower-House Seats', Associated Press, 30 July 2000.
83 'Haiti en État d'Anarchie Institutionnelle', Haiti en Marche, 3 Septembre 1997, p.6.
84 Interviews with civil society, human rights organisations and political opposition, 1997–98.
85 Freedom House, Haiti, 2002, <https://freedomhouse.org/report/freedom-world/2002/haiti> (accessed 4 January 2016).
86 See e.g. Faubert, Carroll 'Evaluation of UNDP Assistance to Conflict Affected Countries – Human Security' UNDP report, 2005, p.12
87 UN Security Council Resolution, S/RES/1542, 30 April 2004. 7 II (a), (c).
88 UN Secretary-General's Report, S/2004/300, 16 April, 2004, para.1.
89 UN Security Council Resolution, S/RES/1702, 15 August 2006.

90 Reporters without Borders, Haiti Annual Report 2004, <http://www.rsf.org/article.php3?id_article=10005> (accessed 3 December 2008).
91 These increased freedoms arguably changed somewhat with the presidential elections in 2010, when three men putting up posters for presidential candidate Manigat were found dead and mutilated, M. Taft-Morales, 'Haiti's', p.7. This could be interpreted as political intimidation and a more restrictive democratic space, but it is not conclusive.
92 For details on the election process, see International Crisis Group, 'Haiti after the elections: Challenges for Préval's first 100 days', *Policy Briefing*, no.10, May 2006, pp. 2–7.
93 Interview with senior official at MINUSTAH, Port-au-Prince, April 2008.
94 As discussed in Chapter 6.
95 Estimates for participation vary, see e.g. Al Jazeera, 'Haitians shun Senate elections', 20 April 2009, <http://english.aljazeera.net/news/americas/2009/04/2009419224231220542.html> (accessed 7 January 2015). SG report, S/2009/439, 1 September 2009, para. 12.
96 SG report, S/2011/183, 24 March 2011, para.2.
97 M. Weisbrot and J. Johnston, 'Haiti's fatally flawed election', Centre for Economic and Policy Research, Washington DC, 2011.
98 M. Taft-Morales, 'Haiti's national election issues: issues, concerns and outcome', Congressional Research Service, 2011, p.7.
99 See e.g. SG report, S/2012/128, 29 February 2012, para.3.
100 See e.g. F. Robels, 'Haitian leader powers grows as scandals swirl', *The New York Times*, 16 March 2015.
101 SG report, S/2013/139, 8 March 2013, para.29.
102 See e.g. SG report, S/2013/493, 19 august 2013, para.11.
103 SG report, S/2015/667, 31 August 2015, para.2.
104 A.R. Kolbe, N.I. Cesnales, M.N. Puccio, R. Muggah, 'Impact of perceived electoral fraud on Haitian voter's beliefs about democracy', Igarape Institute Strategic Note 20, November 2015. https://igarape.org.br/wp-content/uploads/2015/11/NE-20_Impact-of-Perceived-Electoral-Fraud-on-Haitian-Voter%E2%80%99s-Beliefs-about-Democracy.pdf> (accessed 23 February 2016).
105 M. Deibert, '"Rotten" system blamed as Haiti's election ends in stalemate', *The Guardian*, 14 February 2016.
106 Interviews by phone with civil society, Port-au-Prince, 2015. See also Kolbe et al., 'Impact'.
107 See e.g. IFES, Election guide Haiti, <http://www.electionguide.org/countries/id/94/>, (accessed 16 March 2016).
108 Kolbe et al., 'Impact'.
109 Due to Hurricane Matthew the elections were postponed yet again to 20 November.
110 These are discussed specifically in previous chapters.
111 Armed Conflicts report, 'Haiti', Ploughshares, <http://www.justice.gov/sites/default/files/eoir/legacy/2014/02/25/Haiti.pdf> (accessed 7 January 2016).
112 R. Machado, and D. Robert, 'Haiti: situation economique et perspectives', Inter-American Development Bank, 2001 quoted in Paul Farmer 'Haiti: Short and Bitter Lives', Le Monde Diplomatique, July 2003.
113 Quoted in M. Weisbrot and L. Sandoval, 'Debt Cancellation for Haiti: No Reason for Further Delays' Centre for Economic and Policy Research, December 2007, p.3.
114 SG report, S/2007/503, 22 August 2007.
115 SG report, S/2008/202, 26 March 2008, para. 53.
116 U. Fasanco, 'Haiti/s economic, political turnaround', *IMF Survey Magazine: Countries and Regions*, 17 September 2007.
117 Singh, p.5.
118 See also SG report, S/2009/439, 1 September 2009, para.6. Paul Collier was asked by the SG to undertake an assessment and provide recommendations for socio-economic

184 *Democratisation*

development in 2009. See P. Collier, 'Haiti: from natural catastrophe to economic recovery – a report for the Secretary-General of the UN, January 2009'. But things changed with the earthquake. See also P. Collier, 'Building Haiti's economy one mango at a time', *The New York Times*, 29 January 2010.

119 UN Economic and Social Council, Report of the ECOSOC Ad Hoc Advisory Group on Haiti, 2–27 July 2012, para.8–10. The positive and negative aspects of aid delivery after the earthquake are not discussed here as they have been discussed extensively elsewhere, see e.g. P. Collier, 'Haiti's rise from the rubble, the quest to recover from disaster', *Foreign Affairs*, September/October, 2011. *The Economist*, 'Still waiting for recovery', 5 January 2013.

120 UN fact sheet, 'Haiti moving forward step by step,' <http://www.un.org/en/peacekeeping/missions/minustah/documents/UN-factsheets-2012-en.pdf> (accessed 11 February 2016).

121 IMF, PRSP Haiti, no.14/154, June 2014.

122 Haiti inflation rate, <http://www.tradingeconomics.com/haiti/inflation-cpi>, (accessed 10 February 2016).

123 T. Donais and G. Burt, 'Vertically integrated peacebuilding and community violence reduction in Haiti', CENTER FOR INTERNATIONAL GOVERNANCE INNOVATION papers, no. 25 February 2014, p.7 footnote 2.

124 UNDP, Human Development Report 2015, Work for human development, briefing note for countries on the 2015 Human Development Report, Haiti, p.4.

125 Ibid., p. 2.

126 World Bank state that in 2015, 50 per cent did not attend school, whereas UNICEF states that 77 per cent attended primary school.

127 R.J. Singh and M. Barton-Dock, 'Haiti Toward a New Narrative, Systematic country diagnostic', World Bank Group, 2015, p. 2.

128 Singh, p.3.

129 UNDP,' Haiti MDG report: progress and challenges', 25 June 2014. <http://www.us.undp.org/content/washington/en/home/presscenter/articles/2014/06/25/undp-releases-haiti-mdg-report-significant-progress-has-been-made.html> (accessed 16 March 2016).

130 See also, R.J. Singh and M. Barton-Dock,'Haiti Toward a New Narrative, Systematic country diagnostic', World Bank Group, 2015.

131 See also ibid. Singh, pp. 1–2.

132 The Economist Intelligence Unit, 'The Democracy Index – Democracy and its discontents', 2014, p.7.

133 Ibid. p.12.

134 The BIT Transformation Index Haiti country reports, Bertelsmann Stiftung, <http://www.bti-project.de/> (accessed 4 July 2015).

135 Worldwide governance indicators, Country data report for Haiti, 1996–2013.

136 Buss, 'Why', p.29.

Bibliography

Arblaster, A., *Democracy*, Milton Keynes: Open University Press, 1987.

Armed Conflicts Report, 'Haiti', Ploughshares, <http://www.justice.gov/sites/default/files/eoir/legacy/2014/02/25/Haiti.pdf (accessed 7 January 2016).

Bertelsmann Stiftung, BIT Transformation Index Haiti country reports, <http://www.bti-project.de/> (accessed 4 July 2015).

Chung, D., *The Development Challenge in Haiti*, New York: The World Bank Group, 1997, <http://www.worldbank.org/html/extdr/offrep/lac/haiti.htm> (accessed 3 May 1998).

Collier, P. 'Haiti: from natural catastrophe to economic recovery – a report for the Secretary-General of the UN', January 2009.

Collier, P. 'Haiti's rise from the rubble, the quest to recover from disaster', *Foreign Affairs*, September/October, 2011.
Crisis Group, 'Haiti after the elections: Challenges for Préval's first 100 days', *Policy Briefing*, no.10, May 2006.
Diamond, L. and Morlino, L. 'The quality of democracy', *Journal of Democracy*, vol.15, no. 4, 2004.
Dogan, M. (ed.), *Comparing Pluralist Democracies. Strains on Legitimacy*, London: Westview Press, 1988.
Donais, T. and Burt, G. 'Vertically integrated peacebuilding and community violence reduction in Haiti', Center for International Governance Innovation Papers, no. 25 February 2014.
Dupuy, A., *Haiti in the New World Order, The Limits of the Democratic Revolution*, Oxford: Westview Press, 1997.
Economist Intelligence Unit, 'The Democracy Index – Democracy and its discontents', 2014.
Farer, T. (ed.), *Beyond Sovereignty. Collectively Defending Democracy in the Americas*, London: Johns Hopkins University Press, 1996.
Fasanco, U. 'Haiti/s economic, political turnaround', *IMF Survey Magazine: Countries and Regions*, 17 September 2007.
Freedom House, Haiti, 2002, <https://freedomhouse.org/report/freedom-world/2002/haiti> (accessed 4 January 2016).
Haitian Constitution 2012.
Hippler, J. (ed.), *The Democratisation of Disempowerment. The Problem of Democracy in the Third World*, London: Pluto Press, 1995.
Hurbon, L. 'The hope for democracy', *The New York Review of Books*, 3 November 1994.
IFES, Election guide Haiti, <http://www.electionguide.org/countries/id/94/>, (accessed 16 March 2016).
International Coalition of Independent Observers, 'Pre-election statement', 19 May 2000.
International Monetary Fund, 'Poverty reduction strategy paper, Haiti', no.14/154, June 2014.
Khouri-Padova, L. 'Haiti lessons learnt', UN Best Practices Unit, Discussion Paper, March 2004.
Kolbe, A.R., Cesnales, N.I., Puccio, M.N. and Muggah, R., 'Impact of perceived electoral fraud on Haitian voter's beliefs about democracy' Igarape Insitute Strategic Note 20, November 2015 <https://igarape.org.br/wp-content/uploads/2015/11/NE-20_Impact-of-Perceived-Electoral-Fraud-on-Haitian-Voter%E2%80%99s-Beliefs-about-Democracy.pdf> (accessed 23 February 2016).
Nicholls, D., *From Dessalines to Duvalier: Race, Colour and Independence in Haiti*, London: Macmillan, 1996.
Ministry of Planning and External Cooperation, 'Growth and poverty reduction strategy paper', 2008–2010, November 2007. <http://siteresources.worldbank.org/INTPRS1/Resources/Haiti-PRSP(march-2008).pdf> (accessed 3 February 2016).
Oyugi, W., Odhiambo, A., Chege, M. and Gitonga A. (eds), *Democratic Theory and Practice in Africa*, London: James Curry, 1988.
Parry, G. and Moran, M. (eds), *Democracy and Democratization*, London: Routledge, 1994.
Pastor, R.A. (ed.), *Democracy in the Americas. Stopping the Pendulum*, London: Holmes & Meier, 1989.
Perusse, R.I., *Haitian Democracy Restored 1991–1995*, London: University Press of America, 1995.

Plamenatz, J. *Democracy and Illusion: An Examination of Certain Aspects of Modern Democratic Theory,* London: Clarke, Double and Brendon, 1973.
Potter, D., Goldblatt, D., Kiloh, M. and Lewis P. (eds), *Democratization,* London: Polity Press, 1997.
Reporters without Borders, Haiti Annual Report 2004, <http://www.rsf.org/ article.php3?id_article=10005> (accessed 3 December 2008).
Singh, R.J. and Barton-Dock, M., *Haiti Toward a New Narrative, Systematic Country Diagnostic,* New York: World Bank Group, 2015.
Taft-Morales, M., 'Haiti's national election issues: issues, concerns and outcome', Congressional Research Service, 2011.
The Peasant, 'Special MKNKP congress and march: Peasants demand justice, land reform, political participation', vol. 2, no.1, spring 1995.
Torres, J.C. 'The politics of economic crisis in Latin America', *Journal of Democracy,* vol. 4, no. 1, January 1993.
Trading Economics, 'Haiti inflation rate', <http://www.tradingeconomics.com/haiti/inflation-cpi>, (accessed 10 February 2016).
Trouillot, M., 'Aristide's challenge', *The New York Review of Books,* 3 November 1994.
USAID 'FY 1998 Congressional Presentation, Haiti', <http://www.info.usaid.gov/pubs/cp98/lac/countries/ht.htm> (accessed 23 July 1999).
Weisbrot, M. and Johnston, J. 'Haiti's fatally flawed election', Centre for Economic and Policy Research, Washington DC, 2011.
Weisbrot, M., and Sandoval, L., 'Debt cancellation for Haiti: No reason for further delays', Centre for Economic and Policy Research, Washington DC, December 2007.
Werleigh, C., 'Democracy and political empowerment', Catholic Institute for International Relations Conference, London, 19 November 1998.
World Bank, 'Worldwide governance indicators, Country data report for Haiti', 1996–2013.

UN documents

Faubert, C., 'Evaluation of UNDP Assistance to Conflict Affected Countries – Human Security' UNDP report, 2005.
SG report, S/2007/503, 22 August 2007.
SG report, S/2008/202, 26 March 2008.
SG report, S/2009/129, 6 March 2009.
SG report, S/2009/439, 1 September 2009.
SG report, S/2011/183, 24 March 2011.
SG report, S/2012/128, 29 February 2012.
SG report, S/2013/139, 8 March 2013.
SG report, S/2013/493, 19 august 2013.
SG report, S/2015/667, 31 August 2015. UN Economic and Social Council, Report of the ECOSOC Ad Hoc Advisory Group on Haiti, 2–27 July 2012.
UN fact sheet, 'Haiti moving forward step by step,' <http://www.un.org/en/peacekeeping/missions/minustah/documents/UN-factsheets-2012-en.pdf> (accessed 11 February 2016).
UN Secretary-General's Report, S/2004/300, 16 April 2004.
UN Security Council Resolution, S/RES/940, 1994.
UN Security Council Resolution, S/RES/1542, 30 April 2004.
UN Security Council Resolution, S/RES/1702, 15 August 2006.
UN Security Council Resolution, S/RES/1780, 15 October 2007.

UNDP, Human Development Report 2015, 'Work for human development', briefing note for countries on the 2015 Human Development Report, Haiti.
UNDP, Haiti MDG report: progress and challenges, 25 June 2014. <http://www.us.undp.org/content/washington/en/home/presscenter/articles/2014/06/25/undp-releases-haiti-mdg-report-significant-progress-has-been-made.html> (accessed 16 March 2016).

Media

AFP, 'Aristide set to announce solution to electoral crisis', Paris, 27 July 1995 as translated in FBIS-LAT, 27 July 1995.
Collectif Haiti de France, 'Rosny Smarth arrête de traiter les affaires courantes et quitte la primature', Une semaine en Haiti, no.385, 28 October 1997.
Collier, P. 'Building Haiti's economy one mango at a time', *The New York Times*, 29 January 2010.
Daniel, T., 'Haitian opposition leaders attack electoral process', Reuters, 5 June 2000.
Daniel, T., 'Haiti election chief: Urged to change results', Reuters, 21 June 2000.
Deibert, M. '"Rotten" system blamed as Haiti's election ends in stalemate', *The Guardian*, 14 February 2016.
Economic and Political Weekly, 'Not for Democracy', 1 October 1994.
EFE News Agency, 'Aristide wants talks to ensure better organisation of second round of elections', Madrid, 28 June 1995, as translated in SWB part 5, 29 June 1995.
Farmer, P., 'Haiti: Short and bitter lives', *Le Monde Diplomatique*, July 2003.
Haiti-Correspondance, 'Race against time until the elections', serie 2, no.52, 28 February 2000.
Haiti en Marche, 'Haiti en état d'anarchie institutionnelle', 3 Septembre 1997, p. 6.
Haiti Observateur, 'The results of an imposed democracy', 28 August – 3 September 1996.
Haiti Progrès, 'The "electoral coup d'etat" takes shape', 23–29 February 2000.
Haiti Progrès, 'OAS rubberstamps CEP election figures', 10–16 May 2000.
Le Matin, 'Vingt-deux partis réclament l'annulation des élections', 5 July 1995.
Le Nouvelliste, 'Alliés d'hier, adversaires d'aujourd'hui', 12 November 1996.
Le Nouvelliste, 'La démocratie en cours, sans le peuple', 7 April 1997.
Norton, M., 'Haiti postpones elections', Associated Press, 3 March 2000.
Norton, M. 'Blast damages Haiti election HQ', Associated Press, 18 May 2000.
Norton, M., 'Haitian groups condemn election', Associated Press, 24 June 2000.
Norton, M., 'Haitians vote for lower-house seats', Associated Press, 30 July 2000.
Notimex News Agency, 'Low voter turnout reported in second round of elections', Mexico City, 17 September 1995 as translated in SWB part 5, 19 September 1995.
Orenstein, C. 'The roads built in haiti only go so far', *The Washington Post*, 30 January 2000.
Radio Metropole, 'Electoral Council confirms case of electoral fraud, but denies pro-Lavalas claim', Port-au-Prince, 5 April 1995, as translated in SWB part 5, 7 April 1995.
Radio Metropole, 'MRN leader calls for boycott of elections and dissolution of Electoral Council', Port-au-Prince, 21 June 1995, as translated in SWB part 5, 24 June 1995.
Radio Metropole, 'Report on growing differences between pro-Aristide organisations', Port-au-Prince, 21 January 1997, as translated in SWB part 5, 25 January 1997.
Reuters, 'Protesters block Haiti national highway', Port-au-Prince, 9 February 2000.
Reuters, 'Just weeks away Haiti's election cloaked in doubt', Port-au-Prince, 25 February 2000.

Robels, F. 'Haitian leader powers grows as scandals swirl', *The New York Times*, 16 March 2015.

Signal FM Radio, 'Prime Minister says low voter turnout result of lack of information', Port-au-Prince, 7 April 1997, as translated in SWB part 5, 9 April 1997.

Signal FM Radio, 'MPP leader explains reasons for withdrawing from Lavalas Movement', Port-au-Prince, 17 March 1998, as translated in SWB part 5, 19 March 1998.

The Economist, 'Still waiting for recovery', 5 January 2013.

9 Violence, democracy and development
Concluding thoughts

There have been vast developments in UN peace operations since the mid-1990s. Policies have been significantly strengthened, a framework for peace operations has been put in place and there have been notable improvements in implementation. Haiti contributed in many ways to the developments of these polices, as the numerous peace operations there threw in sharp relief multi-faceted peacekeeping challenges.

Haiti exemplifies the changes and lessons learnt by the UN in this period and the significant progress in the peace operations from 1994 to 2004, although in Haiti sadly much also remained the same. Support for police reform and capacity-building through to an increased focus on judicial and penal reform improved these sectors. With stronger mandates in conjunction with human and financial resources came greater success of operations. Yet others lagged behind. A persistent difficult political environment with spoilers working to undermine democratic change complicated the efforts. There are six areas that deserve further mention in these concluding thoughts as they in particular were pertinent to peace operations in Haiti: strategic approaches; coordination and integration; economic development; justice and reconciliation; context and politics; and realistic expectations and objectives.

Strategic approaches

There was no strategic approach addressing the mandated tasks cohesively, and which considered the interdependencies of the issues such as democratisation and the rule of law. The UN acknowledged and understood these interdependencies, but in practice they were not implemented as part of a strategic approach. The objectives, particularly early on, were vague such as 'return of democracy' or 'peace'. Consequently, the absence of such a strategy led to 'silo-ed' approaches in each sector; this in turn meant that each sector could improve, but the extent of that improvement was always limited by the fact that there was no overall strategic goal.

For example, MINUSTAH addressed violence perpetrated by armed gangs in the neighbourhoods of Port-au-Prince very effectively and ensured a stability dividend. But they did not seek to solve the problem that these gangs were linked to the political and economic elites, as well as people in government. The root causes of the gangs' continued existence were therefore left unaddressed. These operations notably increased security in gang-held territories but the longevity and sustainability were undermined by not dealing with these connections. It is doubtful whether the government would have agreed to MINUSTAH taking on such a role and addressing these connections. It was outside the mandate and the resources of the mission. Yet it would be impossible to solve the issue of armed gang violence separately from the political and economic agendas in Haiti.

A critical lesson from the interventions in the 1990s was that judicial reform requires to be tackled at the same time as police reform, or police reform increasingly runs the risk of failure. An effective functioning judicial system is critical to the police. Although importantly judicial reform was part of the mandates after 2004, there were insufficient resources to adequately boost support. Moreover, the question of how disarmament, demobilisation and reintegration (DDR) is intimately linked with economic development, justice, reconciliation and security sector reform (SSR) was not a key consideration when developing the DDR programmes in Haiti. All these connections, albeit understood, at least after 2004, and emphasised in policies and reports, were not sufficiently taken advantage of when designing programming and in everyday implementation of the missions' mandates.

The absence of a strategic approach was also further complicated by bilateral national objectives, which frequently led not only to an unwillingness to coordinate, but also to obstruction of UN objectives. This was particularly evident in the rule of law sector, as cooperation and coordination of police support met with severe problems early on. This adversely affected implementation and in some cases delayed reform. Even if structures meant to guarantee coordination were in place, in practice they did not function adequately.

The sectors of security sector reform, security and stability, DDR, transitional justice and democratisation are inherently political and thus it is exceptionally difficult both to operationally support and to ensure a strategic vision to that support by multiple actors. Yet to succeed it is essential. The peace operations in Haiti underscore the critical importance of implementing a strategic cohesive approach in these areas to consolidate support and therefore provide for sustainable successful operations.

Coordination (in the absence of integration)

The concept of integration was not developed until the last peace operations in Haiti; the focus was on the need to coordinate UN efforts. Coordination of UN efforts however, can at best be described as poor and ad hoc. Parallel interventions took place in the police, justice and penal sectors, where occasional collaboration was based on personalities rather than strategic objectives aimed at maximising outcomes and value added.

The peace operations in Haiti underscore the desperate need and importance of integration and the fundamental difficulties with integration of UN agencies. Emphasis was placed on integrating the work of the UNDP and MINUSTAH, in particular on DDR and the rule of law. In practice, it was not an integrated mission. Integration in Haiti was hampered by numerous factors. From both the UNDP and the mission there was unwillingness to integrate and institutional mistrust. In part, this was based on the perceived short-term objectives of the mission versus the long-term development goals of UNDP as well as a perceived more intrusive approach by the mission versus the perceived 'softer' approach to the government by the UNDP. Practically integration was impeded by different budget cycles, reporting lines, timelines and experience.

The numerous problems with integration in Haiti led one senior MINUSTAH staff member to conclude that 'the institutions are not ready for formal integration'. There were no effective management structures to integrate the different sectors, particularly the security sector, together into one strategic framework. The DDR section attempted this where the Chief and his Deputy were from MINUSTAH and UNDP respectively. Yet it only partially worked. The working relationship between the UN agencies, especially UNDP and the mission, was too dependent upon personalities and there was no effective mechanism in place to ensure greater cooperation, leading to lost opportunities and wasted resources.

In many ways, this is an example of the difficulties that integrated field missions face. Sections that had the same strategic vision were complicated through the two organisations' very different approaches, short versus longer term mandates, and management, budget and reporting structures. More notably, this underscores the critical importance of ensuring closer, if not integration, then coordination of UN efforts. This has come a long way since the 1990s with joint work plans and internal coordination fora, but it is critical to minimise duplication and maximise results to improve coordination still further.

Economic development

UN peace operations cannot do long-term sustainable economic development. However, integrating efforts in peace operations much more substantially with economic development programming is critical for democratisation efforts and support to the security sectors. No changes are sustainable, and hard-pressed to succeed, without a comprehensive approach to these issues placed firmly within a broader economic development framework. Placing the peace operations within the broader context of the economic situation in Haiti was important as it was so closely connected with instability and insecurity, as well as with DDR, democratisation, police reform and justice. Regrettably, programming in these areas is rarely, if ever, implemented as part of a whole.

When the UN deployed in 1994 and in 2004 the economic situation in Haiti was one of extreme poverty, disparity, inequity and despair. Haiti was, as it always had been, the poorest country in the Western Hemisphere. Economic equity and equality lie at the heart of democracy, as does the ability to participate, none of which improved much in Haiti. A much more level playing field needed to be established economically, politically and socially. The political legitimacy of all governments was damaged by the lack of progress in these areas. The consistent dwindling participation in elections in both the 1990s and the 2000s was in part a reflection of the complete lack of economic development, and a core factor in continued violence and conflict.

The mission and UNDPKO clearly saw socio-economic disparity, extreme poverty, and the inability of the government to deliver services as root causes for the insecurity and instability, and development as necessary to consolidate sustainable stability, but shorter-term mission projects were not linked to other longer-term economic programming. No peace operations have a mandate to implement economic development, nor should they. However, this is where a strategic objective would have been useful, ensuring that the stability dividend established by the missions was effectively used by international and national development actors, as well as the UN Country Team.

The missions' programming suffered particularly in the areas of DDR and SSR for not taking sufficiently into consideration the direct link between poverty, lack of development and violence. Timeframes are an important issue in this context – sustainable economic recovery and growth will inevitably take longer than DDR. This does not mean that efforts should be delayed for economic recovery to take place. It does mean that efforts need to be re-thought. If a DDR programme leads to improved economic status for its participants in a context of extreme poverty, there will be no support for it in civil society. MINUSTAH therefore changed its programming and introduced the CVR programme, which was a significant improvement as the communities also benefitted from the reintegration programmes and there was a focus on local economic recovery. Yet it was still not sufficiently tied to longer-term economic programming and therefore the sustainability was undermined.

The security sector reform programmes mirrored in many ways the experiences of DDR, where limited economic development contributed to delaying progress. The national budget was not able to support the required changes in the security structures. After 2004 for example, the state was not able to cover even the salaries of the number of police officers that the police plan outlined. The planning process of police reform needed to be more closely coordinated with efforts in the economic development sector. Police and other rule of law plans need to be sustainable within the current economy and state budgets. Equally important however, is that economic development programmes and international financial institutions understand the needs of the rule of law better and ensure that some of their efforts are tailored accordingly. Unfortunately neither was reflected in Haiti.

Justice and reconciliation

Transitional justice was not part of any of the UN mandates in Haiti and the Haitian government lacked the political will to implement it. Unfortunately, non-existent, at best poor, transitional justice set a precedent for impunity and lack of accountability, and contributed to insecurity as impunity encouraged the different armed elements to undermine security and stability. It led to problems within the criminal justice system and in part bad governance. It also meant that there was no reconciliation; in Haiti, a sense of justice was necessary for a process of reconciliation.

Justice in Haiti was also essential for democratisation, but instead because of amnesties and coup supporters living in impunity, there were untouchables in Haitian society. To consolidate the democratic process, both the Haitian government and the international community should have prioritised some form of justice for the coup era. By not having any adequate process of justice rather than reinforcing democracy, it was reminiscent of dictatorial regimes as impunity has always been the prerogative of dictatorships. In many ways, reconciliation of Haitian society was a prerequisite for the process of democratisation. But as reconciliation could not be obtained without some form of justice, justice would have been necessary for the continued process of democracy.

Because there was no effective transitional justice mechanism, people stopped believing in change. Initially justice was on the agenda, but then reconciliation became the priority of the government – yet neither came about. This signalled that no real change was about to take place. Simply put, people needed to feel secure and in order to feel secure some form of justice was required. Without it, the very same actors who had instigated the political violence in 1991–94 became part of politicised armed gangs thereafter, as well as criminal gangs connected with drugs trafficking. It also meant that these actors took part in the democratisation process, both standing in the elections and seeking to influence the democratic process, not only after 1994 but also in 2016. Impunity for crimes committed during the junta years contributed to an unravelling democratisation process, insecurity and fear.

Context and politics

Good national leadership is needed to break the cycle of violence and poverty, and is critical to effectuate change. The UN or any other international entity, however, cannot provide good national leadership. The UN can only strive to provide an environment in which good leadership can take root. There needs to be national political will by the government and political and economic elites to enhance and consolidate that environment and leadership. There has not as yet been a leader who has had the ability, or perhaps the will, to bring the different political, economic and social actors together in a united vision for a better Haiti.

In Haiti, there has never been a social contract between the state and its citizens. It suffers from inequity and inequality, and many would want it to remain that way. This has meant that there has been resistance to the rule of law and democratisation, and key actors have wanted to control the security forces and therefore attempted to hinder reform. The basis for reform is that all must see the benefits of such reform; in Haiti, many actors still thought the advantages of controlling the rule of law continued to outweigh the disadvantages. For example, historically leaders have always sought to control the security forces. After 1994, this did not change; to varying degrees leaders at national and local levels still sought to influence the police, and other armed elements, even in 2016. These authorities consolidated power through the support of the police and armed gangs, intimidating and harassing political opponents, thus undermining the very fragile democratisation process. Solid and effective police reform support programmes matter little if the political system as a whole does not seek a similar change. The Haitian security sector has always been susceptible to politicisation because certain sectors feel they should control it for their own political and economic gains, and for the security forces it has meant power, money and control. Ultimately, this has led to disillusionment and disrespect for the rule of law by the security services and civil society.

Transitioning from authoritarianism to a stable democratic society takes time. A culture of pluralism and equity needs to take root. Haitians have fought for a democratic society for a long time, yet changes have been slow, in part non-existent. The political will has been limited to change. The spoilers of democratisation and change in Haiti have sadly been consistent and persistent in their efforts.

Realistic expectations and objectives

No UN mission can solve, or should be expected to solve, all the problems of any given mission country. Missions operate within the parameters set by mandates and resources. Mandates should be clear, achievable and thus not overly ambitious. Objectives need to be well defined. There needs to be realism about what the UN can achieve in any peace operation given its constraints. This must be clearly articulated to, and understood by, both governments and countries in fragile states.

This does not mean that UN missions cannot do better. They can and, as strongly exemplified by Haiti, they need to improve in many areas including integration, coordination and ensuring cohesive strategic approaches, as well as in the sectoral areas of DDR, SSR, democratisation and transitional justice. Haiti also importantly underscores that missions need to more effectively apply lessons from previous operations, there needs to be better knowledge retention and understanding of the context. In short, in several areas the UN in Haiti could have done much better. Yet it is neither the task nor sole responsibility of a peace operation to establish a democracy, but only to ensure that the aspects facilitating the process of democratisation are in place. Ultimately, the responsibility to build that democracy rests with the Haitian people.

Appendix A
UN missions to Haiti

International Civilian Mission in Haiti, OAS/UN (MICIVIH)

MICIVIH was established in February 1993, it was the United Nations' first joint mission with a regional organisation. MICIVIH was mandated to ensure respect for the human rights inscribed in the Haitian Constitution and in the international instruments which Haiti was party to; and contribute to the strengthening of judicial, police, and prison institutions important for the promotion and protection of human rights. On 20 April 1993, the General Assembly adopted, without a vote, its resolution 47/20B authorising United Nations participation, jointly with OAS, in MICIVIH. Its headquarters was established at Port-au-Prince with 14 regional offices and sub-offices across the country.

MICIVIH's mandate expired on 15 March 2000.

United Nations Mission in Haiti (UNMIH)

UNMIH was established on 23 September 1993 by Security Council Resolution 867. UNMIH was mandated to implement provisions of the Governor's Island Agreement and to assist in modernising the armed forces of Haiti and establishing a new police force. The mandate was revised by Security Council Resolutions 940 (1994) and 975 (1995) to enable the mission to support the Government of Haiti in sustaining a secure and stable environment; professionalising of the Haitian armed forces and the creation of a police force separate from the armed forces; and establishing an environment conducive to the organisation of free and fair elections.

UNMIH's mandate expired on 30 June 1996.

United Nations Support Mission Haiti (UNSMIH)

UNSMIH was established on 28 June 1996 by Security Council Resolution 1063 UNSMIH was mandated to assist the Government of Haiti in the professionalisation of the Haitian National Police (HNP); to assist Haitian authorities in maintaining a secure and stable environment; and to coordinate United Nations' system activities to promote institution-building, national reconciliation and economic rehabilitation.

UNSMIH's mandate expired on 31 July 1997.

United Nations Transition Mission in Haiti (UNTMIH)

UNTMIH was established 30 July 1997 by Security Council Resolution 1123. UNTMIH was mandated to assist the Government of Haiti by supporting and contributing to the professionalisation of the Haitian National Police (HNP). The mandate was limited to a single four-month period.

UNTMIH's mandate expired on 30 November 1997.

United Nations Civilian Police Mission in Haiti (MIPONUH)

MIPONUH was established on 28 November 1997 by Security Council Resolution 1141. MIPONUH was mandated to continue to assist the Government of Haiti in the professionalisation of the Haitian National Police.

MIPONUH's mandate expired on 15 March 2000.

International Civilian Support Mission in Haiti (MICAH)

MICAH was established on 17 December 1999 by General Assembly Resolution A/54/193. It was launched on 16 March 2000. MICAH was mandated to consolidate the results achieved by MIPONUH and its predecessor missions; to support the democratisation process; to strengthen Haitian justice and penal institutions; to support the professionalisation of the Haitian National Police; and to promote human rights. MICAH formulated three pillars to carry out its mandate: the Justice Pillar, the Police Pillar, and the Human Rights Pillar.

MICAH's mandate expired on 6 February 2001.

United Nations Stabilisation Mission in Haiti (MINUSTAH)

The United Nations Stabilisation Mission in Haiti (MINUSTAH) was established on 30 April 2004 by Security Council Resolution 1542. MINUSTAH took over from the Multinational Interim Force on 1 June 2004. Initially MINUSTAH was mandated to support the Transitional Government in ensuring a secure and stable environment; to assist in reforming the Haitian National Police; to support a Disarmament, Demobilisation and Reintegration (DDR) process; to assist with the restoration and maintenance of the rule of law; to protect civilians under imminent threat of physical violence; to support democratisation processes; to promote and protect human rights. MINUSTAH's concept of operations and the authorised strength have been adjusted by the Security Council on several occasions to reflect changes in environment. For details, see Security Council resolutions 1608 (2005), 1702 (2006), 1743 (2007), 1780 (2007), 1840 (2008). After the earthquake in January 2010 there was an increase in force levels to support the immediate recovery, reconstruction and stability efforts, see Security Council Resolutions 1908 (2010) and 1927 (2010). Subsequently as security improved, force levels were reduced, see Security Council Resolutions 2012

(2011), 2070 (2012), 2119 (2013), 2180 (2014). In October 2015, the Security Council asked the Secretary-General to conduct a Strategic Assessment Mission to Haiti to consider the possible withdrawal of the Mission.

MINUSTAH's mandate was extended until 15 October 2016 by Security Council Resolution 2243 (2015).

Appendix B
Haiti timeline
A chronology of key events

1492	Christopher Columbus lands and names the island Hispaniola.
1697	Spain cedes western part of Hispaniola to France, and this becomes Haiti.
1791	The slaves revolt.
1801	Toussaint Louverture a former slave and leader of the Haitian revolution, conquers Haiti, abolishing slavery and proclaiming himself governor-general of an autonomous government.
1802	French forces fail to conquer the Haitian interior.
1804	Haiti becomes independent; former slave Jean-Jacques Dessalines declares himself emperor.
1806	Dessalines is assassinated and Haiti divided into a black-controlled north and a mulatto-ruled south – a civil war ensues.
1818–43	Pierre Boyer becomes President of Haiti. He unifies Haiti in 1820, but excludes blacks from power.
1915	US invades Haiti.
1934	US withdraws troops from Haiti, but maintains fiscal control until 1947.
1956	Francois Duvalier (Papa Doc) seizes power in a military coup
1959	Duvalier establishes the Tontons Macoutes militia, officially called Volontaries de la Securité Nationale (VSN).
1964	Duvalier declares himself president-for-life.
1971	Duvalier dies and is succeeded by his 19-year-old son, Jean-Claude Duvalier (Baby Doc), who also declares himself president-for-life.
1986	Baby Doc flees Haiti in the wake of mounting popular discontent and is replaced by Lieutenant-General Henri Namphy as head of a governing council.
1988	Leslie Manigat becomes president, but is ousted in a coup led by Brigadier-General Prosper Avril, who installs a civilian government under military control.
1990	16 December, Jean-Bertrand Aristide is elected president in Haiti's first free elections with 67.5% of the votes.

Haiti timeline

1991	Aristide is inaugurated on 7 February and ousted in a coup on 30 September, led by Brigadier-General Raoul Cédras, triggering sanctions by the US and the Organisation of American States. Aristide goes into exile.
1993	The joint UN-OAS International Civilian Mission in Haiti (MICIVIH) deploys in February.
1993	UN imposes sanctions in June in reaction to the junta rejecting an accord facilitating Aristide's return.
1993	September, The Security Council establishes the first peacekeeping operation.
1994	September, The military regime relinquishes power in the face of an imminent multinational invasion authorised by the UN.
1994	15 October Aristide returns.
1995	UN peacekeepers begin to replace US troops; Aristide supporters win parliamentary elections.
1995	28 April, Aristide abolishes the National Army.
1995	December, Rene Préval, from Aristide's Lavalas party, is elected to replace Aristide as president.
1997–99	Characterised by political deadlock.
1999	Préval declares that parliament's term has expired and begins ruling by decree following a series of disagreements with deputies.
2000	November, Aristide is elected president for a second non-consecutive term, amid allegations of irregularities and low participation.
2001	July, Presidential spokesman accuses former army officers of trying to overthrow the government after armed men attack three locations, killing four police officers.
2001	December, 30 armed men try to seize the National Palace in an apparent coup attempt; 12 people are killed in the raid, which the government blames on former army members.
2002	July, Haiti is approved as a full member of the Caribbean Community (Caricom).
2004	January–February, Violent uprising spreads throughout the country and escalates.
2004	29 February, President Aristide is forced into exile. The Security Council authorises the Multilateral Interim Force to deploy to Haiti.
2004	17 March, Interim Prime Minister Gerard Latortue forms a transitional government.
2004	30 April, The Security Council establishes MINUSTAH.
2004	June, First UN peacekeepers arrive to take over security duties from the US-led force.
2004–05	Rising levels of deadly political and gang violence in the capital.

2006	7 February, General elections. Rene Préval emerges as the winner of the presidential vote.
2006	21 April, Second round of parliamentary elections.
2006	10 June, A new government headed by Prime Minister Jacques-Edouard Alexis takes office.
2006	29 August, The government establishes the National Commission on Disarmament, Dismantlement and Reintegration.
2006	October, US partially lifts an arms embargo, imposed in 1991.
2007	January, March, MINUSTAH and the PNH launch new offensive against armed gangs.
2007	November, Allegations of sexual misconduct by Sri Lankan peacekeepers leads to repatriation of 108 soldiers (including three commanders).
2008	February, Parliamentary vote of no confidence in Prime Minister Jacques-Edouard Alexis, protesting the government's economic policies, fails.
2008	April, Violent demonstrations and riots in several cities as a result of the rising cost of living. Government announces emergency plan to cut price of rice in bid to halt unrest.
2008	12 April, Parliament dismisses Prime Minister Alexis.
2008	August–September, Four consecutive hurricanes and storms cause severe damage, an estimated 800 killed and hundreds injured.
2008	5 September, The Haitian Parliament approves a new government, ending a five-month impasse. Michele Pierre-Louis succeeds Jacques-Edouard Alexis as prime minister.
2009	19 May, Former US President Bill Clinton is appointed UN Special Envoy to Haiti.
2009	July, World Bank and International Monetary Fund cancel $1.2bn of Haiti's debt, 80% of the total, after judging Haiti to have fulfilled economic reform and poverty reduction conditions.
2009	11 November, Jean-Max Bellerive becomes prime minister after the Senate passes censure motion against his predecessor, Michelle Pierre-Louis.
2010	12 January, An estimated 300,000 people are killed when a magnitude 7.0 earthquake hits the capital Port-au-Prince and region.
2010	31 March, International donors pledge $5.3 billion for post-quake reconstruction at a donor conference.
2010	October–December, Cholera outbreak claims some 3,500 lives and triggers violent protests.
2010	28 November, Presidential and parliamentary elections.
2010	December, Announcement of inconclusive provisional results of presidential election triggers violent protests.

2011	January, Former president Jean-Claude Duvalier returns from exile, faces corruption and human rights abuse charges.
2011	March, Legislative and presidential run-off elections. Michel Martelly wins second round of presidential election.
2011	14 May, Michel Martelly is sworn in as president.
2011	July, Death toll from cholera outbreak climbs to nearly 6,000.
2011	18 October, President Martelly appoints Garry Conille as his prime minister, after parliament rejected his two previous nominees.
2012	January, Presidential Martelly proposes reviving Haiti's army, which was disbanded in 1995 because of its role in coups and its history of human rights abuses.
2012	24 February, Prime Minister Garry Conille resigns in protest at the refusal of many of his ministers and the presidential administration to cooperate with a parliamentary inquiry into dual citizenship among senior officials.
2012	16 May, Parliament approves Laurent Lamothe as prime minister.
2012	October, Hundreds protest against the high cost of living and call for the resignation of President Martelly. They accuse the president of corruption and failure to deliver on his promises to alleviate poverty.
2013	16 September, Martelly greets the first 41 recruits of the new armed forces after they return from eight months of training in Ecuador.
2013	November–December, Street protests in Port-au-Prince and other major cities, with marchers voicing discontent about various issues including an overdue election, unemployment and corruption.
2014	April, Further anti-government protests begin in Port-au-Prince.
2014	December, Prime Minister Lamothe is forced to resign after weeks of protests and failing to reach agreement over elections.
2015	January, Martelly appoints Evans Paul as Prime Minister.
2015	9 August, First round of delayed parliamentary elections are held.
2015	25 October, Second round of parliamentary elections, first round of presidential elections – second round postponed until 24 April 2016.
2016	2 February, Evans Paul resigns as Prime Minister.
2016	7 February, President Martelly ends his term without handing over power.
2016	14 February, Interim President Jocelerme Privert is sworn in.
2016	24 April, The presidential run-offs are again postponed.
2016	25 April, Interim President Privert suggests that the presidential run-offs should be held at the end of October.

Index

Note: Page numbers in *italic* refer to illustrations; page numbers followed by an 'n' refer to notes.

affranchis 18
agricultural sector 26
Alexandre, Boniface 25
Alexis, Jacques 93–4
amnesties: defined 150n20; vs. expectations 142
anciens libre 18
Andrésol, Mario 92–4
anti-UN demonstrations 45–6
Aristide, Jean-Bertrand: changes to the army 63–4; coup of September 1991 22–3; demonstrations against 24; leadership of 17, 20; National Truth and Justice Commission 143; run-off elections 160
armed forces *see also* Forces Armées d'Haiti (FAd'H); changes to 63–4; history of 20–2; kingmaker role 21; retraining 65
armed gangs 36–41
Assistance to Penitentiary Reform (*Assistance a la reforme pénitentiaire*) 123
attachés 22, 23, 44, 58
authoritarianism: coup of September 1991 22–3; history of 14–17; reemergence 23–5
Avril, Prosper 17

blancs 18
Boyer, Jean-Pierre 19
Brahimi report 83
buy-back scheme 59

Canada 27
Canadian International Development Agency (CIDA) 99

Capstone doctrine 50n26
Caribbean Community (CARICOM) 25
Carter, Jimmy 23
CAU (Corrections Advisory Unit) 124–6
CDCs (Community Development Committees) 69
Cédras, Raoul 22, 23, 147
Celestin, Jude 170, 171
CEP (Civilian Electoral Council) 16–17
Charles, Moise Jean 171
chefs de section 22, 66
children 37
cholera outbreak 46
Christophe, Henry 19
CIDA (Canadian International Development Agency) 99
CIMO (*Compagnie d'Intervention et de Maintien d'Ordre*) 89–90
Cité Soleil 36
civil society 6
civil society oversight 98–9
civil unrest 44–7
Civilian Electoral Council (CEP) 16–17
class divisions 18–20
colour divisions 18–20
Commission for Reflection on National Security 72
Committees for the Prevention of Violence and for Development (CPVDs) 69
Community Development Committees (CDCs) 69
Compagnie d'Intervention et de Maintien d'Ordre (CIMO) 89–90
Conflict Violence Reduction (CVR) 63, 69–72
Conseil des Sages 25

Conseil National de Gouvernement (CNG) 16–17
Conseil Superieur du Pouvoir Judiciaire (Superior Council for the Judiciary) (CSPJ) 119
Consensus on the Political Transition Pact 25
Constant, Emanuel 'Toto' 75n31, 76n59, 115, 147, 152n46
constitution: of 1987 59; 1987 64; judicial reform 129
construction 26
consumer prices 26
context, and politics 193–4
coordination: overview 7; and integration 190–1
Corrections Advisory Unit (CAU) 124–6
corruption 119–20
coup of September 1991 22–3
CPVDs (Committees for the Prevention of Violence and for Development) 69
crime, types of 41–4
criminal prosecutions 146–8
CVR (Conflict Violence Reduction) 63, 69–72

DAP 125–6
DDR (disarmament, demobilisation and reintegration): and armed gangs 40; development of 56–8
deforestation 27
demobilisation *see also* disarmament, demobilisation and reintegration (DDR); defined 57; process of 63–72
democracy: and the democratisation process 156–8, 160–1; promotion of 160–8
Democracy Index 178
democratisation process: and democracy 156–8; and elections 166–8; and *Famni Lavalas* 168–78; and judicial reform 128–30; and security 164–5, 173–4; Security Council Resolution 1542 168
demonstrations 44–7
Dessalines, Jean-Jacques 14
diaspora 27
dictatorships 15–16
disarmament: defined 57; process of 58–63
Dominican Republic 27
donors: overview 27; judicial reform 113; police reform 88–9, 91, 92; and security sector reform (SSR) 99
drug trafficking 43–4, 65, 98
Dupuy, A. 20
Duvalier, François (Papa Doc) 15–17, 20

Duvalier, Jean-Claude (Baby Doc) 15–16, 20

École de la Magistrature 114
Ecole de la Magistrature (School for Magistrates) (EMA) 119
L'Ecole National de Police (ENP) 96
economic development: overview 7–8; and the democratisation process 174–6; importance of 190–1
economic situation, overview 25–7
elections: and armed gangs 38; and the democratisation process 166–8; and elections 170; post-occupation 17
employment 26–7, 65
ENP (L'Ecole National de Police) 96
environmental degradation 27
Estimé, Dumarsais 16
expectations: vs. amnesties 142; and objectives 194
exports 26
external influences 6–7

Famni Lavalas (Lavalas Family): creation of 162; and the democratisation process 168–78; leadership of Aristide 17; Multination Force (MNF) 58; political violence 23; support of 93
'flap-flap' republic, Haiti as 161–2
Forces Armées d'Haiti (FAd'H): and insecurity 36; Multination Force (MNF) 58; political violence 23; reintegration *see also* armed forces 64–6
Forst, Michel 45
France 14–17
Le Front pour l'Avancement et Progres d'Haiti (FRAPH): and DDR 66; and insecurity 22, 23, 36, 115

gangs, armed *see armed gangs*
Garde d'Haiti 20–2
Gendarmerie *see Garde d'Haiti*
Global Focal Point (GFP) 100
governance, structure *159*
Governor's Island agreement 22
grands blancs 19
Gross Domestic Product (GDP) 26–7, 175–6
Gross National Product (GNP) 26
Group of Six 25

Haitian National Police (PNH) *see also* police reform; census 95–6; disarmament operations 61; expectations of 90–1;

204   Index

history of 87–8, 92–101; human rights abuses 89–90; international support 91–2; reform plan 94–5; security operations 38; structure *84–6*; training 88–9
Hippo report 83
history: of the armed forces 20–2; of authoritarianism 14–17; of the Haitian National Police (PNH) 87–8, 92–101; of the prison system *123*; timeline 198–201
homicide 42–3
human rights abuses: *Le Front pour l'Avancement et Progres d'Haiti* (FRAPH) 115; post-occupation 17; training on 89; vigilante groups 24

ICRC (International Committee of the Red Cross) *123*
imports 26
infant mortality 27
integrated missions, concept of 3
integration, and coordination 190–1
interim police force 86–7
internally displaced (IDP) resettlement camps 37
International Civilian Mission in Haiti (MICAH) 112, 196
International Civilian Mission in Haiti (MICIVIH) 23, 59, 112, 144, 195
International Committee of the Red Cross (ICRC) *123*
International Criminal Investigation, Training and Assistance Programme (ICITAP) 86, 89
International Institute for Democracy and Electoral Assistance (IDEA) 116
International Monetary Fund (IMF) 165
International Organization of Migration (IOM) 65
International Police Monitors (IPMs) 87
international policing *see UN police officers (UNPOL)*

Joint Mission Analysis Centre (JMAC) 39
judicial reform: overview 110; context for 111; and the democratisation process 128–30; historical account 111–22
judicial system, structure *112*
jury trials 121–2
justice, vs. reconciliation 141, 192–3
Jwèt Pa Nou (It's Our Turn) television programme 46

kidnapping 41–2, 97, 98

la vie chère riots 45
Latortue, Gerard 25, 94
Lavalas *see Famni Lavalas* (Lavalas Family)
Lavalas Family (*Famni Lavalas*): creation of 162; and the democratisation process 168–78; leadership of Aristide 17; Multination Force (MNF) 58; political violence 23; support of 93
law reform 120–1
Leopards 21
Lescot, Elie 16
liberated slaves 19
life expectancy 26–7
Louverture, Toussaint 28n2

Magloire, Paul 16
Manigat, Leslie 17
Manigat, Mirlande 170
manufacturing 26
Martelly, Michel: candidacy of 47, 170; DDR efforts 72; judicial reform mandate 118, 120–1; presidency of 43, 44
MICAH (International Civilian Mission in Haiti) 112, 196
Michel, Smarck 166
MICIVIH (International Civilian Mission in Haiti) 23, 59, 112, 144, 195
minimum wage 26
Ministry of Justice and Public Security (MOJPS) 94, 116–17
MINUSTAH (UN Stabilisation Mission in Haiti): overview 196–7; establishment of 25; and insecurity 36, 62; law reform 120–1; mandate for judicial reform 116–17; police reform 92–3; security operations 38
MIPONUH (UN Civilian Police Mission in Haiti) 112, 196
Mirebalais 46
missions: overview 195–7; integrated 3
Mouvman Péyizan Papaye (MPP) 181n49
Mulet, Edmond 40, 120
Multination Force (MNF) 58–61
Multinational Force (MNF) 35
Multinational Interim Force (MIF) 25

Namphy, Henri 16–17
Narcisse, Maryse 171
National Disarmament Commission (NCD) 62
National Truth and Justice Commission 142–4
Noirisme 16, 19–20

nouveaux libre 19

Office of Transition Initiatives (OTI) 65
Operation Baghdad 41–2
Organisation of American States (OAS) 25

Pascal-Trouillot, Ertha 17
peace operations, historical account 8–9
penal reform *see prison reform*
pépé democracy, Haiti as 161–2
Péralte, Charlemagne 28n10
Perry, William 58
Pétion, Alexandre 19
petits blancs 19
Pierre-Louis, Jean 49n11
Pierre-Louis, Michèle 170
PNH (Haitian National Police) *see also* police reform; census 95–6; disarmament operations 61; expectations of 90–1; history of 87–8, 92–101; human rights abuses 89–90; international support 91–2; reform plan 94–5; security operations 38; structure 84–6; training 88–9
police reform *see also* Haitian National Police (PNH); overview 81–2; interim police force 86–7; plan 94–5
policy guidance, evolution in 2
political legitimacy 163–4
political violence 23, 34–6 *see also* violence
politics, and context 193–4
population, increase in 26
Port-au-Prince: security in 37–8; violence in 43
Port-au-Prince agreement 23, 58, 60
poverty 26–7
Poverty Reduction Strategy Paper 176
Preparatory Commission on Legal and Justice Reform (*Commission préparatoire à la réforme du droit et de la justice*) 113
pre-trial detention 121–2
Préval, Rene 35, 43, 46, 72, 93, 163
prison reform: overview 110, 122; post-2004 124–8
prison system: conditions in 123–4, 127–8; history of *123*
privatisation 165–6

Raboteau massacre 22–3, 147
raids 59–60
Rassemblement des Militaires Démobilisés (RAMIDEM) 47
Rassemblement des Militaries Révoqués Sans Motif (RAMIRESM) 47

reconciliation, vs. justice 141
reintegration: defined 57–8; process of *see also* disarmament, demobilisation and reintegration (DDR) 63–72
remittances 27
retraining, armed forces 65
Rome Statute 145
Rule of Law Indicator Project (ROLIP) 98
rules of engagement (ROEs) 35
rural police 66

Sachs, Jeffery 175
Sam, Vilbrun Guillaume 15
School for Magistrates (*Ecole de la Magistrature*) (EMA) 119
security: and the democratisation process 164–5, 173–4; in Port-au-Prince 37–8
Security Council Resolution 940: and the disarmament process 58; and the Governor's Island agreement 23; judicial reform 112; mandate 34–6, 83; promotion of democracy 160
Security Council Resolution 1542: and the democratisation process 168; judicial reform mandate 116–17, 124; police reform 83
Security Council Resolution 1702 69
security sector reform (SSR): overview 3–4; and armed gangs 40; civil society oversight 98–9
slavery, historical account 18–20
Smarth, Rosny 163
socio-economic differences: historical account 18–20; post-2004 176–7
St Jean Bosco massacre 17
state capacity 163–4, 174
Statute de la Magistrature 119
strategic approaches, importance of 189–90
summary 'justice' 115
Superior Council for the Judiciary (*Conseil Superieur du Pouvoir Judiciaire*) (CSPJ) 119

Ti Legliz (little church) 17
Tontons Macoutes, establishment of 21
trade embargo 26
training, human rights abuses 89
transitional justice 140–1, 192–3 *see also* justice
Transparency International 119
trials 121–2
truth commissions 142–4

UDMO (*Unités Départmentales de Maintien d'Ordre*) 89–90
UN Civilian Police Mission in Haiti (MIPONUH) 112, 196
UN Department of Peacekeeping Operations (UNDPKO) 39
UN Development Programme (UNDP) 61, 125
UN High Commission for Refugees (UNHCR) 25
UN Mission in Haiti (UNMIH): overview 195; establishment of 23; rules of engagement 35
UN Office of Drugs and Crime (UNODC) 42–3
UN peace operations, historical account 8–9
UN police officers (UNPOL): statistics 82; training 96–8
UN Stabilisation Mission in Haiti (MINUSTAH): overview 196–7; establishment of 25; and insecurity 36, 62; law reform 120–1; mandate for judicial reform 116–17; police reform 92–3; security operations 38
UN Support Mission in Haiti (UNSMIH) 35, 112, 195
UN Transition Mission in Haiti (UNTMIH) 112, 196
unemployment 26–7, 65
United States, occupation of Haiti 15, 20–2
Unités Départmentales de Maintien d'Ordre (UDMO) 89–90
Unity 170
US Agency for International Development (USAID) 60, 65
US Institute for Peace (USIP) 116
USS Harlan County 23

vigilante groups 24, 67, 114–15
Vincent, Stenio 15–16
violence: changes in 24–5, 38; defined 35–6, 48n1; political nature of 34–6; statistics 37, 42–3; types of 41–4
vocational training 65

weapons 59–61 *see also* disarmament, demobilisation and reintegration (DDR)
Wimhurst, David 50n23
World Bank 26, 178
World Food Programme 26

youths 37